The Interior Design Productivity Toolbox

Checklists and Best Practices to Manage Your Workflow

Phyllis Harbinger, ASID, CID, NCIDQ

WILEY | AMERICAN SOCIETY OF INTERIOR DESIGNERS

Cover Design: C. Wallace
Cover Images: Fabric Swatches and Office Design Drawing © iStockphoto/DigiClicks;
Wood Samples © iStockphoto/joecicak

This book is printed on acid-free paper. ∞

Published by John Wiley & Sons, Inc., Hoboken, New Jersey
Published simultaneously in Canada

For general information about our other products and services, please contact our Customer
Care Department within the United States at (800) 762-2974, outside the United States
at (317) 572-3993 or fax (317) 572-4002.

Wiley publishes in a variety of print and electronic formats and by print-on-demand. Some
material included with standard print versions of this book may not be included in e-books or in
print-on-demand. If this book refers to media such as a CD or DVD that is not included in the version
you purchased, you may download this material at http://booksupport.wiley.com. For more
information about Wiley products, visit www.wiley.com.

Library of Congress Cataloging-in-Publication Data:

Harbinger, Phyllis, 1962-
    The interior design productivity toolbox : checklists and best practices to manage your workflow /
Phyllis Harbinger.
        pages   cm
    Includes bibliographical references and index.
    ISBN 978-1-118-68043-8 (pbk.), ISBN 978-1-118-89694-5 (ebk.); ISBN 978-1-118-89696-9 (ebk.).
        1. Interior decoration—Practice—Handbooks, manuals, etc.   2. Interior decoration firms—
Management—Handbooks, manuals, etc.   I. Title.
NK2116.H37   2014
729—dc23
                                                                                        2013051308

Printed in the United States of America
V10011704_062819

Contents

Acknowledgments

This book would not be possible were it not for the intervention of a wonderful and supportive group of people.

First, I would like to thank my first design business mentor, David Shepard, for being the person who started the evolution of this book by tasking our Best Practices Network with creating an "evergreen" product that would enhance the lives of other professionals in our field. I would also like to thank BPN members Laura Britt and Cathy Davin, my soul sisters and confidantes. You have both held me accountable for creating this book over the past two years.

Thank you to my design colleagues Shannon Leddy, Audra Canfield, Nicole Cavanaugh, and Katie Leede for participating in the early focus group work. To Francine Martini, Jennifer Carnivale-Hollinger, Laura Robertson, Judy Girod, and Annie Coggan who reviewed a great deal of the content of this book and gave me such wonderful notes and feedback, especially on the contract design sections. You are all treasures in my life.

To Fabienne Fredrickson, Donna Cravotta, and Teri Goetz for empowering me and challenging me to take risks and grow and change—I love you!

To all of my family and friends who have waited patiently for me to finish this book so I can be more involved in your lives again—thank you!

To my wonderful and supportive husband, Ross Jurman. You are my love and my life, and I thank you for putting up with the late nights and countless weekends of writing, and for your patience and belief in me. You are my Rock!

I would like to close by acknowledging the greatest contributor to the successful completion of this work. To Charity Turner, my wonderful, beautiful, and über talented colleague and design associate. You have been a true partner in the creation of this book, and I owe you the world for all you have done to help me turn the DCI checklists into a resource that will truly help other designers.

Online Resources on the Companion Website

The Interior Design Productivity Toolbox includes access to interactive, online versions of all of the checklists featured in the book, as well as to an Excel budgeting tool to track project expenses. These resources are fully downloadable and can be customized for your own projects.

To access the online resources, you will need the unique access code printed on the card included in the back of this book. Follow these steps:

1. Navigate your web browser to: www.wiley.com/go/interiordesigntoolbox

2. In the "Please enter your access code" section, enter your access code and click submit.

3. If you've never registered for a Wiley Companion site before, click on "Create New Account." If you are an existing Wiley user, follow the log-in instructions provided on the site.

4. New Wiley Users, please fill out the registration form, choosing your username and password.

5. Click the "Log-in" button when you have completed the registration form.

6. Once you have completed the registration process, you will arrive at the Companion Site for this book. We recommend that you bookmark this site for easy access throughout your work.

If you have purchased an ebook version of this title or if your access code is not working, please contact Customer Care at 877-762-2974 or at http://support.wiley.com to receive a unique access code for the web resources.

Introduction and How to Use This Book

The business of interior design is so complex. I believe that the design/build industry is crying out for a clear and concise method for procedures and accountability in all phases of a project. To answer this need in the marketplace, I have designed a system of checklists to provide interior designers, architects, and builders, as well as design students, a methodology for facilitating their workflow whether they are just beginning or sustaining their practice.

When I started out in the industry, I really had to fly by the seat of my pants. I had interned for a design firm, but my life circumstances forced me to hang out my shingle much sooner than I would have preferred. I yearned for a manual that would teach me how to run a design business and help me teach new employees what I had learned, while also empowering them to do their jobs more effectively.

Nothing that I have found offered the small firm or the budding interior design student and entrepreneur a foolproof method to carry out operating procedures while providing complete step-by-step guidelines with supporting examples. We all know from our research that you cannot put a price on efficiency, systems, and procedures. This system will help you to document the most important aspects of your projects.

In the design world, some things are common sense and others are not. The methodology provided in this book will help you avoid what could otherwise be costly mistakes and will save you both time and money. It will essentially pay for itself!

This workbook will allow you to keep a watchful eye over important details in your practice while maintaining accountability from your employees as various phases of the project are being completed. Whether your team is surveying a project, creating drawings, or specifying and ordering materials and furnishings, the checklists will help you to avoid missing important items and steps that might otherwise be overlooked.

Using this system of checklists will ease your workflow, as it addresses everyday tasks and protocols of best business practices and allows your team to track the progress at each phase of the project.

Builders and contractors will also benefit! In speaking to a few of my trusted vendors, I've found that they are all in need of an accountability system. Think of this book as a way to effectively communicate and maintain protocols and systems when working with architects and designers on a project.

Students will be empowered with the step-by-step guide to drawings and specifications that are hard to access "under one roof." This workbook gives students who are studying to obtain a degree in interior design the tools they will need to ease the transition from academia to the professional world. It provides an opportunity to up-level individual skill sets and better prepare students for work in an interior design firm, offering a leg up on the competition in this competitive job market. This will be a lifesaver for both students and professors. Having clear systems to follow with accountability at each step, supplemented by visual examples for each topic, allows students to complete drawings and surveys with fewer edits and to understand what exactly is being asked of them.

The Interior Design Productivity Toolbox can change the way a designer runs a business, making both the owner and the staff more efficient and better organized, while also providing clear and concise methodologies to improve and enhance the tasks and workflow.

The book is set up to guide you through the entire design process—from the moment you get a lead to the final punch list. Each section not only has the all-important checklists but also contains valuable information based on my twenty-plus years of experience in the field and in the classroom.

I truly want to share this system that I have created over the years with as many people as possible to streamline your processes and provide you with added accountability and great value. Why should everyone reinvent the wheel? It is said that it takes at least ten thousand hours to master a task. I have spent twenty years doing so and have taken all of this knowledge and created this workbook so that you could benefit from my experience.

This book has a few different platforms. Those of you who have purchased the hard copy will also have access to a web portal where you and your team will be able to download individual checklists. To access the checklists online, visit www.wiley.com/go/interiordesigntoolbox and follow the instructions found on the registration card in the back of this book.

If you are downloading the e-book, you will still be able to get PDF versions of the checklists so that you and your team can download or use them in the cloud to communicate your project management and progress goals more effectively. If you purchased an ebook version of this book, please contact Customer Care at 877-762-2974 or at http://support.wiley.com for a unique access code to take advantage of the web resources.

The web portal is also the home of our proprietary budget cost estimate system, which we are providing as an additional resource to all who purchase this book. Our budget cost estimate system was developed in response to our clients' need to understand the budget at each phase of the project.

In most cases, the designer is given an initial budget and a scope of work. We have taken the scope of work and broken it out by the type of space being designed. The system has an overall scope of work cost outline when you open the program. From there, tabs have been created that identify each room/space to be designed; you will also be able to add to this as you see fit. As you specify furniture, fixtures, finishes, and equipment (FFF&E), you and your team will begin to populate the project document. We suggest that you share this document with your clients at least once a week or whenever you have added elements that will affect the overall budget. Our clients have been thrilled with this offering, as it keeps the entire collaborative team "in the know" and allows the client to really have a sense of the expenditure at each phase of the project.

My hope is that each and every one of you gets at least one "nugget" or "aha!" moment from this book, but my true wish for you is that it will provide you with an all-in-one go-to resource for your team's systems and accountability.

Now let's get started!

PART I

Beginning a Project: Meetings and Surveys

CHAPTER 1

Meetings

Meeting with Clients

How do you meet your ideal client? Many of you who will read and use the material in this book are seasoned professionals, while others are emerging professionals or just now hanging your shingle out for the first time and entering the world of entrepreneurship.

Since 2008, the interior design industry has changed. Clients expect a lot more value for a lot less of an investment. At DCI Studio, we run a luxury design firm and have spent numerous years honing our client attraction skills, learning new ways to preselect our clients, and developing systems that automate the process.

Courting and beginning a relationship with a new client involves certain critical components. First, how do you acquire new business? Does it come from referrals, advertising, the Web, or your networking efforts? Are you tracking the sources of your new business? Doing so is a very good idea. Start an Excel spreadsheet or create a Word document, if you prefer to work that way.

When an e-mail or telephone inquiry comes in from a prospective client, having a protocol in place can help you determine whether this prospect would be an ideal client and a good fit for your firm. We have devised an excellent system for weeding out the "tire kickers" and the less-than-ideal clients.

Whether the inquiry is received via the Internet or by telephone, we have a corporate "signature" e-mail that we personalize and send out to the prospect. We also have fine-tuned a form, which we call the Client Lifestyle Questionnaire (included in this chapter), that addresses the perennial question of *the budget*. This questionnaire can be e-mailed to prospective clients, or you could create a web-form on a cloud server such as Woofu.com so that the form is evergreen and results are e-mailed to you directly. Our firm requires a minimum project investment, and we make prospects aware of this before we engage in a phone call or further correspondence. The next step is to ask the prospective client to start a folder(s) on Houzz.com, Pinterest.com, or Evernote.com categorizing the spaces to be designed with annotated notes on each image detailing what the client likes/dislikes so that you get a feel for the client's style before the "get acquainted" call. Doing this can save you a lot of time.

Now you have a vetted prospect. The prospect has read your introductory materials, done the homework on the Web, and filled out the Lifestyle Questionnaire. Once all of the materials are received, we send an e-mail with a series of available time slots for an initial call. You may use a scheduling app or a Web service, which is even better.

Be very clear that the initial call will last only 15 to 20 minutes, to prevent you from getting involved in a long conversation prior to seeing the space that needs to be designed. During this call with the prospect, outline the requirements and discuss the project approach.

This chapter provides a checklist of questions and notes that we use during the "get acquainted" call. It is very important that you have this list to make sure you cover all the bases. Also, I highly recommend that you take notes on a tablet or on your computer during the call so that you can repeat back to the prospect what he or she is saying. Acknowledging the client's "pain" with regard to design dilemmas is affirming and can be extraordinarily valuable to them. It shows that you are listening, which is one of the most important skills a designer can develop. In addition, you can share the notes with your team via e-mail and create a file for the prospect to assist in developing other material if he or she does become a client.

After we have established that a prospect is excited to work with us *and* that the prospect is our ideal client type, we will set up an appointment for an in-home or office consultation.

We always charge a fee for an initial consultation, as it constitutes an expenditure of our time and the sharing of our expertise and intellectual property. If a prospect signs on with us, we credit the consultation fee to the initial design fee. If the prospect does not engage our services, we still get paid for the time we've invested.

Next comes the initial client meeting. This meeting is very different from subsequent meetings. It is more of a "getting to know you" meeting—a time to see the space that needs to be designed, assess the client's body language, ask defining questions, and get a feel for their personalities and how the space is currently used. All decision making parties should be present for this first meeting.

In the event that all parties cannot be present at the first meeting, we advise that you meet one of the clients and request that at the follow-up meeting, where the *design services proposal* is presented, that all parties be present. I have postponed meetings if both parties cannot make it, as I believe that attendance by all involved parties is critical to my success in landing a project.

After the initial meeting, we come back with a design proposal and review three options with our clients. We go through each option step-by-step and answer any questions the clients may have. Once they have signed the design proposal, we again meet with all decision makers to review the *Letter of Engagement,* answer any questions, and revise scope where necessary. All parties should sign the Letter of Engagement before moving on to the design phase.

Example Letters of Engagement are provided in this chapter (see Figures 1.1 and 1.2), which you may make your own and use in your practice. You should have your own legal counsel review the document before you send it to a client, as every design firm works differently and different laws, rules, and regulations may be in force where you do business.

The following checklists give you the tools you need to travel seamlessly through the process of qualifying and meeting with your clients. To achieve stellar results, please pay special attention to each step of the process.

　　　　　　　　　　　　　　　　　　　NEW PROSPECTIVE CLIENT PROTOCOLS CHECKLIST

BEFORE YOU SET UP A "GET ACQUANTED" CALL

Before you set up a call with a prospective client, make sure you do the following:

☐ **Have someone on your staff call the client and say something like the following:**

"Hi, (*Prospective Client's Name*),

Thank you for your interest in (*Your Company Name*)! My name is (*Your Name*), (*Your Title*) of (*Your Company Name*). Before we set up a "get acquainted" call with you and our principal (if you have staff), we ask that you please visit our website, if you have not done so already, and read through the About Us section as well as our Testimonials page. Can we have your e-mail address so that we can send our New Client Lifestyle Questionnaire? We ask that you complete this so we can learn a little more about you and what you are looking for assistance with on your project."

If the prospective client does not answer and you go to voice mail, you could conclude by saying: "We look forward to hearing from you! Have a great day!"

☐ **Send an e-mail with the Client Lifestyle Questionnaire attached. The e-mail can read:**

Dear (*Prospective Client's Name*):

I/We hope you have taken the time to log on to our website and read through the About Us section as well as our Testimonials. This should give you a clear idea of how we work with our clients and what to expect during the design process. I/We should also mention that the minimum investment to engage our services on a project is $_____ (*insert your minimum fee*), so you may want to review your budget before we connect.

I/We also ask that all prospective clients begin an idea folder on Houzz.com after we set up our call time and invite me/us to view the folder. You can make notes on the images about what you like and the spaces in which you see inspiration. This allows me/us to see your taste and style so that we can have a more informed discussion and make the best use of our time together.

Last, would you kindly fill out the attached Lifestyle Questionnaire and e-mail it back to our team so that I/we can review your style, needs, and wishes for your new project.

If all of this resonates with you, please be back in touch once you have completed the above-referenced items, and we will be happy to set up a "get acquainted" call.

I/We look forward to speaking with you soon, (*Prospective Client's Name*)!

☐ **Spend time looking through the Houzz.com folder the prospect has put together.**

GET ACQUAINTED CALL

Every "get acquainted" call is different, but the flow loosely follows this outline below:

☐ **Introduce yourself and your company.**

☐ **Discuss exactly what it is that the potential clients are looking for your assistance with: a one-time consultation or a more long-term design solution?**

☐ **Discuss how you work (what you do on the project, the service packages you offer, how your fees are structured, etc.).**

☐ **Discuss the budget. You will have prequalified them in the e-mail you sent, but we advise addressing this matter again to be sure they are your ideal client(s).**

☐ **If you and the potential client(s) seem to have common ground and you feel you are a good fit for each other, then set up a date/time to meet for your first in-person consultation.**

(*Your Logo Here*)

Client Lifestyle Questionnaire

The purpose of this questionnaire is to help our design team have a better understanding of your goals, desires, and objectives for your project. We also feel that by completing this questionnaire, you will have a clear idea of your needs and you will be able to articulate them more succinctly. If you are uncertain of the answer to a question, simply leave it blank or make a note/ask a question and we will address it when we speak. We ask that you endeavor to be as specific as possible—clear communication will go a long way toward ensuring your vision is achieved.

Contact Information

Project Address

Street Address _____

City _____ State/Province/Region _____

Postal/Zip _____

Home Phone _____

Fax _____

Client Name #1 _____

Cell Phone _____

E-mail _____

Client Name #2 _____

Cell Phone _____

E-mail _____

How would you prefer to be contacted? (Circle one) Home Phone, Cell Phone #1, Cell Phone #2, E-mail

Who is responsible for project decisions? _____

Have you ever hired an interior designer? If yes, when did this take place, and were you pleased with the results and experience?

_____

_____

_____

How did you hear about us? (Circle one) Internet, Houzz.com, Referral, Other

If other, please elaborate here _____

Why are you looking to design or redesign your space now? _____

_____

_____

About Your Project

Project Type: (Circle all that apply) New Construction, Remodel, Design/Decorating

Project Investment: (Circle one) $20,000–$30,000 (our project minimum), $30,000–$50,000, $50,000–$100,000, $100,000–$250,000, $250,000–$500,000, $500,000+, Other (please elaborate) _____

If other, please specify:

Project Square Footage: _____

What best describes your ideal timeline for your project? (Circle one) Immediately—I'm sitting on boxes!, Within 3 months, 3–6 months, Other

Rooms to be included in your project: (Circle all that apply) Entire Home, Entry Hall/Foyer, Living Room, Dining Room, Family/Great Room, Kitchen, Nook, Office/Study, Laundry Area, Powder Room, Master Bedroom, Guest Bedroom, Master Bathroom, Guest Bathroom, Home Theater/Media Room, Lower Level/Basement, Outdoor Area

Enhancements being considered: (Circle all that apply) Furniture, Reupholstery, Flooring, Window Treatments, Window Replacements or Changes, Appliances, Plumbing Fixtures, Interior Paint, Exterior Paint, Wallcovering, Space Planning, Lighting, Artwork and Accessories

What best describes your style? (Circle all that apply) Traditional, Contemporary, Transitional, Eclectic/Mix, Formal, Casual

Colors you like: _____

Colors you don't like: _____

What is your favorite room in your home? _____

Why? _____

_____

_____

_____

_____

_____

_____

What don't you like about your current home? _____

_____

_____

_____

_____

_____

_____

What part of your home do you use the most? _____

What part of your home do you use the least? _____

How long do you plan on staying in your home? _____

Are there any pieces of furniture or collections that must be worked into the new plan? Please explain: _____

_____

_____

_____

_____

_____

_____

Do you need sun control from your window treatments? Please explain: _____

_____

_____

_____

Are there any technical needs associated with your project scope? (Circle all that apply) Computers, Wireless/DSL/cable, Home theater/surround sound, Music, Other

Your Family

List household members and requirements: _____

_____

_____

_____

_____

Are there any physically challenged or elderly people living in the home? If yes, please explain any special requirements: _____

_____

_____

_____

_____

_____

_____

Household Pets and Special Needs: _____

_____

_____

_____

Your Lifestyle

Our entertaining style is: (Circle one) Formal, Informal, Combination/both

Average number of guests: (Circle one) 1–6, 7–12, More than 12

Average guest age: (Circle one) Adults, Teenagers, Children, All ages

Entertaining preference: (Circle all that apply) Sit-down meals, Buffet-style meals, Watching TV/movies, Games/cards, Music

Do you have any hobbies/interests we should consider when designing your spaces? Do you need an area to accommodate your hobby?

_____

_____

_____

_____

Thank you for your input. Please e-mail this questionnaire back to us at (info@yourcompany.com). We look forward to speaking with you about your project!

Your Company Name
Your Company Address
Your Company Phone Number
Your Company E-mail Address

The day before the meeting:

- ☐ **Confirm the appointment time and date with the prospect. Ask that he or she respond via e-mail or phone as necessary.**
- ☐ **Review the Houzz.com files and your call notes to reacquaint yourself with the prospect's style, scope of work, etc.**
- ☐ **Leave extra time to get to the appointment. Do *not* be late!**
- ☐ **Be sure to charge all electronic devices.**

Typically, the principal of the firm would attend the initial consultation, sometimes with a team member, oftentimes without. Be sure to bring the following to this first meeting:

- ☐ **Camera (or smartphone that takes good-quality photos)**
- ☐ **Tablet with portfolio (This works really well when your portfolio is divided into different presentations by category.)**
- ☐ **Brochure to leave behind with a list of your services and a business card with all of your contact information**
- ☐ **Tape measure (for any quick measurements that you wish to take)**
- ☐ **Scale to measure drawings/architectural plans the prospect may have from the builder/architect**
- ☐ **Voice recorder (An iPad® can also be used for this and the information transcribed into a note, which makes writing the letter of engagement easier.)**
- ☐ **Notepad or tablet for taking notes (A tablet or phone app is a quick and easy way to take notes and immediately transfer them into an e-mail to send to other employees, contractors, etc.)**
- ☐ **Fan decks (for any quick references for color families or color consultations)**

In the initial meeting, be sure to do the following:

- ☐ **Determine the siting of the home. Where does the sun rise and set?**
- ☐ **Check the curb appeal and condition of the exterior before you ring the bell. The exterior can give you valuable information about the prospect's taste and style, lifestyle habits, etc.**
- ☐ **Walk through the entire home/apartment/office. Often, there are clues in areas not within the scope of work that will inform your design approach.**
- ☐ **Keep track of your time, especially if you are billing for the consultation.**
- ☐ **If you still think the prospect is a good fit, set up a date for your next meeting, to present the formal design proposal.**

After the initial meeting:

- ☐ **Write a short thank-you note to the prospect for inviting you into their home/apartment/office. Let the prospect know you will be creating a proposal for the project and that you look forward to meeting again soon.**
- ☐ **Transfer all your notes from your tablet to your computer and review them.**
- ☐ **Compose the design proposal. Sleep on it, and then review it again. A bit of time and some tweaking results in a more refined proposal. Print multiple copies for all parties to review.**
- ☐ **Download all photos from the initial meeting, and share them with your team. Label each photo by room/space.**
- ☐ **Get ready for your meeting to review the design proposal.**

MEETINGS   **PROPOSAL CHECKLIST**

The following is a list of elements to include in your proposal:

Date

Prospect name(s)

Current address

Future address (If different from current address)

Write a brief paragraph here describing your mission, what you will do for the prospect, and what the prospect can expect.

Entry Level

Describe what will be included in this package, which might be any of the following:

- ☐ **Construction documents**
- ☐ **Drawings**
- ☐ **Elevations**
- ☐ **Conceptual drawings and sketches**

Midrange

Describe this package. You may wish to include all services in the entry-level package and then add to the list using some of the following ideas:

- ☐ **Installation coordination, direction, and supervision**
- ☐ **White-glove cleaning services upon completion of the project**
- ☐ **Problem resolution**
- ☐ **Purchasing management to include the following: Budgets, pricing, proposal, expediting, scheduling**
- ☐ **Punch list preparation and oversight**
- ☐ **Project coordination and management**
- ☐ **Meetings with general contractors and subcontractors**
- ☐ **Selection review with clients**
- ☐ **Product recommendations and specifications**
- ☐ **Selections**
- ☐ **Conceptual sketches and drawings**
- ☐ **Elevations**
- ☐ **Scope of work**

Highest Tier:

Here you would include **all** elements from the entry-level and midrange service offerings but add perhaps turnkey service, art installations, organizer services, and/or host a wine and cheese party. It's a great networking opportunity and you can give guided tours. Hire help to prepare platters and serve drinks. You may want to include a housecleaning on the day of the party or a cooking lesson for the clients in their home. This is the package where you pull out all the stops.

- ☐ **Outline your terms and conditions and your fee structure.**
- ☐ **Be sure to include tax applicable to your services.**
- ☐ **Have the clients sign and date the proposal.**

LETTER OF ENGAGEMENT CHECKLIST

Here is a list of items to include in your Letter of Engagement.

- ☐ **A header/footer on every page with the client's name, the name of your company, and the page number**
- ☐ **A space for each party (designer/client A/client B) to initial at the bottom of each page**

Scope of Services

- ☐ **Initial design:** Discuss what is included in the initial design phase, such as the following:
  - Palette of materials
  - Color recommendations
  - FFF&E
  - Space plans/elevations (list each space)
  - Window treatments
  - Number of shopping days included

- ☐ **Interior specifications and purchase management services:** Discuss what is included in this phase, such as the following examples:
  - FFF&E
  - Refurbish existing pieces
  - Prepare purchase orders
  - Place orders (upon approval and payment)
  - Receive any invoices and/or acknowledgments
  - List frequency of job site visits when you will be there to check progress and quality of work
  - Prepare preliminary budget
  - Clause: Your services do not include responsibility for anything structural, HVAC, plumbing, electric, or other mechanical systems installed or to be installed at the site.

Fees and Expenses

- ☐ **Creative services fee (design fee), before the drawings for the project are started**
- ☐ **List of spaces for which drawings will be generated (Design fee is separate from other fees outlined in the Letter of Engagement.)**
- ☐ **Tax for service if applicable**
- ☐ **Number of drawing revisions included and fee for additional revisions**
- ☐ **Purchase management services: Outline what you are billing the client for (purchase management of FFF&E and services performed by any trade contractors) and how you will bill the client.**
- ☐ **Fees for accessories purchased at retail stores and/or AV components and consultation**
- ☐ **Restocking fees for orders that are canceled**
- ☐ **Independent purchasing clause**
- ☐ **Consultation services**
- ☐ **Disbursements/reimbursable expenses**

Engagement of Third Parties

- ☐ **Discuss other trades and professionals involved in all aspects of the project.**
- ☐ **Discuss how these services will be billed.**

Limitation of Liability

- ☐ **Use a "hold harmless" clause in your Letter of Engagement.**

Drawings and Specifications

- ☐ **Drawings created are conceptual and are for design intent purposes only.**
- ☐ **The designer does not provide architectural or engineering services.**

Termination

- ☐ **Either party can terminate the Letter of Engagement with written notice, and each party is responsible for any outstanding obligations.**

Other Matters

- ☐ **The client will permit the designer to take any photos of the project for use in a portfolio or for other business purposes.**
- ☐ **The contract should be interpreted under the laws of your state and be subject to arbitration, not courts of law.**
- ☐ **The client is to sign and initial the Letter of Engagement on all pages and submit payment for the design fee/percentage of the project.**

Letter of Engagement References

SAMPLE LETTER OF ENGAGEMENT

YOUR LOGO GOES HERE

Date

Client Name
Current Address
New Address (If applicable)
City, State, Zip

Interior Design Services – Terms of Engagement

The purpose of this letter is to set out the terms under which **YOUR FIRM** (the "Designer") is to provide interior design services to **CLIENT NAME(S)** for your home/apartment/offices.

SCOPE OF SERVICES

Initial Design: In this phase of the project (the "Initial Design Services"), we will discuss with you the scope of the project, your design ideas and color and style preferences, your budget, and any additional requirements you have for the project. Upon signing of the Agreement, we will conduct an initial design study, which shall include surveying and measuring the (LIST SPACES) in your home/office/apartment.

We will then prepare for you a palette of materials to generally illustrate Designer's suggested interior design scheme (the "Design Concepts"), including color recommendations, interior finishes, and Merchandise (as defined below).

We will also prepare space plans to illustrate our recommendations for (LIST SPACES) and window treatments in (LIST SPACES). We will prepare elevation(s) for new built-in cabinetry for (LIST SPACES AND DETAILS OF LOCATIONS ON WALLS).

We have included ___ (INSERT #) shopping days for furniture selection. Also included in our scope of work will be ___ (INSERT #) trip(s) to the design buildings where Designers will source fabrics and other textiles and lighting to be used for the conceptualization of the project. We will meet with you at your home/office/apartment to review the options.

Interior Specifications and Purchase Management Services ("Purchase Management Services"): Upon your approval of the Design Concepts, Designer shall, as and where appropriate:

1. Select and/or specially design required interior installations and all required items of furniture, furnishings, custom cabinetry, hardware, floor coverings, ceiling treatments, window treatments, and accessories ("Merchandise"). When requested by you, the Designer shall prepare specifications for the refurbishment of existing pieces and new furnishings and shall liaise with third parties regarding such refurbishments.
2. Prepare and submit for your approval purchase orders for completion of interior installations and purchase of merchandise.
3. Upon receipt of your approval and appropriate initial payment (as described in "Ordering of Merchandise and Interior Installations" below), Designer will place orders for Merchandise and Interior Installations.
4. Receive all correspondence, such as acknowledgments, invoices, and shipping notices related to the project and shall promptly process all such information on your behalf and shall keep you apprised of any issues that arise. The Designer shall provide supervision in the installation of such furniture and furnishings.
5. Visit the location on a periodic basis, at your request, to become generally familiar with the progress and quality of the work and to determine in general if the work is proceeding in accordance with Designer's concepts. Constant observation of work at the location is not part of Designer's duties but Designer will be on-site for all major milestone installations at various phases in the project. If General Contractor or any of his trades request our presence at meetings, Designer will be on-site. If there are questions that arise on the job site, Designer will come to the site and address any issues. Designer is not responsible for the performance, quality, timely completion or delivery of any work, materials, or equipment furnished by contractors pursuant to direct contracts with you but will be your advocate and liaison and work with them to complete in a timely manner.
6. Preparation of preliminary budget after selections are made.

Designer's services shall not include undertaking any responsibility for the design or modification of the design of any structural, heating, air-conditioning, plumbing, electric, ventilation, or other mechanical systems installed or to be installed at the location.

PH___ BG___ DG___

Figure 1.1 Residential Sample Letter of Agreement

(NAME OF CLIENT) AGREEMENT Page 2   **YOUR FIRM NAME**

FEES AND EXPENSES

You agree to pay to Designer, prior to the commencement of the drawings and Design Concepts, a nonrefundable initial creative services fee of $_____$, which shall compensate the Designer for the drawings for the (LIST SPACES). This fee is in addition to any other compensation payable to Designer under this Agreement. Tax for this service will also be due. As part of the preparation of drawings, the Designer, at your request, shall prepare one revision. Additional revisions requested by you will be billed to you as Additional Services at the Designer's hourly rate of $_____$.

In addition to the Initial Design Fee, you agree to compensate the Designer for Purchase Management Services as follows:

1. _____ percent (__%) of the cost of merchandise, fixtures, furniture, built-in cabinetry, wall and flooring materials, and furnishings purchased by you, whether via designer showrooms, catalogs, or retail stores; and
2. _____ percent (__%) of the cost of all work or services performed by trade contractors and artisans recommended by the Designer.

This fee (the "Purchase Management Fee"), although calculated on the value of the items and the cost of services coordinated, is a fee for professional services rendered by the Designer and is not a commission. The Purchase Management Fee will become due and payable at the time you are required to pay for the underlying merchandise or service on a pro rata basis and shall not be refundable, even if the order is canceled, except in the case of the negligence of the Designer. The Purchase Management Fee for any canceled order will be credited against any replacement item ordered. All vendor discounts extended to the Designer for merchandise, furniture, and furnishings shall be passed on to you. The Purchase Management Fee shall be calculated without regard for any shipping, handling, applicable tax, delivery, and/or storage charges. Where you request the Designer's assistance in selecting accessories purchased at retail stores or audio/visual components, you agree to compensate the Designer at a rate of $\_\_\_\_$ per hour plus travel time for shopping and placement of such items in the home. You will be responsible for any restocking fees or penalties incurred as a result of the cancellation of an order by you except in the case of the negligence of the Designer.

If you, independently of the Designer, purchase furniture, furnishings, or services based on the general design scheme as prepared by the Designer under this Agreement and have already asked Designer to search for said furniture, furnishings, or services on your behalf, you agree to pay the Designer for the time spent researching or shopping for such items at the Designer's hourly rate of $_____$.

Where you request consultation by the Designer, but the Designer is not acting as the agent/liaison in the purchase, you will be billed at the Designer's hourly rate of $\_\_\_\_\_$ plus travel time. These services may include meetings regarding work/progress of the general contractor or builder; telephone liaison with You or builder/contractor on general contracting items, in-home accessorizing of space on behalf of you, accessory shopping, electrical concerns such as switching, receptacles, etc. (**excluding** track and new recessed lighting, decorative pendants, ceiling fixtures, wall sconces, table and floor lamps **suggested by Designer**).

If the Designer needs to create any additional drawings, designs for cabinetry, or if additional space plans are requested, there will be an additional fee to be negotiated at that time with you.

Disbursements incurred by the Designer and their staff in connection with the project, shall be promptly reimbursed by you upon receipt of Designer's invoices. Reimbursements shall include, among other things, costs of messenger services made at your request, postage, express mail at your request, local and long distance travel, and the like.

Payments for services of the Designer shall be made upon receipt of presentation of a statement for services rendered. For fees delinquent more than thirty days from due date, a charge of 1.5% per month will be added.

You shall be responsible for payment of all state and local sales taxes on merchandise, interior installations, and design fees as applicable. The Designer shall collect the sales tax on all fees as part of regular monthly invoicing.

ENGAGEMENT OF THIRD PARTIES

Merchandise and interior installations specified by Designer shall, if you wish to purchase them, be purchased solely through the Designer, who will act as the agent in the sale. Designer may, at times, request you to engage others to provide merchandise or interior installations. The Designer will assist you in obtaining bids or negotiating proposals and in the awarding of contracts at your request. However, agreements with trade contractors will be entered into directly between you and such contractors and you shall be solely responsible for the payment of all fees to such contractors.

Should the nature of Designer's design concepts require the services of any other design professional, such professional shall be engaged directly by you pursuant to separate agreement as may be mutually acceptable to you and such other design professional.

ORDERING OF MERCHANDISE AND INTERIOR INSTALLATIONS

Merchandise and interior installations to be purchased through Designer will be specified in a written purchase order prepared by Designer and submitted in each instance for your written approval. Each purchase order will describe the item and its price to you (F.O.B. point of origin) ("Client Price"). The client price for each item of merchandise and interior installations is subject to the Designer's fee for services rendered in this phase of the project, as described in "Fees and Expenses" above. Designer shall provide supervision in the installation of merchandise and interior installations.

PH___ BG___DG___

Figure 1.1 Residential Sample Letter of Agreement (*continues*)

(CLIENT NAME) AGREEMENT Page 3   **YOUR FIRM NAME**

Once you have approved the purchase order in writing and have returned it to Designer with Vendor's required initial payment equal to fifty percent (50%) of the client price, Designer will place the order. The balance of the client price, together with delivery, shipping, handling charges, and applicable taxes, is payable prior to delivery to and/or installation at the Location or to a subsequent supplier for further work upon rendition of Designer's or vendor's invoice. Purchase orders for fabrics, wall coverings, accessories, antiques, and items purchased at auction or at retail stores will require full payment (100%) at time of signed proposal.

LIMITATION OF LIABILITY

You agree that the Designer shall not have any liability to you for any losses, claims, damages, liabilities, or expenses arising out of or relating to the project or the services to be rendered by the Designer under this Agreement unless such losses, claims, damages, liabilities, or expenses resulted directly from the gross negligence or willful misconduct of the Designer. Furthermore, you agree to indemnify and hold harmless the Designer against any losses, claims, damages, liabilities, or expenses to which the Designer may become subject arising out of or relating to the project or the services to be rendered by the Designer under this Agreement unless such losses, claims, damages, liabilities, or expenses resulted directly from the gross negligence or willful misconduct of the Designer.

The Designer shall not be responsible for any malfeasance, neglect, or failure of any contractor, vendor, supplier, or other service provider to meet their schedules for completion or delivery or to perform their respective duties, services, and responsibilities in a manner satisfactory to you.

DRAWINGS AND SPECIFICATIONS

Designer's drawings and specifications are conceptual in nature and intended to set forth design intent only. They are not to be used for architectural or engineering purposes. Designer does not provide architectural or engineering services.

TERMINATION

Either party may terminate this Agreement upon written notice to the other party. Termination shall be without prejudice to any and all other rights and remedies of Designer or you. In the event of termination by either party, you shall remain liable for all outstanding obligations owed by you to Designer and for all items of merchandise, interior installations, expenses, and other services on order as of the termination date and Designer shall remain responsible for completion of work and delivery of services for which you have previously paid.

OTHER MATTERS

You agree to provide Designer with access to the location and all information Designer may need to complete the project. It is your responsibility to obtain all approvals required by any governmental agency (permits) or otherwise in connection with this project.

At Designer's request, you will permit Designer or Designer's representatives to photograph the project upon completion for its own use and inclusion in the Designer's portfolio and for business purposes. The Designer shall not disclose the location or your name without your prior written consent.

In addition to all other legal rights, Designer shall be entitled to withhold delivery of any item of merchandise or the further performance of interior installations or any other services, should you fail to timely make any payments due Designer.

This contract shall be interpreted under the laws of the State of New York, without regard to its conflicts of law principles. Any controversy or claim arising out of or relating to this Agreement or breach thereof, shall be settled by arbitration in the city of the Designer's office, in accordance with the Commercial Arbitration Rules of the American Arbitration Association then in effect, and judgment upon award rendered by the arbitrator(s) may be entered in any court having jurisdiction hereof.

Neither Client nor Designer may assign their respective interests in this Agreement without the written consent of the other.

This Agreement represents the entire understanding between the parties concerning the particular project to which it refers and supersedes all prior negotiations, understandings, and agreements concerning the same. This Agreement may be amended only in writing, executed by both parties.

If the above is satisfactory to you, please sign and initial this Agreement and return to me with your check for the 50% of the design fee in the amount of $_____ which includes sales tax of _____%. I will sign and give you a copy for your records when we come to survey the space.

Thank you very much.

Sincerely yours,   ACCEPTED & AGREED

_____   _____   __/__/__

NAME   CLIENT 1   Date
Principal Designer

                                              ____ _____   __/__/__

                                              CLIENT 2   Date

Figure 1.1 Residential Sample Letter of Agreement

Your Company Name
Company Address
Company Phone Number
info@yourcompanyname.com

Date

Client name and address

Re: project name and address

Dear Client,
The following is our proposal for Design and Architectural services as you have requested for the proposed (insert size and location of project).

INTENT

It is my understanding that you are requesting that we work in conjunction with you to fully develop and document for construction of the proposed scope of project (e.g., 30 unit residential development with ground-floor commercial).

DESIGNER'S/ARCHITECT'S RESPONSIBLITIES

Our proposed architectural design services are divided into the following 8 phases:
Preplanning, Preliminary Schematic Design, Final Schematic Design, Design Development, Construction Documents, Bidding and Permitting, Construction Administration.

PHASE 1: PREPLANNING PHASE

The Designer/Architect will:
> a. Review the preliminary program, site information, architectural plans, and/or other documents that pertain to the project site.
> b. Review all relevant planning, zoning, building department, multiple dwelling law, landmarks, and other agency requirements which have bearing on the project.
> c. Review proposed and potential building size, unit allocations, and associated zoning and planning department issues to help the owner determine and or confirm maximum and reasonable potential development parameters for the project.
> d. Conduct field survey of existing structure and prepare measured drawings of existing conditions.

PHASE 2: PRELIMINARY SCHEMATIC DESIGN

The Architect/Designer will:
> a. Produce diagrammatic/ schematic design and documentation for the proposed project, conforming to the guidelines established in Phase 1.
> b. Meet with consultants (expeditor, structural engineer, mechanical, electrical, and plumbing engineer, and others as required) to establish design direction.
> c. Meet with City of New York Department of Buildings personnel to review proposed design for plan consistency with all relevant City of New York Building Code parameters.
> d. Meet with City of New York City Department of City Planning Staff, local community board, Landmarks Preservation Commission Staff, and others as pertinent to this project to review proposal and determine final requirements for approval of interpretive design features including building height, building setbacks, floor area ratios, and parking allocations.

Figure 1.2 Contract Sample Letter of Agreement

PHASE 3: FINAL SCHEMATIC DESIGN

The Designer and Architect will:

   a. Complete the preliminary/schematic design based upon the owner's direction and as required to meet with the final requirements of city agencies.

   b. Provide drawings, computer models and other documentation as required to establish a clear description and understanding of the proposed design for client's review and approval.

PHASE 4: DESIGN DEVELOPMENT

Based upon the approved schematic design, the Designer and Architect will:

   a. Provide drawings and other documentation as required to establish a clear description and understanding of the architectural, structural, mechanical and electrical systems, materials and other such aspects of the proposed project for your review and approval.

   b. Propose finish materials for your review and approval.

PHASE 5: CONSTRUCTION DOCUMENTATION:

Based upon your approved Design Development documents, the Designer and Architect will:

   a. Coordinate and direct the work of the project consultants including, but not limited to: expeditor, surveyor, civil, structural, mechanical, electrical, and geotechnical engineers in regards to the proposed building.

   b. Create construction drawings including but not limited to: Site plans, floor plans, reflected ceiling plans, exterior elevations, building sections, interior elevations, and details as necessary to provide a clear description of the construction required to complete the proposed work.

   c. Create schedules and specifications for the proposed project.

   d. Cooperate with client's cost consultants, if any, in determining the cost of the proposed work.

PHASE 6: DEPARTMENT OF BUILDINGS APPROVALS AND BIDDING:

This phase involves the simultaneous activities of submitting documents to the Department of Buildings (DOB) and associated agencies for approval, and submitting documents to contractors for bids.

It is understood that obtaining DOB approvals is a multitiered and complicated process. The expediter and other consultants as required direct the Architect in this process. It is understood that the owner will employ an expeditor, lawyer, and real estate consultants whose responsibilities will be to expedite and coordinate all regulatory processes. The Designer and Architect will follow the directions of the owner's consultants and produce documents to support the required processing. **[Note: This is not usually an issue for single building development. It may be for multiple-unit housing.]**

The Designer and Architect will aid you in the solicitation of bids for the successful contracting for the construction of the proposed work. Three contractors will be solicited for bids.

It is understood that, depending on construction bids, changes to the plans may be required at this time.

PHASE 7: CONSTRUCTION OBSERVATION:

It is assumed that the standard AIA document: A-101, "Standard Form of Agreement Between Owner and Contractor", will be the basis of the contract between you and your contractor and or subcontractors. In that respect, we will aid you in the administration of the construction of the proposed structure as follows:

   a. At your request, we will review and comment on your relations to the general contractor and/or subcontractors performing work on your building, including:

      1. Construction and payment schedules

      2. Applications and/or Certificates for payment

      3. Change orders

      4. Review of technical documents submitted by the contractors for review and approval, including: shop drawings for steel, cabinets, or other shop-built items; manufacturer's literature for specified items and samples

   b. We will visit the site at intervals appropriate to the stage of the construction and report to you on the progress and status of the work. Our proposal includes weekly site visits for one hour per week for the duration of construction. Site visits beyond this number shall be billed on an hourly basis.

Figure 1.2 Contract Sample Letter of Agreement

c. We will endeavor to guard you against defects and deficiencies in the work and determine in general if the work is being performed in a manner consistent with the construction documents. However, we shall not be required to make exhaustive or continuous on-site inspections, nor shall we be required to have continuous representation on-site during construction. Also, the Designer and the Architect shall not have control over or charge of, nor be responsible for, the construction means, methods, techniques, sequences of procedures, or safety precautions in connection with the work, as these are the responsibilities of the Contractor.

d. We shall report to you any deviations from the contract documents; however we shall not be responsible for the Contractor's failure to perform the work in accordance with the contract documents.

e. The Designer and the Architect shall have access to the work at all times whenever there is work in preparation or progress.

f. In reviewing requests for payments submitted by the Contractor, we will endeavor to provide you with an estimate of the progress of the work to date for your evaluation of the requests for payment.

g. The Designer and the Architect shall have the authority to reject work that does not conform to the contract documents.

PHASE 8: LETTERS OF COMPLETION, SIGN-OFFS, AND CERTIFICATES OF OCCUPANCY

This is the final phase of the project and is typically managed by the Expediter. This involves coordination of the Architect and design consultants, and the Contractor and subcontractors. Work includes final construction inspections, surveys, and final amendments to DOB documents.

OWNER'S RESPONSIBILITIES

The Owners agree to:

1. Provide the Designer and the Architect with a full architectural survey(s) from a licensed Surveyor, legal descriptions, and title reports as necessary to complete our work.

2. Provide the Designer and the Architect with the services of engineering consultants or specific design consultants when reasonably requested, including but not limited to: geotechnical, structural, mechanical, electrical, plumbing, civil, or other relevant engineering services; kitchen design consultants; lighting designers; landscape designers or architects; or similar specialties.

3. Provide the architect with structural, mechanical, geotechnical or other such tests and inspections as may be necessary.

4. Provide all legal and insurance services that may be necessary for the project to meet your needs and interests.

5. Keep the Designer and the Architect informed of any relevant issues concerning the successful completion of the project.

6. Keep the Designer and the Architect informed of any faults or defects in the project that you may discover, including any errors, omissions, or inconsistencies in our documents or service.

CONSTRUCTION COST

1. The construction cost shall be the total cost of all elements of the project designed and specified by the Designer and Architect and shall include costs of management or supervision of construction, but shall not include design costs (the Architect, engineering consultants, or other consultants), nor cost of property acquisition.

2. Evaluations of the project budget represent the Designer/Architect's best judgment as a design professional. It is understood that neither the Designer, Architect nor the owner has control over the cost of labor, materials, equipment, or market nor negotiating conditions which may affect the cost of the work. Therefore, we make no warranties that bid or negotiated prices will not vary from your proposed budget.

USE OF DOCUMENTS

Drawings, specifications, and other documents of service that we prepare shall be used solely for this project. The rights to these documents remain ours.

DISPUTE RESOLUTION

Any claim, dispute, or other matter in question, unresolved by common agreement shall be subject to mediation as a condition precedent to arbitration. Arbitration shall be in accordance with the rules of the American Arbitration Association.

Figure 1.2 Contract Sample Letter of Agreement (*continues*)

TERMINATION

This agreement may be terminated by either party upon not less than seven days' written notice should the other party fail substantially to perform in accordance with the terms of this agreement through no fault of the party initiating the termination. You may terminate this agreement with not less than seven days' notice at your convenience and without cause. In the event of termination, which is not the fault of the architect, the Designer and Architect shall be compensated for all services performed to the date of termination.

ADDITIONAL PROVISIONS PROPOSAL: (Insert Owner & Project Name)

1. The Owner, the Designer and Architect, respectively bind themselves, their partners, successors, assigns, and legal representatives to the other party to this agreement. Neither the Owner nor the Architect shall assign this agreement without the written consent of the other, except that the Owner may assign this Agreement to a lender providing financing for the project.

2. This represents the entire agreement between us and may be changed only by written agreement by both parties.

3. The Designer and Architect has no responsibility for the discovery, handling or removal or disposal of, or exposure of persons to hazardous materials or toxic substances at the project site.

4. The maximum financial liability that the Designer and Architect may be held responsible for in regard to work performed under this contract shall not exceed the maximum fee paid to the Designer and Architect.

PAYMENTS AND FEES

Our proposed fee for the services described above is 18% of cost of construction/a maximum not to exceed cost of $xxx,xxx.xx. (Insert your company name) will bill the owner on an hourly basis against this maximum. If a previous phase is billed below the maximum stated, that portion remaining may be allocated to subsequent phases. If earlier phases are exceeded, this may be deducted from subsequent phases. In no event shall the total maximum hourly fee billed exceed $xxx,xxx.xx without owner's approval based on the scope of work outlined in this proposal. Our hourly billing rates are described below. All amounts shown are maximum not to exceed values.

	Phase	Percentage	Fee
1	Preplanning	2%	
2	Preliminary Schematic	5%	
3	Final Schematic	8%	
4	Design Development	20%	
5	Construction Documents	40%	
6	Approvals/Bidding	10%	
7	Construction Administration	10%	
8	Completion	5%	

We will bill hourly based upon these estimates. Our hourly rates are listed below.

Additional work:

Work outside of that described above shall be billed on a time and material basis. Our hourly rates are:
Principal Designer $150.00/hr.
Architect or Job Captain $90.00/hr.
Draftsman $60.00/hr.

Figure 1.2 Contract Sample Letter of Agreement

Changes in Scope of Work.

Design is a process of constant refinement. It is understood that design changes are expected during phases 1, 2, and 3. Changes during this period are generally included in the estimated fee. However, significant changes made by the Owner to agreed-upon direction, or that result from significant changes in program, project scope, or budget, are subject to fees for additional services. Design changes made by the owner commencing with Design Development (Phase 4) will result in fees for additional services. Should the owner's requested changes result in hourly billings exceeding the maximum fee established in the fee structure listed above, the owner shall be billed as additional work beyond that maximum.

Reimbursable Expenses:

Over and above the stipulated contract sum, the owner will reimburse (Insert your company name) for the following expenses at cost plus 15%:
   1. CAD plotting of drawings @ $12.00 per sheet (except those for house coordination)
   2. Blueprinting and reproductions (except those for house coordination)
   3. Long-distance phone calls
   4. Messenger and delivery services
   5. Travel @ $0.50/mi. plus parking
   6. Renderings and models
   7. Professional liability insurance dedicated exclusively to this project
Total reimbursable expenses for a job of this generally amount to approximately $2,000.

PAYMENTS:

1. (Insert your company name) will bill the Owner solely based upon direct expenses and our hourly billing rates, outlined above, during the development of the project.
2. Payments are due upon presentation and are considered past due after 10 days. Payments delinquent for more than 30 days will be charged interest at 1 1/2% per month. (Insert your company name) reserves the right to terminate this agreement, upon giving a written notice, if payments are delinquent for more than 60 days past the invoice date.
3. In the event that the Owners elect to suspend the project, or if the owner's do not maintain progress such that there is no progress for more than 6 months, then this agreement shall be reestablished and updated as required.
4. In the event that the Owners elect to terminate the project, or if the project is terminated due to circumstances unrelated to the architect's performance, then the Designer and Architect shall be compensated in full for services performed prior to termination, together with reimbursable expenses then due.

SCHEDULE:

1. It is understood by all parties that time is a critical component of this Agreement.
2. The Designer and Architect agree to make every reasonable effort to meet the Owner's stated schedule.
3. It is understood by all parties that the work of others, beyond the immediate control of the Designer and/or Architect, may affect the timely completion of documents. The Designer and Architect cannot be held responsible for the timely completion of work by other consultants.

Commencement Date of Work shall be the date when all required information for the successful completion of the work described above is with the Designer and Architect. Required information includes, but is not limited to:
a. Updated soils and geotechnical reports.
b. Updated architectural survey, complete with easements, and utilities.
c. Owner's description of the project, and approved programming document.
d. Retainer fee of $xx,xxx.xx

Agreed this day, _____.
By:
_____
_____

Figure 1.2 Contract Sample Letter of Agreement (*continues*)

Meeting and Survey Materials

I believe that the Meeting and Survey Materials Checklist is one of the most important checklists our firm has created. How many times have you or a member of your team arrived at a job site to survey and discovered that you neglected to bring one very important tool? I would cringe when this happened, as it meant that someone would have to return to the site, wasting both travel time and productive billable hours. No doubt you can relate to this.

Meeting notes have been a savior for us. We can always refer to the history and be reminded of tasks that may otherwise slip through the cracks. Years ago I began to bring an assistant or a junior designer with me to meetings so that I could be totally present and engaged with the client and not worry about missing a function, a wish list item, or a detail. Until recently, notes from meetings would be taken manually and then typed up and e-mailed to the team and the client within 12 to 24 hours of the meeting so that we could respond to the tasks at hand. Now I suggest that you record the meeting on a smartphone or tablet, or take notes on a tablet during the meeting, so that you do not have to rewrite everything, reducing the hours you spend on double-tasking. Once meeting notes are completed, action items may be recorded in your preferred project management software tool. We recommend Basecamp®, Asana, or TeamworkPM™ project management software. This will foster more awareness for your team on who is responsible for individual tasks and follow up and create better accountability practices.

We have also created a "toolbox" of items that we always have with us. We suggest using a clear, zip locked pouch (you can purchase these at an office supply store with a scale and compass inside), as it makes it so easy to find the items you need at a glance. We have become superefficient with our toolbox, and it has been a lifesaver on many occasions. Figure 1.3 shows an example of a toolbox.

I strongly recommend that every designer carry a high-resolution pocket camera or a smartphone so that they can take good quality photos during the meeting. Our designers do this using tablets and/or smartphones. I use an app called Photogene® to make notes on the photos on-site so I have everything I need in one place. Documenting the conditions from the onset allows you to accurately recall and quote a particular space, detail, or the like. I suggest that you start on a large window wall when taking photos and work clockwise around the room so that later you will be able to identify your photos and match them to room elevations. You may wish to label the photos as east, west, north, or south elevations to make it easier for team members to use the information.

Documenting existing furnishings and fixtures is also of key importance. Many times, clients want these pieces out of the way so they disappear to a warehouse during renovation and the client fails to communicate that to you. Having the relevant measurements and photos from the outset is critical to achieving a successful outcome with repurposing in a project.

One of the key components of a successful delivery is making sure all pieces ordered will fit through elevators, door openings, hallways, stairwells, and so on. *This is critical!* We offer a suggestion: Take detailed measurements of these areas even if you are not designing that space. Any traffic pattern that impacts a delivery must be noted. We generally take these measurements on day one of the survey. The specifications checklists for upholstery, case goods, cabinetry, and appliances provided in subsequent chapters will help you do a thorough access measurement prior to placing an order.

As a project moves forward, there will be a series of meetings for you and your team members to attend. The final section of the Meeting and Survey Materials Checklist provides notes and tips on documenting a successful meeting.

MEETING AND SURVEY MATERIALS CHECKLIST

BEFORE MEETING

For every survey (and subsequent meeting), you should come prepared with the following materials. We suggest that you have these items in your dedicated bag at all times in case a situation arises for which you might need any of these tools. That way, you will never have to scramble to find things.

- ☐ **Tape measure/measure gun/measure App**
- ☐ **Architectural scale**
- ☐ **Masking or painter's tape**
- ☐ **Packing tape**
- ☐ **Utility, matte, or Olfa® knife**
- ☐ **Sharpie® markers**
- ☐ **Smartphone or Camera and camera cord**

- ☐ **Flash drive**
- ☐ **Notebook and tracing paper**
- ☐ **Pen and pencil with eraser**
- ☐ **Furniture glides**
- ☐ **Furniture markers**
- ☐ **Printouts of drawings**
- ☐ **Computer or tablet**

During Meeting

At every meeting/initial survey appointment, you should be prepared to do the following:

- ☐ **Take meeting notes and e-mail them to your supervisor and other team members.**
- ☐ **If an item requires measuring at the home** (for clearance, for window treatments, etc.**) take measurements on-site before the end of the meeting.**
- ☐ **Be sure to take photos and measurements of any existing furniture that will be repurposed.** (Get a few photos of different views of each piece of furniture.)
- ☐ **Always take elevation photos of windows and existing window treatments for reference.**
- ☐ **Take progress photos of rooms and areas being renovated to document the project.**
- ☐ **Take photos of any areas you need to document for damage repair, new work, etc. Always be sure to include photos of architectural and electrical details.**
- ☐ **If you or the client references a problem or damage to something already installed or delivered, document it in your meeting notes and by taking photos so you can contact the manufacturer with the necessary information.**
- ☐ **If a delivery is scheduled, follow the Delivery Protocol Checklist** (see Chapter 6—Residential and Contract Renovations).

Meeting Notes Should Include the Following

- ☐ **Date, time, and duration of meeting**
- ☐ **Topics/overview list**
- ☐ **Name of person who recorded the notes**
- ☐ **Fabrics or furnishings selected with item/color numbers, finish selections, etc.** (Order a set of samples of all the fabrics for the client and a second set for the firm for reference.)
- ☐ **Any necessary measurements of furniture and/or clearances**
- ☐ **Anything that the client is newly interested in having specified and any specific details about how the client wants that item to look (finish, style, etc.)**
- ☐ **Any items selected and for which the client is ready to place an order**
- ☐ **Any items that you need to discuss with the GC, lighting designer, cabinetmaker, etc.**
- ☐ **Any questions that the client has for the manufacturer of an item (cleaning instructions, etc.)**
- ☐ **Tasks moving forward/dates due/who is responsible**
- ☐ **Next meeting date and topics to discuss at next meeting**

Meeting and Survey Materials References

Use a small clear plastic bag with a zipper closure as your toolbox. This keeps your items in one place, its transparency enables you to see through to your items which will ensure that you know the contents of your toolbox at all times and can easily access each item.

Always bring a scale with you so you can easily read your drawing measurements.

It's a good idea to bring along a roll of packing tape. You never know when you will need it. You may need to repack a box to be sent back to a company as a return.

You should always carry a pack of felt furniture glides, especially on delivery days, to put on the bottom of any chair and/or furniture legs to protect the floor.

It is a good idea to bring along furniture markers on delivery days. They are a quick fix for discoloration of furniture or even small scratches. They can really save the day!

Figure 1.3 Your Toolbox

MEETINGS   **MEETING NOTES EXAMPLE**

2/24/14 – MEETING: SMITH RESIDENCE – 11am to 1pm

In Attendance: Client(s) Name(s), Phyllis Harbinger – DCI, Charity Turner – DCI, Marcie Meyer – DCI, and the Cabinet-maker
Meeting Recorded by Marcie Meyer-DCI

General

- Phyllis presented 2 Contractor bids; Client selected Carmine

Hall Bath

- Phyllis presented 3 bathroom drawing iterations for client to select from; Client chose drawing P-3
- Phyllis presented bathtub selections – Client would also like to include the bathtub she had selected on Houzz
- Polished chrome to be specified for all fixtures
- Specify handhelds in addition to shower head (Phyllis commented that she is against a rain head in ceiling)
- Specify a tub filler with a handheld
- Specify under-mount sinks
- Determined that both faucets will be deck mounted – TBD if single or double

Master Bath

- Polished chrome to be specified for all fixtures
- Specify handhelds in addition to shower head (Phyllis commented that she is against a rain head in ceiling)

Dining Room

- Approved built-in cabinetry designs.
- Looked at chair selections. Clients like the model A side and arm chairs from Baker, Style #2031 and are ready to place an order for two arm chairs and four side chairs.
- Narrowed arm chair fabrics to two choices:
  - Kravet-11846-04 (54" wide vertical repeat 0" horizontal repeat 0")
  - Robert Allen-Night-Fog (55" wide vertical repeat 0" horizontal repeat 0")
- Selected side chair fabric
  - Kravet-27968-8 (54" wide vertical repeat 1.5" horizontal repeat 1.5")

Action Items:

- Phyllis to get quote from cabinet-maker (within a week)
- Marcie to add bathtub that client had selected on Houzz to client project file
- Charity to search for hardware for dining room cabinetry

Next Meeting:

- A shopping trip has been scheduled at Klaffs for Thursday, 3/6/14 @ 10am where clients will make their selections for tile, plumbing, and lighting.

CHAPTER 2

![grey blocks]

Residential and Contract Surveys

Introduction

As a designer, I believe one of the most critical phases in a project is the survey. The most valuable information regarding the "bones" of the project is collected and documented in this stage of the design process.

Here we have the opportunity to really "feel" the space—the existing conditions. I urge you and your team to take note of the architecture, the way light enters the space, the ceiling height, molding details, and other architectural elements such as the soffit, a tray ceiling, a cove, or nib walls.

Photos are a crucial component of a survey. They will be referenced throughout the initial drawing process and again in almost every phase of the project. Documenting the existing conditions of your project in drawings as well as photographs both enriches and informs your design experience and practically eliminates the need for revisits to the site to get information about missed elements. Your photos should be carefully organized into folders and titled as follows:

- Initial Survey—Existing Conditions: Document every single element in your photos and your hand-drawn survey.
- Demolition: This folder should contain photographs of each demo'd space.
- Construction: This folder gets quite large, containing documentation of rough-in for electrical and plumbing, tile, finish trims for fixtures, vanities, lighting, etc.
- Scouting Shots: These images detail the finished space.

Photographs document the entire design process, give you useful elements to include in a renovation blog post or article submission, provide the basis for a progress meeting with clients and the contractor, and also make fabulous before-and-after documentation to use on your website!

If you are a true collaborator, you may wish to share the photos from your surveys on a cloud-based server such as the Apple® Photo Stream, Basecamp®, or Evernote® and invite all interested parties to view the folders you have created. This has been an invaluable tool for our firm, keeping all parties informed and allowing for quick reference in the cloud wherever we are, regardless of the time. We can pull up the information on our phones, tablets and computers, 24/7.

When I first began practicing, I had my routine when it came to a survey. Even though I had been trained, knew the process, and knew how to measure, sometimes I would get back to the drafting table (yes, I am dating myself!) and realize that I did not have enough information to complete my drawing. This was truly maddening, as I was forced to go back to the job site, wasting both travel time and important billable hours, retracing my steps and filling in the blanks. This adversely affects your bottom line.

So, I thought, I really must figure out a way to streamline this process. Creating checklists that you can use and also provide to your entire staff prevents these snafus. These checklists are also appropriate for use when training interns and emerging professionals. While we all learn the basics of how to perform a site survey in design school, most projects are assigned as plans and students are not required to actually go out and physically measure a space. The three-dimensionality of a physical survey can be daunting, as it is so easy to miss an important detail.

Chapter 2 of this book provides you with a variety of survey checklists to assist you and your team in everything from initial survey of a "TYP" or typical room to the specifics involved when surveying for a kitchen or a bathroom. We have also included some images that help to clarify these details.

General Room Survey

During a general room survey, you must take note of critical elements such as existing vents, wiring, cable and electrical outlet locations, ceiling electrical junction J-boxes, exposed pipes, and HVAC units.

Make every attempt to note demising walls in apartment buildings and townhomes. Note ceiling heights and whether the ceiling is slab or has a plenum, which may allow for recessed lighting and other wiring possibilities.

What about built-in cabinetry? This is a critical and specific survey item. In Chapter 3, you will find a checklist for the kitchen survey that details all of the components of cabinetry to be included in your survey. You must be very precise in your measurements of the walls, ceiling height, existing baseboard molding, and depth of the opening to receive the built-in.

Be sure to also measure the width wall to wall, at the bottom, middle, and right before the ceiling. Why do this? Because, in many cases, the existing walls are not plumb. Wood and other building materials are, for the most part, straight. You should speak to your contractor and have the walls plumbed before installing any built-in cabinetry, for a quality finish and seamless installation.

SURVEYS   **GENERAL ROOM CHECKLIST**

Measurements

- ☐ **Measure space**
- ☐ **Baseboards and crown**
- ☐ **Window and door frame** (width and depth)
- ☐ **Ceiling height above finished floor (AFF)** (Note if no finish floor exists at survey date.)
- ☐ **Ceiling details and dimensions** (soffit, slope, tray, and beams)
- ☐ **Wall/ceiling pocket details for drapery** (Measure width, length, and depth.)
- ☐ **Note and dimension furnishings remaining in the space or being repurposed.**
- ☐ **Note and dimension existing exposed wiring** (cable, wire chase, etc.).
- ☐ **Note and dimension any floor outlets.** (Note shape, size, location, and number of outlets.)

Elevations

- ☐ **Measure wall length and ceiling height AFF.** (Note if no finish floor exists at survey date.)
- ☐ **Measure baseboards and crown.**
- ☐ **Measure HVAC and/or radiators.** (including surrounding built-in cabinetry, door swings, etc.)
- ☐ **Measure location of door and overall dimensions on elevation.** (Measure door height and width and trim width and lengths.)
- ☐ **Measure window interior and overall dimensions** (length × width × depth).
- ☐ **Measure mullions and windowsills** (height, width and depth/projection).
- ☐ **Measure height above window to ceiling.** (Note crown height.)
- ☐ **Note the style of the window.**
- ☐ **Measure existing cabinetry.**
- ☐ **Wall pocket details** (Measure width, depth and height.)
- ☐ **Measure interior of all closets including structural elements (columns).**

Electrical Measurements

- ☐ **Note and dimension outlets, j-boxes, electrical boxes, cable, Internet, and phone.**
- ☐ **Note and dimension all lighting locations of ceiling lights and wall sconces.**
- ☐ **Note type of outlets and switches** (duplex, quad, combo, dimmers, etc.).
- ☐ **Note and dimension fans, vents, radiators, and HVAC.** (Check walls, ceilings, and floors.)
- ☐ **Note all switches and their dimensioned locations.**
- ☐ **Note switching locations.** (Which switches control which fixtures/outlets?)

Photos to Include

- ☐ **Overall room** (may need two shots from different views)
- ☐ **All elevations in each space surveyed**
- ☐ **Ceiling details** (soffits, slopes, trays, beams, cove details, etc.)
- ☐ **Inside window frames and reveals, window drapery pockets on wall or in ceiling**
- ☐ **Switches, outlets, vents, HVAC, radiators, thermostats, smoke alarms/detectors, security systems**
- ☐ **Crown and baseboards**
- ☐ **Any questionable items for general contractor (GC)**
- ☐ **Any furnishings remaining in the space or being repurposed**
- ☐ **Any lighting remaining in the space or being repurposed**

Hours Spent:

Bathroom Surveys

The following checklist is specifically tailored to the bathroom, which offers up a myriad of challenges. In a bathroom, there are the general survey issues to contend with and numerous little details that must be documented. Existing plumbing fixtures must be documented and provide clues for future renovation concepts.

Always be sure to note the location of existing pipes and fixture locations AFF (above finished floor). I generally do a quick sketch on-site and dimension it. We then put the information into drawings back at the office.

Of equal importance is to note the location of medicine cabinets—whether they are flush-mounted or recessed—and the heights of existing lighting fixtures and vanities.

The tub is the elephant in the room. Always document the dimensions but also the material. Is it porcelain, fiberglass or cast iron? Does it have a removable face? What is the condition? Will the client keep the tub, or is it part of the demolition scope? The color of the tub is critical if it is to remain in place. Also important is the depth of the flange/surround.

The shower: if the bathroom you are surveying has a separate shower stall, make critical notes on all components: height of curb, type of shower enclosure, height of shower enclosure AFF, location of all controls/fixtures, drain type, and so forth.

I like to make special note of outside corners, as they present tiling challenges that I need to be aware of before selecting materials.

It is important to note the ceiling condition—is it a slab or is there room in the ceiling to mount recessed lighting or a J-box?

If you are designing a bathroom compliant with the Americans with Disabilities Act (ADA), make special notes of existing grab bars, supports in the walls (you will see this in the demo phase), wall-mounted fixtures, door openings, and so forth. If the bath was not ADA compliant prior to your survey, pay close attention to details, as you will need to make modifications to the structure in the rough-in and construction phase to accommodate new fixtures and bring the bathroom up to code.

A detailed drawing checklist for ADA-compliant bathrooms can be found in Part II of this book, which can be referenced before completing your survey.

These details will inform future design decisions.

SURVEYS   **BATHROOM CHECKLIST**

Plan Measurements

- ☐ **Measure room** (include HVAC, and radiators)
- ☐ **Baseboards and crown**
- ☐ **Window and door frame** (width and depth)
- ☐ **Measure all shower curbs and saddles** (length and width)
- ☐ **Ceiling height AFF** (Note if no finished floor exists at survey date.)
- ☐ **Ceiling details and dimensions** (soffit, slope, tray, beams)
- ☐ **Sink and gas pipe locations**
- ☐ **Note and dimension toilet pipe and stack locations on-center**
- ☐ **Tub/shower location**
- ☐ **Medicine cabinet** (dimensions and location, recessed or flush-mount, left/right swing)
- ☐ **Note and dimension cabinetry and/or fixtures**
- ☐ **Note and dimension existing exposed wiring** (cable, wire chase, etc.)

Elevations

- ☐ **Measure wall length and ceiling height AFF.** (Note if no finished floor exists at survey date.)
- ☐ **Measure baseboards and crown**
- ☐ **Measure HVAC and/or radiators**
- ☐ **Measure location of door and overall dimensions on elevation**. (Measure door height and width and door trim width and lengths.)
- ☐ **Measure window interior and overall dimensions** (length × width × depth).
- ☐ **Measure mullions and windowsills** (height, width, and depth/projection).
- ☐ **Note the style of the window.**
- ☐ **Measure height above window to ceiling.** (Note crown height.)
- ☐ **Note faucet clearance.** (How much room [height] do you have for a new faucet fixture?)
- ☐ **Medicine cabinet** (dimensions and location AFF)
- ☐ **Measure existing cabinetry and fixtures.**
- ☐ **Wall pocket details** (Measure width and height.)
- ☐ **Location of existing shower, bath, and sink fittings**
- ☐ **Measure existing tub and shower curb heights.** (Note tub orientation – left facing or right facing drain.)

Electrical Measurements

- ☐ **Note and dimension outlets, J-box, cable, Internet, and phone.**
- ☐ **Note and dimension all lighting locations of ceiling lights and wall sconces.**
- ☐ **Note type of outlets and switches and their dimensioned locations** (duplex, quad, GFI, etc.).
- ☐ **Note and dimension fans, vents, radiators, HVAC, thermostats, smoke alarms/detectors, and steam controls.**

Photos to Include

- ☐ **Overall room** (may need two shots from different vantage points)
- ☐ **Each elevation**
- ☐ **Ceiling details** (soffits, slopes, trays, beams, etc.)
- ☐ **Inside window frames and reveals, window drapery pockets on wall or in ceiling**
- ☐ **Switches, outlets, vents, HVAC, radiators, thermostats, steam controls, smoke alarms/detectors**
- ☐ **Crowns and baseboards**
- ☐ **Existing cabinetry and fixtures**
- ☐ **Soil stack location if able to determine**
- ☐ **Any questionable items for general contractor (GC)**
- ☐ **Any items remaining in space or being repurposed**

Hours Spent:

Kitchen Surveys

Kitchens definitely deserve a checklist all their own. They are the heart of the home, a major point of convergence, and a high-traffic area to boot! More often than not, you will find more than one point of entry/exit, especially in larger homes.

Many older kitchens have ceiling soffits or bulkheads running on the perimeter that were used to conceal plumbing and can probably be rerouted during a renovation. We generally have the contractor cut some small and discreet exploratory holes in the bulkheads and other questionable areas to get a feel for what is behind the walls.

You need to consider a myriad of functions in a kitchen while not losing sight of the aesthetics. In my opinion, this is the most critical space to survey. In addition to a plan view, an elevation survey is of equal and sometimes greater significance. The heights of the ceiling, wall-hung cabinetry, countertop, kick base, and existing appliances must be noted. In addition, the thickness of stone countertops, the sill height, and both window and door header heights stimulate critical thinking and inform decisions on new cabinetry design. You must be very precise in your measurements of the walls, ceiling height, existing baseboard molding, and the depth of the opening to receive the built-in.

Carefully document not only existing appliances but also existing fixtures. Call out whether the stove top is gas or electric, and document the fuel source for the oven. In addition, if there are wall ovens, what is their depth and height? Where is the microwave? Is it a built-in style, freestanding, or in a slide-out drawer? How many sinks are present, and what are the depth, shape, and so on? Note the type of faucet—single hole, center-set, or wide spread? Is there a soap dispenser, hot water dispenser, or garbage disposal? You get the idea. All fixture information should be documented. You may even wish to create a schedule for referencing existing fixtures and appliances when you do the initial drawings.

Take note of the existing backsplash. Is it tiled, stone, or back-painted glass? What are the cabinets made of? Are they wood, painted, or stained? Perhaps they are fabricated from Laminate or Therma-Foil, or have a high-gloss lacquer finish. Do the interiors have the same finish? Are there any glass-front cabinets?

Flooring details, especially transitions between spaces, are important to note as well. Are there saddles between the kitchen and the adjoining space(s), or does the flooring continue seamlessly? If saddles are present, what are they fabricated of?

Existing light fixtures and the location of junction boxes (J-boxes) for overhead lighting, pendant lighting, and under-cabinet lighting must also be noted for your electrical drawings of the existing conditions. This drawing is critical in getting a firm quote from the contractor on the electrical work needed in the renovation.

Having these details available makes moving forward, even in a full-gut renovation, a lot more manageable!

SURVEYS   **KITCHEN CHECKLIST**

<u>Plan Measurements</u>

☐ **Measure kitchen**

☐ **Baseboards and crown**

☐ **Window and door frame** (width and depth)

☐ **Ceiling height AFF** (Note if no finished floor exists at survey date.)

☐ **Ceiling details and dimensions** (soffit, slope, tray, and beams)

☐ **Wall/ceiling pocket details for drapery** (Measure width, length, and depth.)

☐ **Note and dimension sink pipe and gas pipe location on-center.**

☐ **Note and dimension cabinetry.**

☐ **Note and dimension furnishings to remain in space or to be repurposed.**

☐ **Note and dimension existing exposed wiring** (cable, wire chase, and so forth).

<u>Elevations</u>

☐ **Measure wall length and ceiling height AFF.** (Note if no finish floor exists at survey date.)

☐ **Measure baseboards and crown.**

☐ **Measure HVAC and/or radiators.**

☐ **Measure location of door and overall dimensions on elevation.** (Measure door height and width and trim width and lengths.)

☐ **Measure window interior and overall dimensions** (length × width × depth).

☐ **Measure mullions and windowsills** (height, width and depth/projection).

☐ **Note the style of the window.**

☐ **Measure height above window to ceiling.** (Note crown height.)

☐ **Note faucet clearance.** (How much room [height] do you have for a new faucet fixture?)

☐ **Measure existing cabinetry, fixtures, and appliances.**

☐ **Wall pocket details for drapery** (Measure width and height.)

<u>Electrical Measurements</u>

☐ **Note and dimension outlets, J-box, cable, Internet, and phone in kitchen.**

☐ **Note and dimension all lighting locations of ceiling lights and wall sconces.**

☐ **Note types and dimension outlets and switches** (duplex, quad, combo, ground-fault interrupter [GFI] for wet locations, dimmers, etc.).

☐ **Note and dimension fans, vents, radiators, HVAC, thermostats, and smoke alarms/detectors.**

<u>Photos to Include</u>

☐ **Overall room** (You may need two shots from different vantage points.)

☐ **Each elevation**

☐ **Ceiling details** (soffits, slopes, trays, beams, etc.)

☐ **Inside window frames and reveals, window pockets on wall or in ceiling**

☐ **Switches, outlets, thermostats, vents, HVAC, radiators, smoke alarms/detectors**

☐ **Crowns and baseboards**

☐ **Existing cabinetry, fixtures, and appliances**

☐ **Sink pipe and gas pipe if able to determine**

☐ **Any questionable items for general contractor (GC)**

☐ **Any furnishings remaining in the space or being repurposed**

<u>Hours Spent:</u>

PART II

Drawings

Drawings

CHAPTER 3

Residential and Contract Drawings

Introduction

Part II explores the details of the drawings. Here you will find checklists to assist all members of the design team in assembling the many details needed for a complete set of drawings.

The checklists are categorized according to the type of space you will be drawing. Then, within each checklist, information is provided on drawing details that are important for the plan and elevation components, facilitating even a new hire in your office culture to quickly learn what is expected of them when creating a drawing.

The goal is for you to select the appropriate drawing checklist, use it either in print or cloud format, and share it with others in your office. It is helpful if the person responsible for the drawing is named. The date the checklist is completed should be documented.

At this point, most design team members use computer-aided drafting (CAD) to develop drawings. It is best to create a template for drawings that contains all pertinent information such as the client's name, the location of the project, your company name, the title of the drawing, the date of the drawing, and any revision date(s). Develop your own nomenclature system for titling and/or numbering drawings. One possibility that works well to identify the appropriate drawings is to use "P" for plans, "E" for elevations, and "S" for sections.

Each space in a residential dwelling or a commercial office requires special considerations. For instance, if you are drawing an ADA-compliant bathroom, you need to be concerned with clearances, door swings, heights of various fixtures, incorporating appropriate blocking in the walls, the appropriate number of grab bars, and so on.

Cabinetry and other millwork designs, including kitchen design, are a subspecialty all their own, yet designers are often required to do the drawings for such cabinetry. The drawings are then refined by a cabinetmaker, depending on whether you are purchasing custom or stock items.

A summary of suggested notes accompanies each checklist presented here. We advise you to read these notes before printing the checklist and beginning the respective drawing. The notes may prompt questions from younger team members and emerging professionals, helping to inform the decisions to be made in creating that particular drawing.

All told, drawings are the key to a successful design solution. They ignite the creative process and provide valuable information and details to the client, the builder, and the permitting authorities, as well as all other members of your team. The more carefully documented the drawing, the better the execution of your design intent.

General Room Drawings

One of the first assignments a design student receives in drafting class is to draw a floor plan of a room. Many readers are already well-versed in this task. The *plan view* should always be drawn first. This is the anchor of the drawing set. Once the plan view is solidified, and you have added all windows, doors, and openings, you can proceed to the elevations.

Drawing sets should always contain existing conditions and then design plans/alternative layouts and other changes you are proposing to the client in your design solution. Perhaps you want to move or take down a non-load-bearing wall? Or maybe you wish to enlarge the size of a window or door? All of these notes must appear in both the plan and the elevation view.

As designers, we have many standards that must be taken into consideration. For example, when drawing a main conversation area in a living room, you should leave adequate clearance for a person to enter the conversation area and also enough space between a cocktail table and seating. You should also make sure no seating components overlap when placed at a ninety-degree angle. You must leave clearance for opening the doors or drawers of all case goods and built-ins. You must not block the flow of air from an HVAC register or unit. If you are floating a conversation area in the center of a room, you must be sure to add floor outlets so that you will have adequate power available for lamps and your client's other media needs.

Because there are so many details involved in creating a drawing, we suggest that you print the following checklist for each and every space. Figures 3.1 to 3.5 show examples of General Room Drawings.

DRAWINGS   **GENERAL ROOM CHECKLIST**

Plan View

- ☐ **Show elevators if applicable.**
- ☐ **Show standard/pocket/sliding door details.** (Show swing or path with a dashed line.)
- ☐ **Show baseboards, radiators, and HVAC.** (Note air-conditioning vents. Look for wall, floor, and ceiling vents and ducts. Show using a dashed line if housed in existing cabinetry.)
- ☐ **Show ceiling details with dashed lines and notations** (soffit, slope, tray, coffers, and beams).
- ☐ **Note flooring transition heights.**
- ☐ **Show all windows and projection of sill/window seat.**
- ☐ **Show overall room dimensions and clearance dimensions.**
- ☐ **Label and dimension all new items** (width × depth × height, including area rugs).
- ☐ **Draw, label, and dimension all existing items to remain in the space** (width × depth × height).
- ☐ **Show wall sconces, table, and floor lamps.**
- ☐ **Show all ceiling lighting using the appropriate lighting layer or line weight.**

Plan View Electrical

- ☐ **Note and dimension all outlets, J-boxes, electrical boxes, cable, Internet, and phone jacks.** (Note existing locations because a location change may necessitate raising the magnetic board due to the switch and telephone jack's new location.)
- ☐ **Note and dimension new/existing outlets and switches.**
- ☐ **Note the type of outlets and switches** (duplex, quad, combo, dimmers, etc.).
- ☐ **Note and dimension fans, vents, radiators, HVAC, and ductwork.** (Call out the location if on wall or floor; should be dashed if on ceiling.)
- ☐ **Note and dimension all ceiling lighting, wall sconces, and under-cabinet lighting.** (This should be on the lighting layers in the drawing.)
- ☐ **Show furniture and/or cabinetry to indicate relationship to lighting and electrical.**

Reflected Ceiling Plan (RCP)

- ☐ **Show and dimension ceiling details with a solid line.**
- ☐ **Show ceiling lighting, label, and dimension.** (Use a lighting layer in the drawing.)
- ☐ **Create a lighting legend.** (See Figure 3.3.)
- ☐ **Show and dimension all built-in cabinetry as a solid line.**
- ☐ **Show any ceiling vents or other items on the ceiling.**

Switching Plan

- ☐ **Show a curved dashed line going from the switch to the coordinating light fixture or outlet.**

Elevations

- ☐ **Show baseboards, crown, door/window framing, HVAC, and radiators.**
- ☐ **Show outlets and switches, new and existing, and dimension on-center (OC).**
- ☐ **Draw and dimension sconces and wall lighting.**
- ☐ **Draw and dimension furniture and cabinetry including built-ins** (width and height).
- ☐ **Dimension ceiling heights and wall lengths in all elevations.**
- ☐ **Show and note the type of switch and/or outlet you will use including the following details where applicable: dimmer, lazy switch, slide; color and finish of outlets or switches.**

Hours Spent

Date Completed: ___/___/___

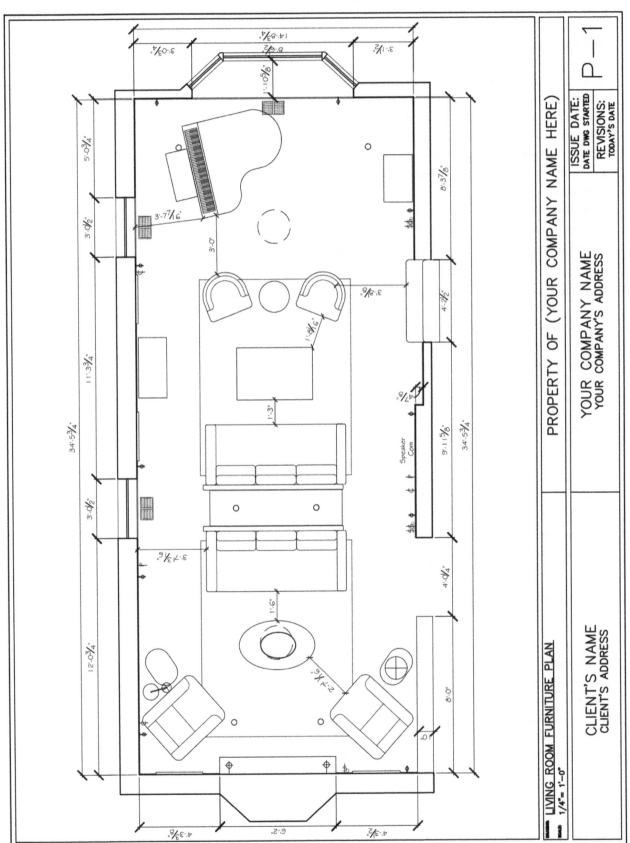

Figure 3.1 Furniture Plan

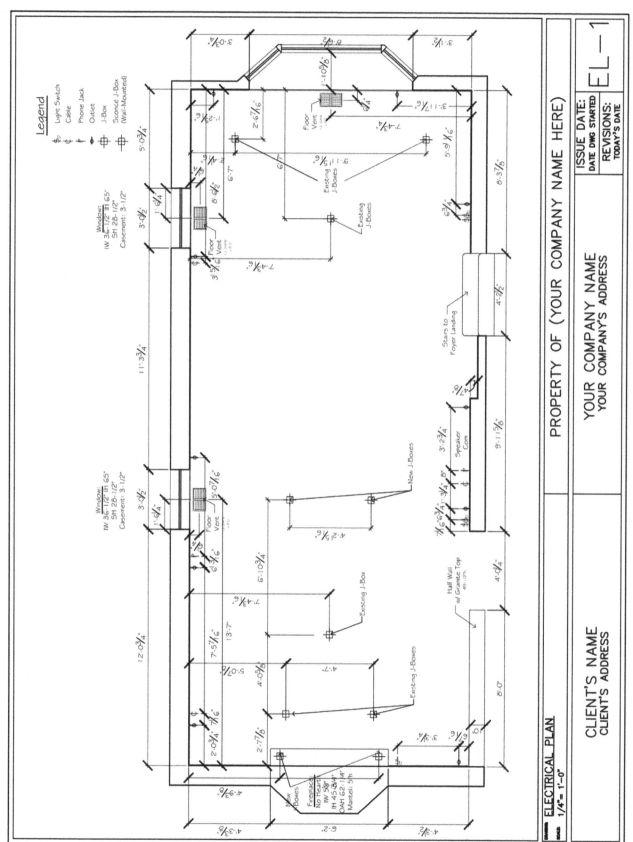

Figure 3.2 Electrical Plan

39

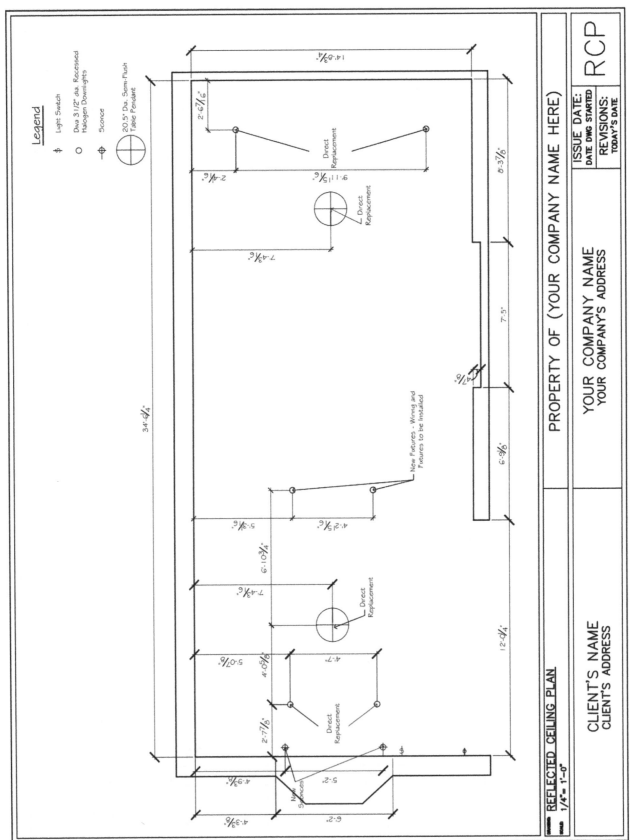

Figure 3.3 Reflected Ceiling Plan

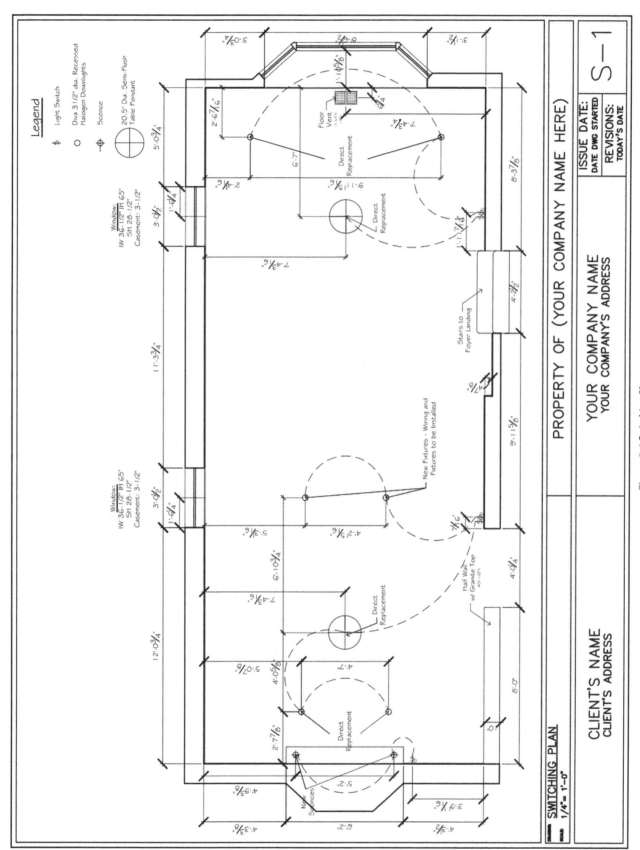

Figure 3.4 Switching Plan

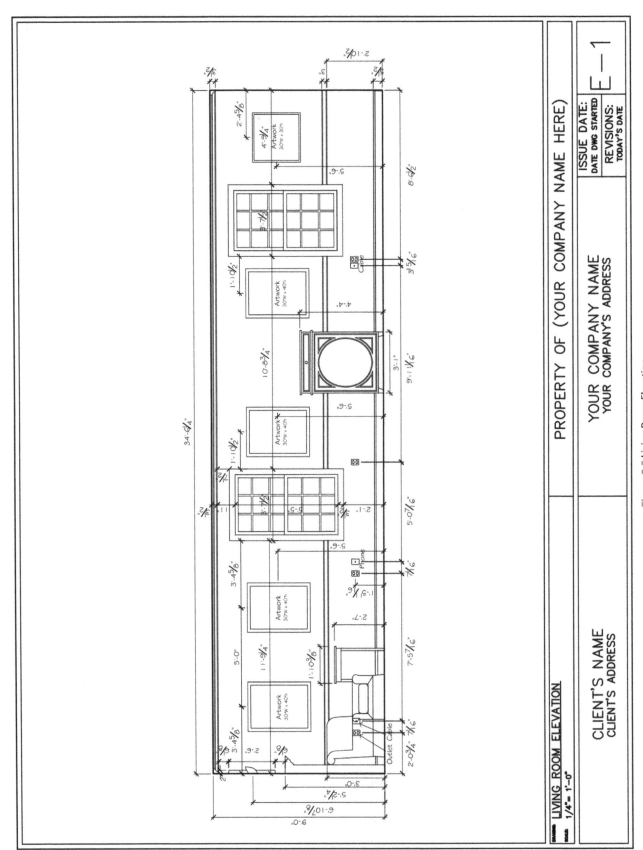

Figure 3.5 Living Room Elevation

Contract General Room Drawings

Contract or commercial drawings require additional details not always found in a residential set of drawings. The spaces are generally larger; thus, designers prefer to use 1/8" scale when printing or drafting a plan for a commercial space that is over 2,000 square feet so that more of the overall space can be easily viewed on one drawing sheet. Of course, larger-scale detail drawings are created for individual spaces and offices, but for an overall view the smaller scale works best.

Who should receive a set of drawings? Depending on your firm's specialty, you may send your drawings to the client; the landlord (if you work on lease projects); an information technology (IT) director and/or vendor; an audiovisual (AV) consultant; the project architect, expeditor, and engineer; and the furniture dealer. As you can see just from these examples, the list is long and each recipient will be interested not only in the plan but also in the schedules and the elevations, depending on their scope of work.

In a contract set of documents, you will generate a multitude of schedules and notes to accompany your plans: door and finish schedules, equipment schedules, and sections where necessary, and, of course, all other information found on a traditional drawing.

Drawings are generally produced by floor. Many corporate clients lease or own multiple floors in a building. Sometimes, a stair connects the spaces, which is a critical point to consider detailing in section and elevation, as well as in plan views.

Contract drawings must pay close attention to ADA requirements. It is now common practice to always shoot for universal design (UD) standards, as they are more generous and create a better design for all. Be sure to indicate the appropriate corridor widths; place signage and wall-mounted lighting at appropriate heights and clearances; and design baths, kitchens, and pantries to comply with Universal Building Code (UBC) requirements for commercial spaces.

You also need to be concerned with the means of egress. All exit doors must open *out*. Has the building been fitted with sprinklers? How many means of egress have been provided? If you are designing from scratch, you will also need to consult the International Building Code (IBC) and the local building codes to determine the appropriate means of egress.

Wheelchair accessibility must be considered when designing a commercial property. The general dimensions of a wheelchair are 30" × 48". Be sure that all design drawings can accommodate the passage of a wheelchair through all doorways/openings and confirm that you have indicated both the push-side (12") and pull-side (18") clearances upon approach to a door. Also determine whether a three-point turn or a 60" turnaround will provide the best transition from space to space.

In addition, consider outlets in private offices for small refrigerators and unusual appliances. Also consider putting all closets on jamb switches so the light comes on automatically when the doors open. These are little luxuries that make a project more special, and clients appreciate the attention to detail.

The checklist that follows gives more guided information about details that must be included in your drawing set. Figures 3.6 to 3.10 show examples of contract drawings.

Construction Plan

☐ **Show standard/pocket/sliding doors.** (Show the swing/path with a dashed line. Minimum clearance of an egress door when open at 90 degrees is 32"; maximum width is 48".)

☐ **Show baseboards, radiators, and HVAC.** (Note AC, wall, floor, ceiling vents, and ducts. Use dashed lines if housed in existing cabinetry.)

☐ **Note flooring transitions.**

☐ **Show ceiling details with dashed lines and notations** (soffit, slope, tray, and beams).

☐ **Show all windows and projection of sills.**

☐ **Show overall room dimensions and clearance dimensions.**

☐ **Be sure to allow for a 60" wheelchair turnaround in all spaces.**

☐ **Doors: Leave 18" minimum clearance on the pull side and 12" on the push side.**

☐ **Show overall corridor dimensions.** (Corridors must be a minimum of 36" wide.)

☐ **Avoid dead-end corridors.** (Check IBC updates for current maximum lengths.)

☐ **A space needs two means of egress if over 7,500 square feet.**

Reflected Ceiling Plan (RCP) and Lighting Specifications

☐ **Show and dimension ceiling details with a solid line and note all ceiling heights.**

☐ **Show ceiling lighting, label, and dimension.** (Use the lighting layer in the drawing.)

☐ **Show all switch locations and note switch type.** (Identify single, three-way, dimmers, etc.)

☐ **Note occupancy sensor locations.**

☐ **Create a coordinating lighting legend.** (See Figure 3.7)

☐ **Show and dimension all built-in cabinetry as a solid line.**

☐ **Show any ceiling grid, ceiling vents, detectors, or other items on the ceiling.**

Architectural Power, and Voice/Data Plan

☐ **Note and dimension outlets, J-box, cable, Internet, and phone in the space.**

☐ **Note and dimension new/existing outlets and switches. Note type** (duplex, quad, etc.).

☐ **Show furniture/systems to indicate relationship to power and data locations.**

Finish Plan

☐ **Using symbols, create a materials specification legend that corresponds with your plan.**

Furniture Plan

☐ **Label and dimension all new items** (all furnishings width × depth × height).

☐ **Draw, label, and dimension all items remaining in the space** (width × depth × height).

☐ **Leave 18" to 24" between any cocktail table and seating. Leave space for a wheelchair.**

☐ **Leave 42" between the back of a desk and the front of a credenza in a workstation.**

☐ **Show ADA-compliant wall sconces, desk and floor lamps.**

Elevations

☐ **Show baseboards, crown, door/window framing, fans, vents, thermostats, smoke alarms/detectors, HVAC, and radiators.** (Use the elevation layers in the drawing.)

☐ **Draw and dimension luminaires, outlets and switches, new and existing, and dimension OC.**

☐ **Draw and dimension systems/furniture and cabinetry including built-ins** (width and height).

☐ **Dimension ceiling heights and wall widths in all elevations.**

Hours Spent

Date Completed: ____/____/____

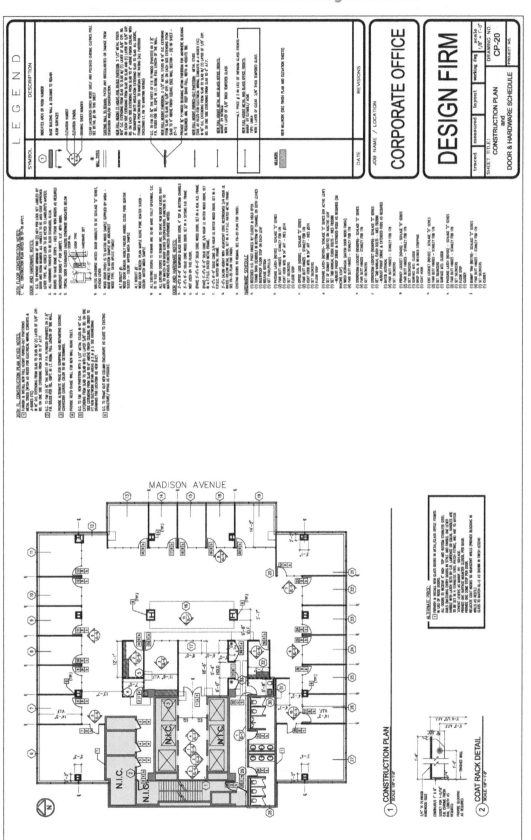

Figure 3.6 Construction Plan

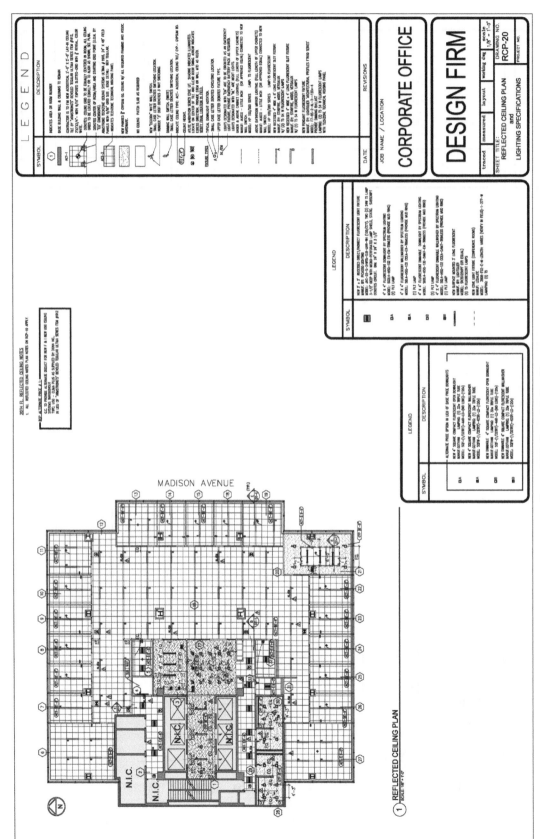

Figure 3.7 Reflected Ceiling Plan

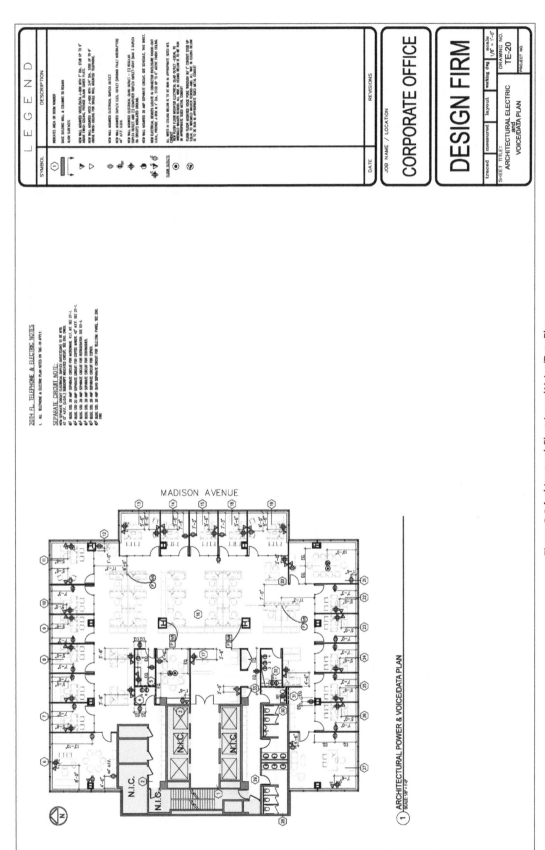

Figure 3.8 Architectural, Electric, and Voice/Data Plan

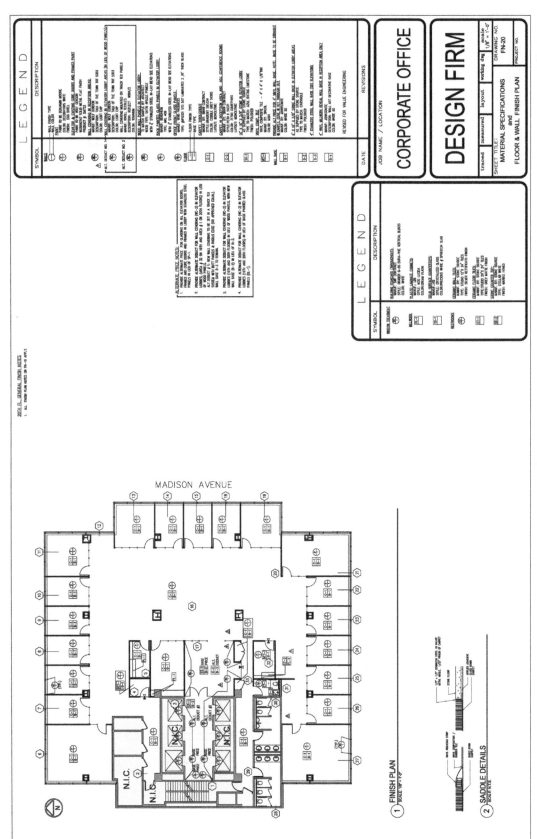

Figure 3.9 Finish Plan

48

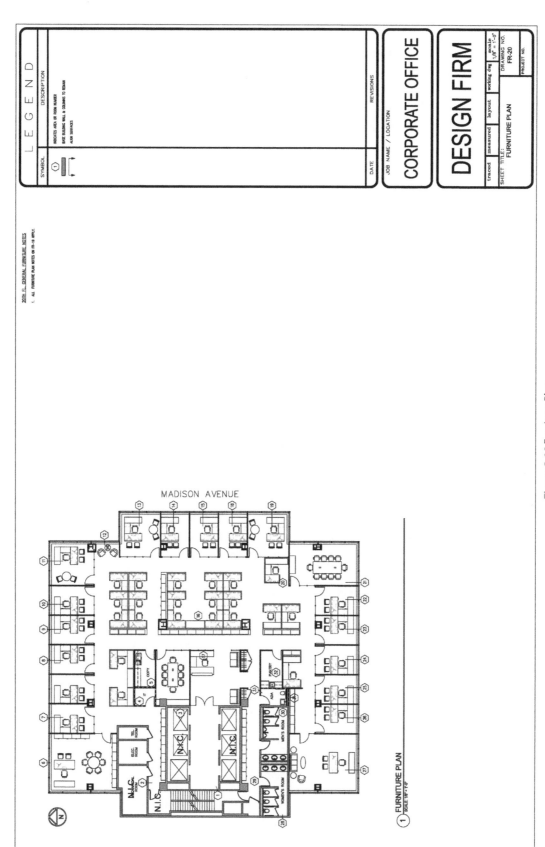

Figure 3.10 Furniture Plan

Residential Bathroom Drawings

Drawing a residential bathroom requires a great deal of attention to detail. Not only are you concerned with the general drawing information, but in a bathroom you are required to note all existing fixtures and locations of pipes, drains, toilet stacks, tile to be saved or demolished, and so on.

You should also know whether or not you have any room in the ceiling to add lighting and investigate whether the wall is thick enough for a recessed/flush-mount medicine cabinet (if one does not already exist) so that you know the design parameters related to this space.

When drawing the existing conditions, note the height of the existing tub, shower curb, towel bars, toilet paper holder, showerhead, and so on, as this information can be helpful in the design intent drawings you will be creating. It is great to have these dimensions for reference, even if your ideas lead you to a different design solution.

When drawing, the plan is, of course, the road map, but the elevations in a bathroom are of equal importance. They are chock full of information. These drawings are most helpful when the design/build team is bringing the project to life through construction.

Be mindful of all electrical components. Always do a switching plan and try to put all sconces and overhead lighting on dimmers for more control. All outlets must be ground-fault interrupt (GFI) and labeled as such. Convenience outlets are also an important component. You may want to specify an outlet near a toilet so an electronically controlled bidet seat (such as the TOTO Washlet®) can be installed. This is important anywhere that the client may need power—for example, for using a blow dryer or electric razor. For illuminated magnifying mirrors, a hardwired installation is preferred.

Of special importance are tile elevations. A tile elevation should be plan projected for each wall, showing details where there are outside corners, necessary bullnose or pencil finishing details, windowsills, vanity heights for chair rails, and so on. Always create a tile RCP if you are tiling for a steam shower. This is a critical element.

Try to align fixtures so that they fall on grout lines wherever possible, and center the shower glass on the curb. Endeavor to plan the shower height to be appropriate for taller/shorter clients for ease of use. Installing a hand shower when the budget permits is highly recommended, as it creates another water source and makes cleaning a tub or shower so much easier for the client. It is also a great assist when bathing children.

Note all fixture and tile info on elevations and plans where appropriate. Figures 3.11 to 3.22 show examples of residential bath drawings.

DRAWINGS   **RESIDENTIAL BATHROOM CHECKLIST**

Plan View

- ☐ **Show standard/pocket/cabinet door.** (Show the swing or path with a dashed line.)
- ☐ **Show baseboards, radiators, and HVAC, fans, thermostat, smoke alarm/detectors, and steam controls.** (Note wall/floor/ceiling vents and ducts.)
- ☐ **Show ceiling details with dashed lines and notations** (soffit, slope, tray, and beams).
- ☐ **Show all windows and projection of sill/window seat.**
- ☐ **Show overall room dimensions and clearance dimensions.**
- ☐ **Show sink pipe location, toilet pipe, and stack locations.**
- ☐ **Show and dimension all wall-mounted and ceiling lighting locations.**
- ☐ **Draw and dimension medicine cabinets:** (Note recess or flush-mount; left/right door swing.)
- ☐ **Indicate locations of shower and tub fixtures.**
- ☐ **Show location of shower/tub drain, curb, saddle, ledge, niches, and accessories.**
- ☐ **Show and dimension the vanity top; add the sink and faucet.** (Check clearances.)

Plan View Electrical

- ☐ **Note and dimension outlets, J-box, electrical box, cable, and phone jack.**
- ☐ **Note and dimension new/existing outlets and switches.**
- ☐ **Note the type of outlets and switches** (duplex, quad, combo, GFI, dimmers, etc.).
- ☐ **Note and dimension fans, vents, radiators, and ductwork.** (Note the location if on a wall or the floor; line should be dashed if on the ceiling.)
- ☐ **Note and dimension all ceiling lighting, wall sconces, and under-cabinet lighting.**
- ☐ **Show fixtures and cabinetry to indicate lighting and fixture/cabinet relationships.**

Reflected Ceiling Plan (RCP)

- ☐ **Show and dimension ceiling details with solid lines.**
- ☐ **Show ceiling lighting, label, dimension, and create a lighting legend.** (See Figure 3.15)
- ☐ **Show and dimension all built-in cabinetry as a solid line.**
- ☐ **Show any ceiling vents or other items on the ceiling.**

Switching Plan

- ☐ **Show a curved dashed line going from the switch to the coordinating light fixture or outlet.**
- ☐ **Make sure to create a coordinating lighting legend.** (See Figure 3.16)

Elevations

- ☐ **Show baseboards, crown, and door/window framing.**
- ☐ **Show outlets and switches, new and existing, and dimension on-center** (OC).
- ☐ **Draw and dimension sconces/wall lighting** (typical height is 5'0" to 5'6").
- ☐ **Draw and dimension furniture, cabinetry, and fixtures** (width and height).
- ☐ **Show and note hardware and hinges** (manufacturer, item number, finish).
- ☐ **Draw and dimension medicine cabinet.** (Typical height to bottom is 48" AFF.)
- ☐ **Draw and dimension shower and tub fixtures.**
- ☐ **Show curb, saddle, ledge, niches, and accessories.** (Include on tile elevations as well.)
- ☐ **Dimension ceiling heights and wall widths.**
- ☐ **Show and note the type of switch(es) and outlet(s) including the following details where applicable: dimmer, lazy switch, slide, color, and finish.**

Hours Spent

Date Completed: ____/____/____

Residential Bathroom Drawing References

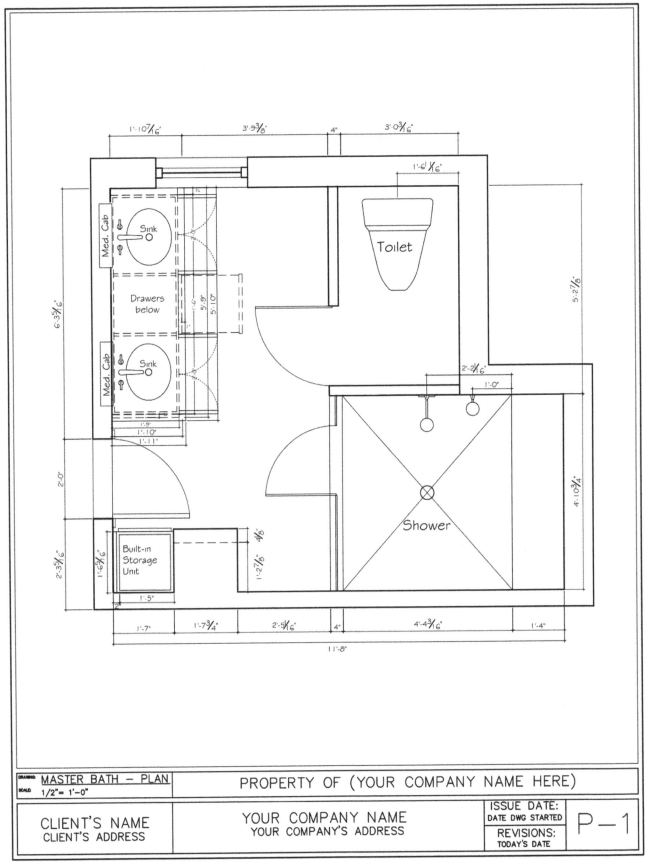

Figure 3.11 Master Bath—Plan

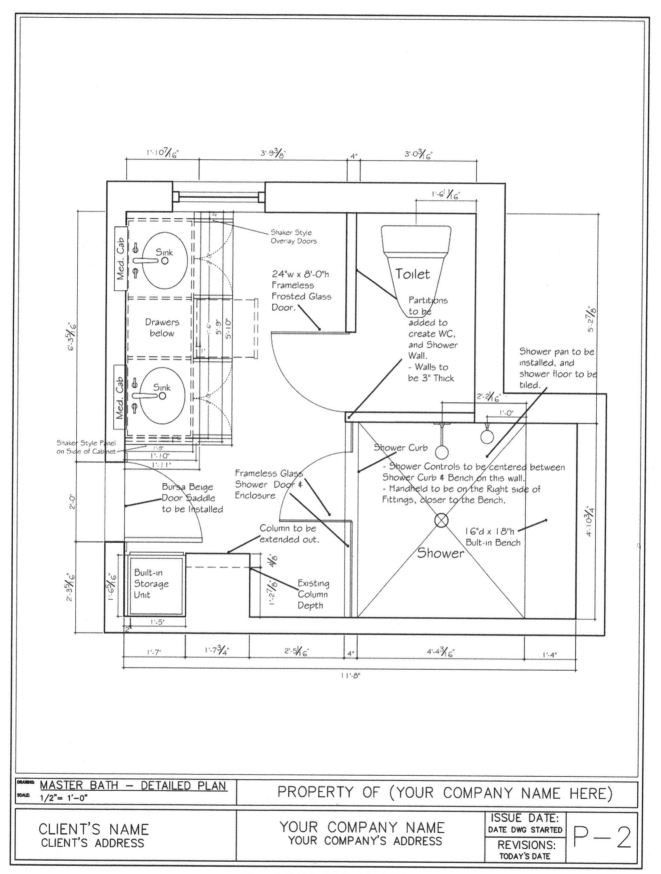

Figure 3.12 Master Bath—Detailed Plan

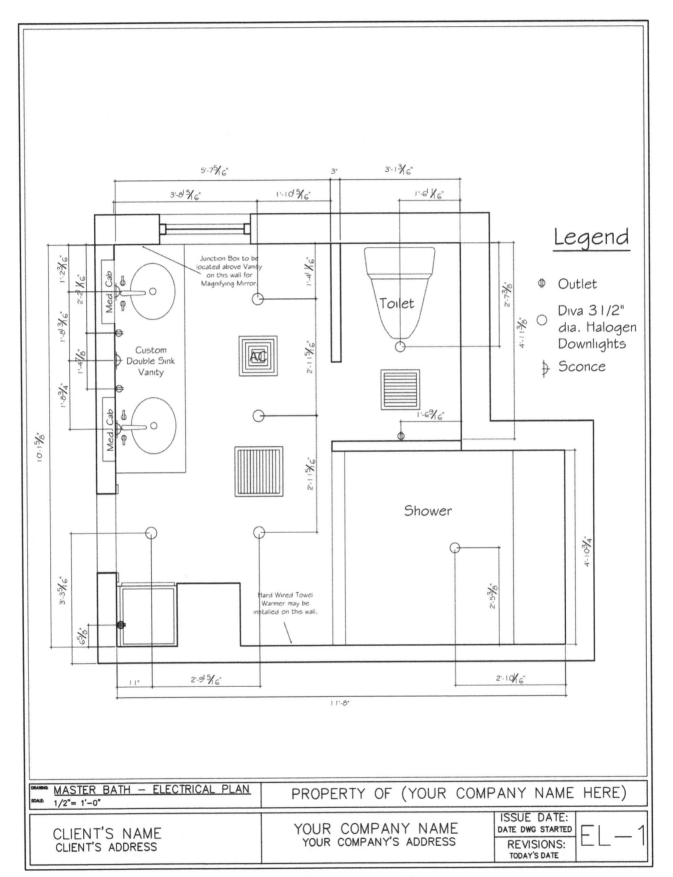

Figure 3.13 Master Bath—Electrical Plan

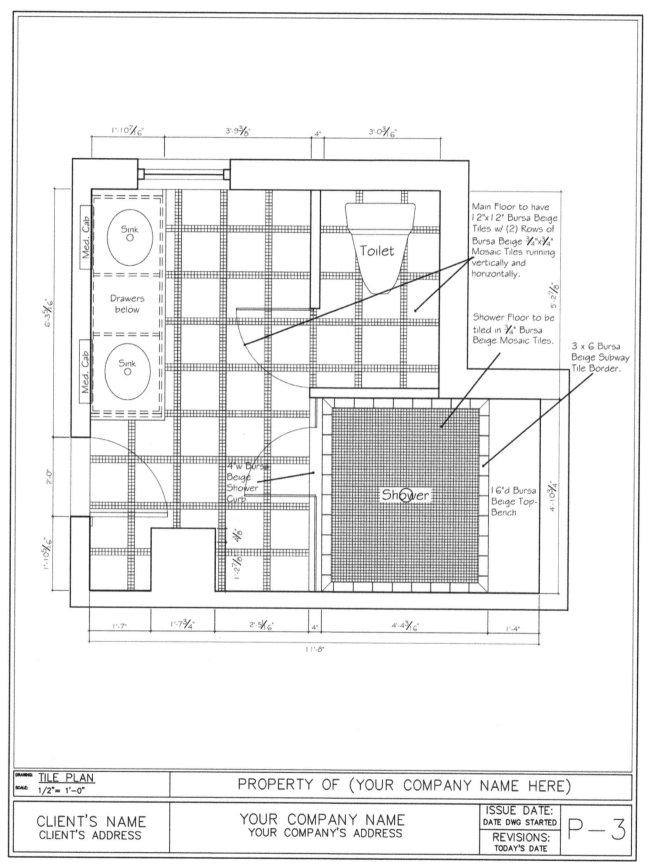

Main Floor to have
12"x12" Bursa Beige
Tiles w/ (2) Rows of
Bursa Beige ¾"x¾"
Mosaic Tiles running
vertically and
horizontally.

Shower Floor to be
tiled in ¾" Bursa
Beige Mosaic Tiles.

3 x 6 Bursa
Beige Subway
Tile Border.

16"d Bursa
Beige Top-
Bench

Med. Cab

Sink

Drawers
below

Med. Cab

Sink

Toilet

Shower

4"w Bursa
Beige
Shower
Curb

1'-10⁷⁄₁₆"   3'-9³⁄₈"   4"   3'-0³⁄₁₆"

5'-2⁷⁄₈"

6'-3³⁄₁₆"

2'-0"

1'-10⁵⁄₁₆"

4⁵⁄₈"

1'-2⁷⁄₈"

4'-10³⁄₄"

1'-7"   1'-7³⁄₄"   2'-5¹⁄₁₆"   4"   4'-4³⁄₁₆"   1'-4"

11'-8"

DRAWING: TILE PLAN	PROPERTY OF (YOUR COMPANY NAME HERE)	
SCALE: 1/2"= 1'-0"		
CLIENT'S NAME CLIENT'S ADDRESS	YOUR COMPANY NAME YOUR COMPANY'S ADDRESS	ISSUE DATE: DATE DWG STARTED
		REVISIONS: TODAY'S DATE

P—3

Figure 3.14 Master Bath—Tile Plan

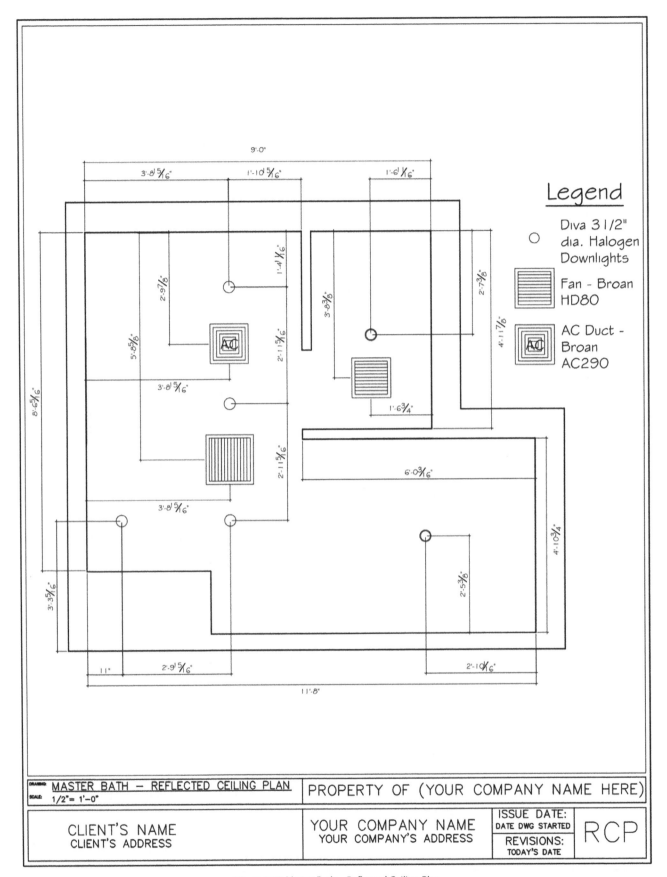

Figure 3.15 Master Bath—Reflected Ceiling Plan

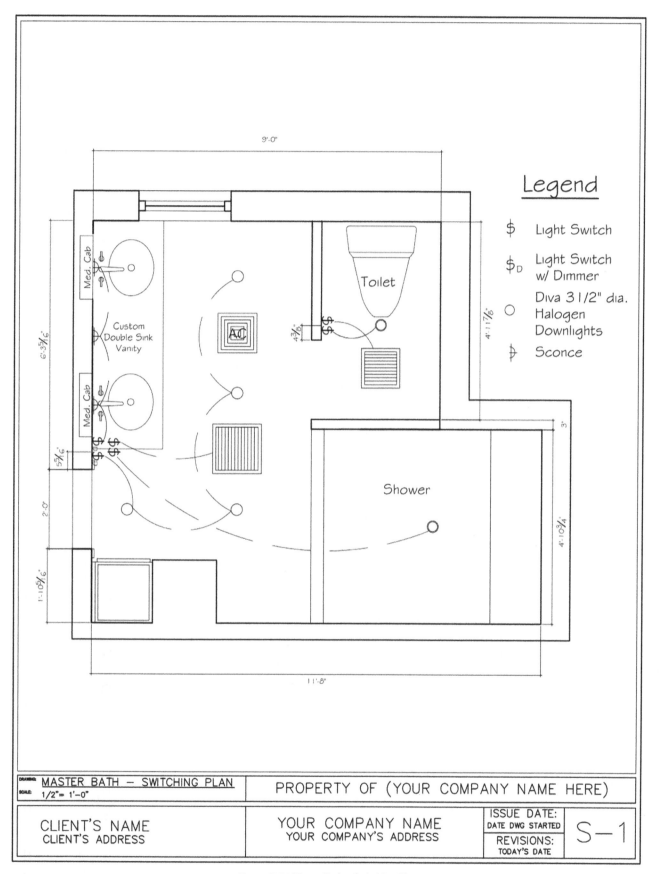

Figure 3.16 Master Bath—Switching Plan

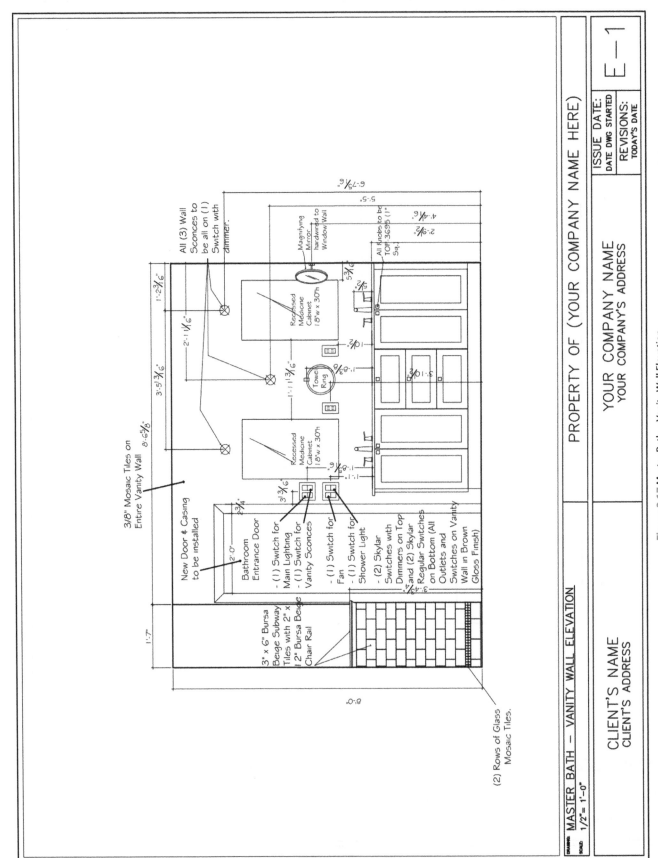

Figure 3.17 Master Bath—Vanity Wall Elevation

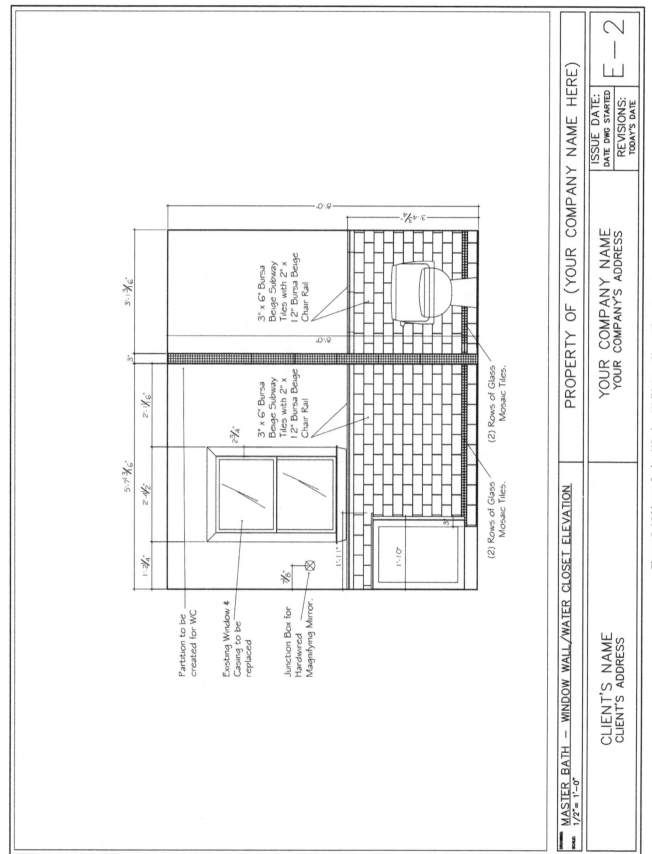

MASTER BATH — WINDOW WALL/WATER CLOSET ELEVATION
SCALE: 1/2" = 1'-0"

3" x 6" Bursa Beige Subway Tiles with 2" x 12" Bursa Beige Chair Rail

3" x 6" Bursa Beige Subway Tiles with 2" x 12" Bursa Beige Chair Rail

(2) Rows of Glass Mosaic Tiles.

(2) Rows of Glass Mosaic Tiles.

Partition to be created for WC

Existing Window & Casing to be replaced

Junction Box for Hardwired Magnifying Mirror.

PROPERTY OF (YOUR COMPANY NAME HERE)

E-2

ISSUE DATE:
DATE DWG STARTED

REVISIONS:
TODAY'S DATE

YOUR COMPANY NAME
YOUR COMPANY'S ADDRESS

CLIENT'S NAME
CLIENT'S ADDRESS

Figure 3.18 Master Bath—Window Wall/Water Closet Elevation

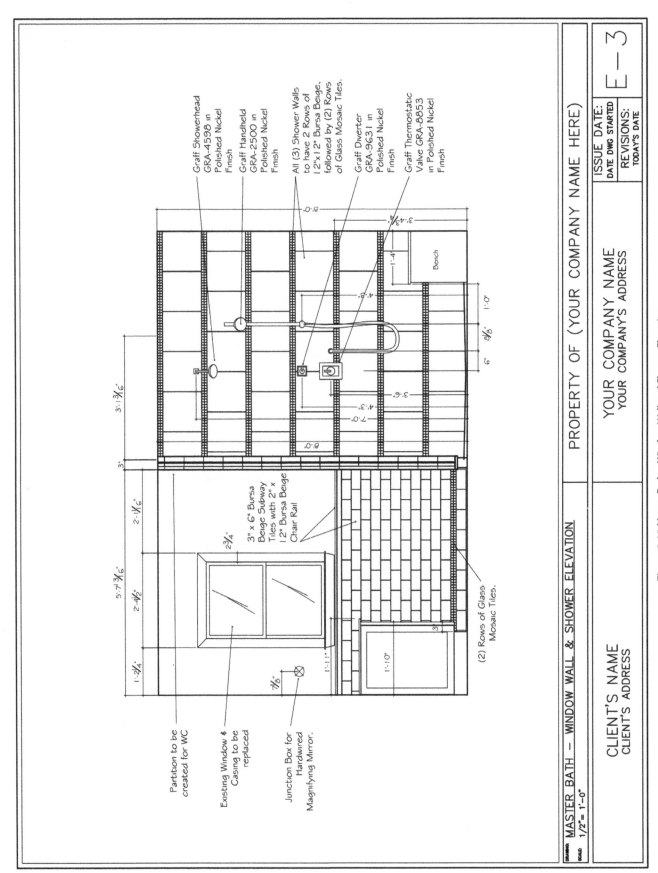

Figure 3.19 Master Bath—Window Wall and Shower Elevation

60

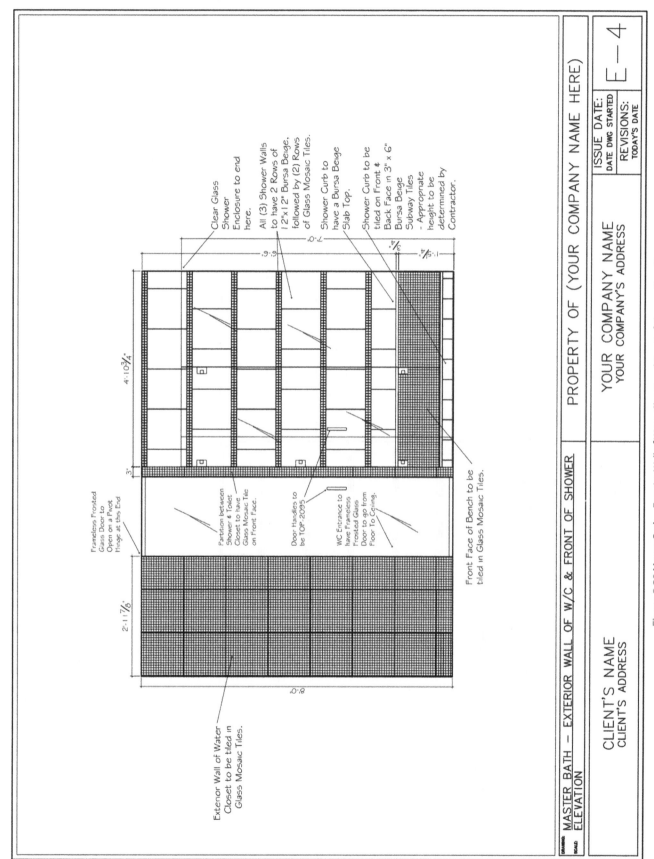

E — 4

ISSUE DATE:
DATE DWG STARTED
REVISIONS:
TODAY'S DATE

Clear Glass
Shower
Enclosure to end
here.

All (3) Shower Walls
to have 2 Rows of
12"x12" Bursa Beige,
followed by (2) Rows
of Glass Mosaic Tiles.

Shower Curb to
have a Bursa Beige
Slab Top.

Shower Curb to be
tiled on Front &
Back Face in 3" x 6"
Bursa Beige
Subway Tiles
- Appropriate
height to be
determined by
Contractor.

Frameless Frosted
Glass Door to
Open on a Pivot
Hinge at this End

Partition between
Shower & Toilet
Closet to have
Glass Mosaic Tile
on Front Face.

Door Handles to
be TOP 2095

WC Entrance to
have Frameless
Frosted Glass
Door to go from
Floor to Ceiling.

Front Face of Bench to be
tiled in Glass Mosaic Tiles.

Exterior Wall of Water
Closet to be tiled in
Glass Mosaic Tiles.

MASTER BATH – EXTERIOR WALL OF W/C & FRONT OF SHOWER
ELEVATION

DRAWING
SCALE

YOUR COMPANY NAME
YOUR COMPANY'S ADDRESS

CLIENT'S NAME
CLIENT'S ADDRESS

Figure 3.20 Master Bath—Exterior Wall of Water Closet and Front of Shower Elevation

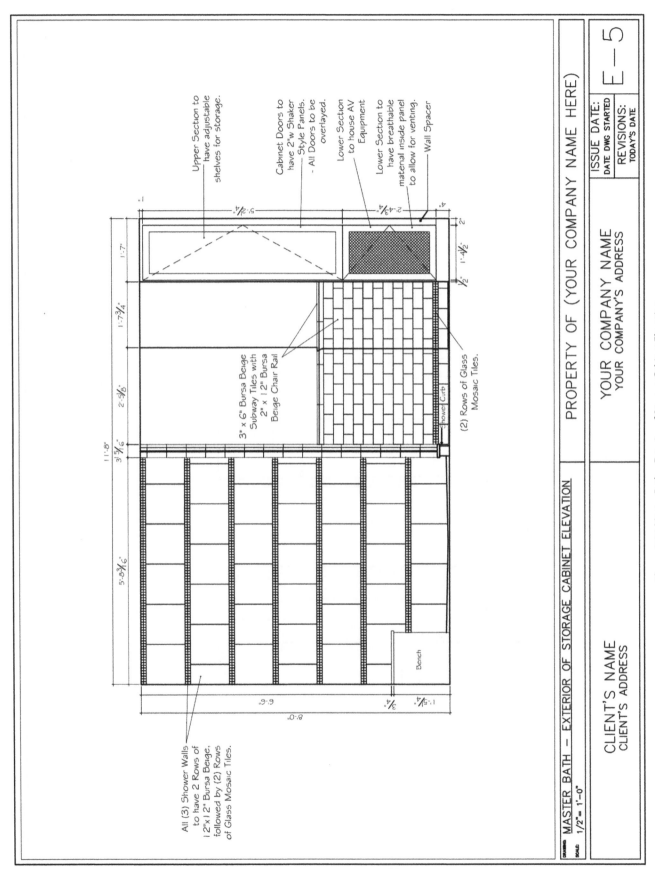

Figure 3.21 Master Bath—Exterior of Storage Cabinet Elevation

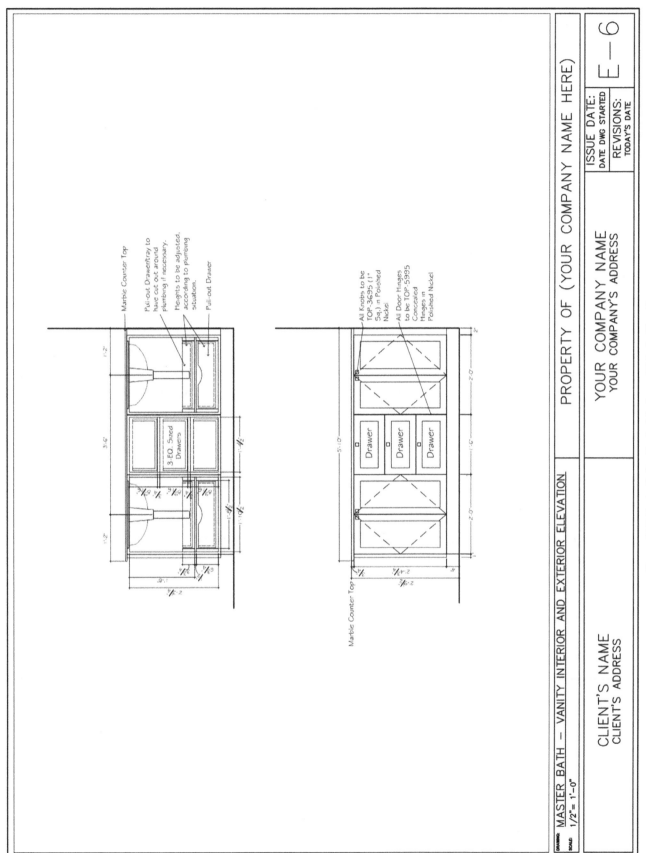

Figure 3.22 Master Bath—Vanity Interior and Exterior Elevation

ADA Bathroom Drawings

In addition to all drawing requirements for residential bathrooms, there are a number of additional steps that must be taken for ADA-compliant bathrooms in order to comply with the building code in the client's jurisdiction. Code requires that certain design elements be provided in both plan and elevation. (Figures 3.23 to 3.25 show examples of ADA-compliant drawings.)

You should begin by referencing the Residential Bathroom Drawing Checklist at the beginning of this section. There is a wealth of information here to help you create a complete set of drawings.

The checklist that follows details information on accessibility issues and appropriate clearances, notes on barrier-free shower enclosures, lighting, sensory cues, and so on. It is important to remember that the ADA references not only persons with mobility challenges but all people with physical and cognitive challenges. The challenge may refer to sight or a hearing impairment, or loss of memory—for example, Alzheimer's patients may lose their ability to remember how to perform basic functions such as bathing.

Elevations are critical in ADA-compliant bathroom drawings. They provide information about necessary heights for mounting lavatories, toilets, grab bars, shower controls, mirrors, and other fixtures and fittings. In the ADA-compliant bathroom drawing, these elements are critical to completing the drawing set.

It is wise to attempt to incorporate the concepts of universal and barrier-free design. This is becoming more commonplace when designing for all persons regardless of their physical and cognitive abilities. Do we not all appreciate the elevator, the motorized walkway, ramps, and curbless shower enclosures? Ease of entry to a space is a welcome and sometimes necessary design element.

Many designers work with clients who are baby boomers, which is a huge demographic in our society. Many baby boomers prefer to age in place and want the comforts of home rather than an institutional feeling in their abode.

By planning the details in the design phase, you can create a bathroom that will be accessible to all people, whether or not they are dealing with a physical challenge. If the bathroom dimensions are tight, space can actually be gained in the footprint of an accessible shower, as the need for a 5″ curb is eliminated. Supports and blocking can be installed behind the Sheetrock so that if grab bars are needed in the future, all current tile work will remain intact, making installation a breeze.

The entire floor should be treated as if it were a "wet" location. Installing an additional drain and creating the appropriate pitch throughout the space, adds to the success of a well-planned design. Custom vanities can be designed or specified as wall-hung, allowing for a wheelchair to comfortably access the controls with adequate clearance for the footrest. Install a convenience outlet near a toilet so an electronic bidet such as the TOTO Washlet® (bidet seat) can be installed.

Universal design allows the designer to program spaces to meet the needs of all users, no matter their physical or mental challenges. This is the wave of our future and the designer's responsibility to the client—great design for *all*!

DRAWINGS

ADA BATHROOM DRAWING CHECKLIST

General

☐ Use a dashed 60"-diameter circle to show the capability for wheelchair turnaround in an open space.

☐ Toilet stalls must have a toe clearance below the front partition and at least one side partition (a minimum of 9" AFF).

☐ Provide a minimum of 32"-width clearance for a straight approach into the bathroom. If the wheelchair needs to turn, a minimum of 36"-width clearance is needed.

Shower/Tub

☐ Draw and dimension the shower with a minimum of 30" × 60" not including a threshold.

☐ Draw and dimension roll-in showers, minimum of 36" × 36" with seat installed (can be a flip-up seat) opposite the shower controls.

☐ The shower seat should be between 17" and 19" AFF.

☐ The curb (if one exists) must not exceed 1/2" in height.

☐ The shower spray must have a 60" hose for fixed or handheld use.

☐ All grab bars should be shown and dimensioned (See Figures 3.23 and 3.24).

Toilet

☐ Urinals should be 17" from the floor to the top of the bowl.

☐ Toilet should be a wall-hung and comfort-height. (Seat must be between 17" to 19" AFF.)

☐ Toilets should be mounted 18" OC from the sidewall.

☐ The grab bars must be mounted horizontally between 33" and 36" AFF.

☐ The side grab bar must be a minimum of 40" long and mounted 12" from the rear wall.

☐ The rear grab bar must be 36" minimum and located at least 6" from the side wall.

☐ Grab bars must have a diameter of 1 1/4" to 1 1/2" and be able to hold a 250-pound load.

☐ In a bathroom stall, you need 60" turnaround for maneuvering a wheelchair.

Sink

☐ The top of an ADA sink must be 34" AFF. The knee-room clearance underneath the sink should be a minimum of 27" high, 30" wide, and 19" deep.

☐ Note that pipes should be insulated and padded (wrapped) if exposed below the sink.

☐ A shallow lavatory should be specified for ease of use (no deeper than 6.5").

☐ Use lever handles for faucets (preferably single handle), or motion-sensors.

Doors, Handles, Locks

☐ The door should not have a raised threshold or saddle. The flooring outside and inside the bathroom should be level.

☐ Door handles and locks should be shown and dimensioned no higher than 48" AFF.

☐ Doors must not require more than 5 pounds of force to open and be 7' high (minimum).

Accessories

☐ Mirrors should be mounted at 40" AFF (to the bottom of the mirror).

☐ Trash receptacle openings should be located between 15" and 48" AFF.

☐ Fixtures should be mounted in lower positions to accommodate limited reach while sitting; 48" AFF is the maximum for any forward and side reaching.

Hours Spent

Date Completed: ____/____/____

ADA Bathroom References

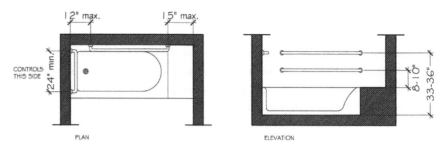

PLAN   ELEVATION

Figure 3.23 ADA Elevation and Plan

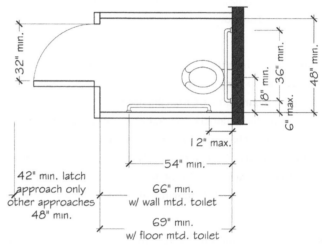

Figure 3.24 ADA Toilet Dimensions

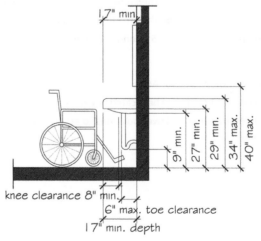

Figure 3.25 ADA Considerations for Sink and Mirror

Kitchen Drawings

Creating a set of drawings for a kitchen is one of the most complex tasks we have as designers. There are so many considerations: cabinetry placement, plumbing, lighting, tile layouts, breakfast area, appliance locations, and so on.

First, you need to document the existing conditions very carefully. This requires a full set of photos from every elevation in addition to close-ups to document any special conditions such as soffits, beams, electrical considerations, and gas pipe locations if visible. Generally, a designer will do the initial planning and offer alternative layouts, but it is highly recommended that the initial plans then be given to a custom kitchen designer or manufacturer so that all the details can be articulated.

Convenience outlets are an important consideration as well in an appliance garage, and inside a cabinet with a slide-out shelf for small appliance connections. Install one on each end of an island or peninsula for ease of use. It makes life so much easier.

All appliances come with certain specifications and clearance guidelines that must be followed in order for them to function properly. Installing a counter-depth refrigerator requires a filler (or two if it is a double-door or French door model) if other cabinetry or a wall is on either side of the appliance. If you are installing a restaurant-quality range, you need to follow the electrical guidelines for power to the range.

Gas lines in apartment dwellings generally cannot be moved, and you must inquire about building regulations on all plumbing and electrical guidelines before designing the space. Many buildings have gas risers and electrical outlet power limitations, and so forth, that must be respected.

The distance between the base cabinets is also an important design detail. Generally, mount a wall-hung cabinet 18" above the countertop. This is a standard, but often in custom cabinetry a client of higher stature or one who is, shall we say, vertically challenged may want to tweak these standard dimensions to their own personal preferences.

Lighting is also a critical element in a kitchen design. Think about a layered lighting solution—one that includes ambient, task, and accent lighting. Ambient or general illumination can be achieved by using overhead lighting, recessed ceiling fixtures, or track lighting. Task lighting will be needed as well. Under-cabinet strip lighting or "hockey pucks" provide illumination for work at the countertop and stove. A pendant provides light for eating and other culinary adventures. Accent lighting is an important layer, providing emphasis and focus in a space. Illuminating the interior of a cabinet or adding directional lighting to highlight artwork or objects above the cabinetry adds excitement and drama to a kitchen. In universal design, many professionals are opting for illuminated kick bases to provide the visually impaired with an illuminated alert as they near the cabinetry. The choices are endless, but the details are imperative.

Figures 3.26 to 3.31 show examples of kitchen drawings, and Figure 3.32 shows an example of a 3D kitchen sketch.

Furniture Plan

☐ **Show standard/pocket/sliding door.** (Show the swing or path with a dashed line.)

☐ **Show baseboards, radiators, and HVAC, fans, thermostat, and smoke alarm/detectors.** (Note wall/floor/ceiling vents and ducts. Use dashed lines if housed in existing cabinetry.)

☐ **Show ceiling details with dashed lines and notations** (soffit, slope, tray, and beams).

☐ **Show all windows and projection of sill/window seat.**

☐ **Note faucet clearance.** (How much room is there for a new faucet?)

☐ **Show overall room dimensions and clearance dimensions.**

☐ **Draw, label, and dimension all new items** (furniture and appliances, width × depth × height).

☐ **Draw, label, and dimension all existing items that will remain in the space.**

☐ **Show appliance door swings and cabinet doors/drawers open using dashed lines.**

☐ **Show cabinet at 24" depth dashed. Use a solid line to indicate counter overhang.**

☐ **Include fillers where needed.** (Check appliance specs for filler and space requirements.)

☐ **Show sink and gas pipe location** (dimensioned on-center [OC]).

☐ **Show lamps, pendants, and wall sconces** (locations to be dimensioned OC).

Electrical Plan

☐ **Note and dimension outlets, J-box, cable, Internet, and phone in the room.**

☐ **Note and dimension outlets and switches. Note type** (duplex, quad, GFI, dimmers, etc.).

☐ **Note and dimension fans, vents, radiators, HVAC, and ductwork/soffits.**

☐ **Note and dimension all ceiling lighting, wall sconces, and under-cabinet lighting.**

☐ **Show cabinetry on this drawing to indicate electrical and cabinet relationships.**

Reflected Ceiling Plan (RCP)

☐ **Show and dimension ceiling details** (including vents and other items).

☐ **Show ceiling lights, label, and dimension. Create a lighting legend.** (See Figure 3.29)

☐ **Show and dimension all built-in cabinetry using solid lines.**

Switching Plan

☐ **Show a curved dashed line going from the switch to the coordinating light fixture or outlet.** (See Figure 3.30 for Switching Plan example.)

Elevations

☐ **Show kick base, baseboards/crown/door/window framing, HVAC, and radiators.**

☐ **Show outlets and switches, new and existing, and dimension on-center (OC).**

☐ **Draw and dimension sconces—wall lighting**

☐ **Draw and dimension furniture, cabinetry, appliances, and fixtures** (width and height).

☐ **Show and note hardware and hinges** (manufacturer, item number, finish).

☐ **Countertop thickness or height is 1.25" typical.**

☐ **Draw cabinet doors/sides. Extend to conceal under-cabinet lighting.**

☐ **Dimension ceiling heights and wall widths.**

☐ **Show and note the type of switches and outlets you will be using, including the following details where applicable: dimmer, lazy switch, slide, color, and finish, etc.**

Hours Spent

Date Completed: ____/____/____

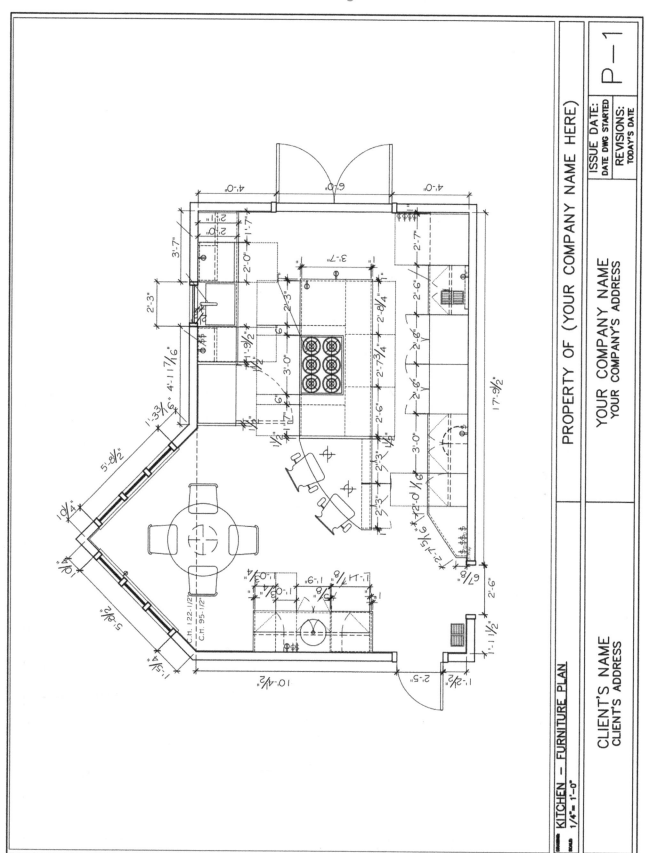

Figure 3.26 Kitchen—Furniture Plan

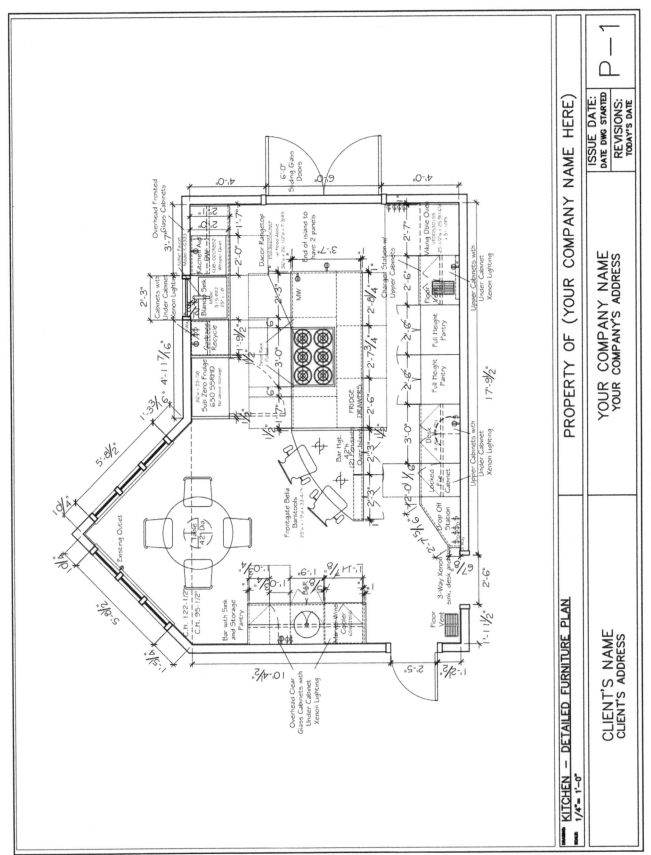

Figure 3.27 Kitchen—Detailed Furniture Plan

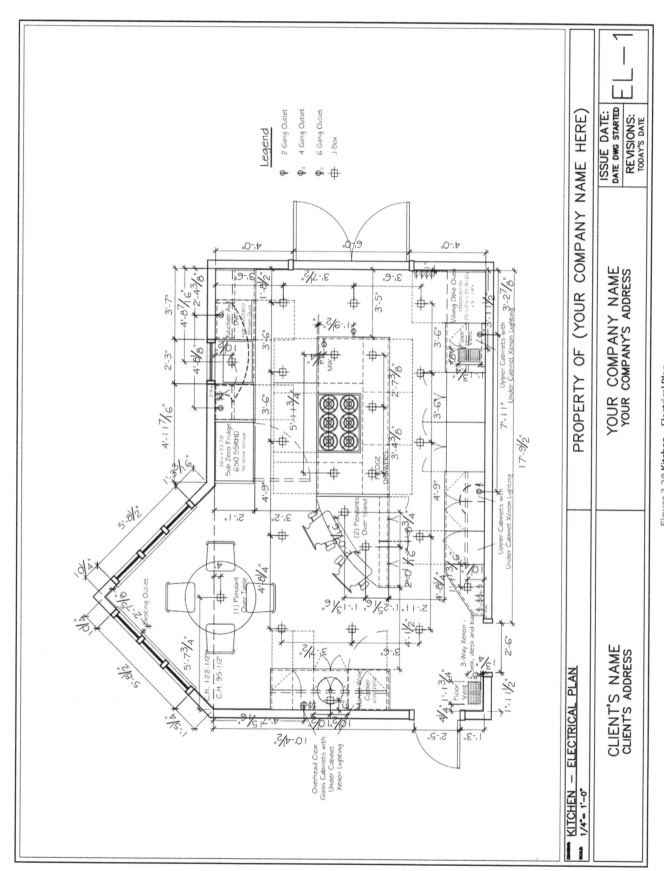

Figure 3.28 Kitchen—Electrical Plan

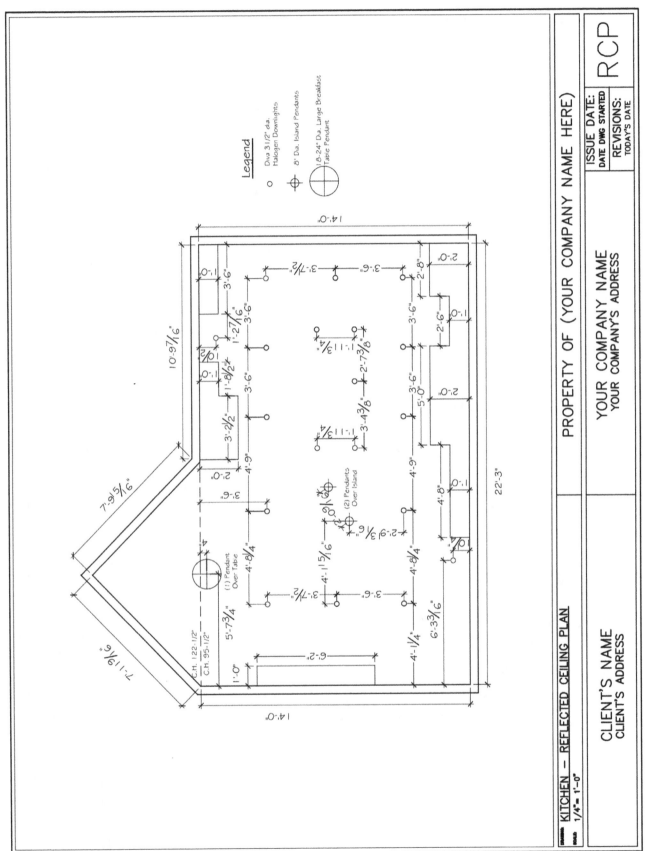

Figure 3.29 Kitchen—Reflected Ceiling Plan

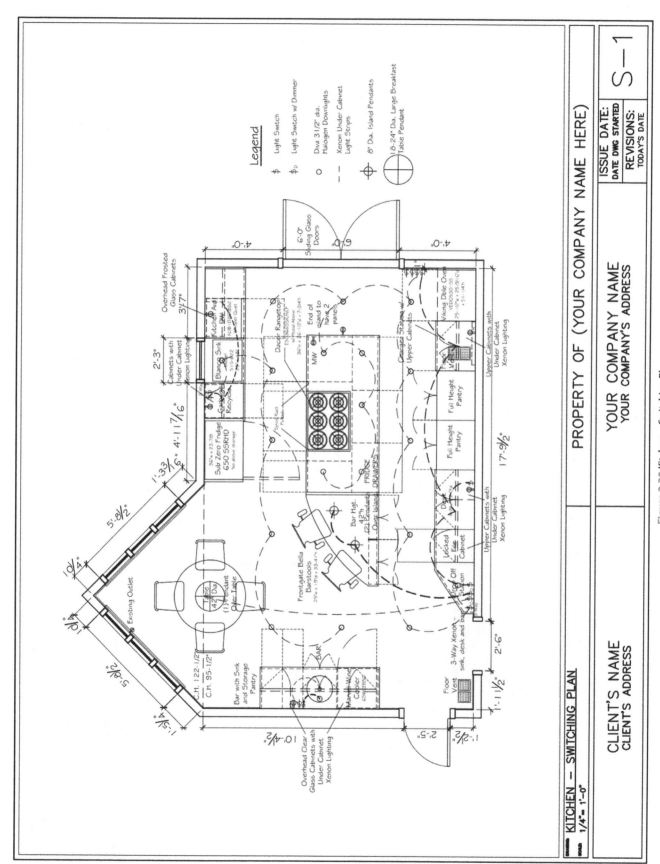

Figure 3.30 Kitchen—Switching Plan

73

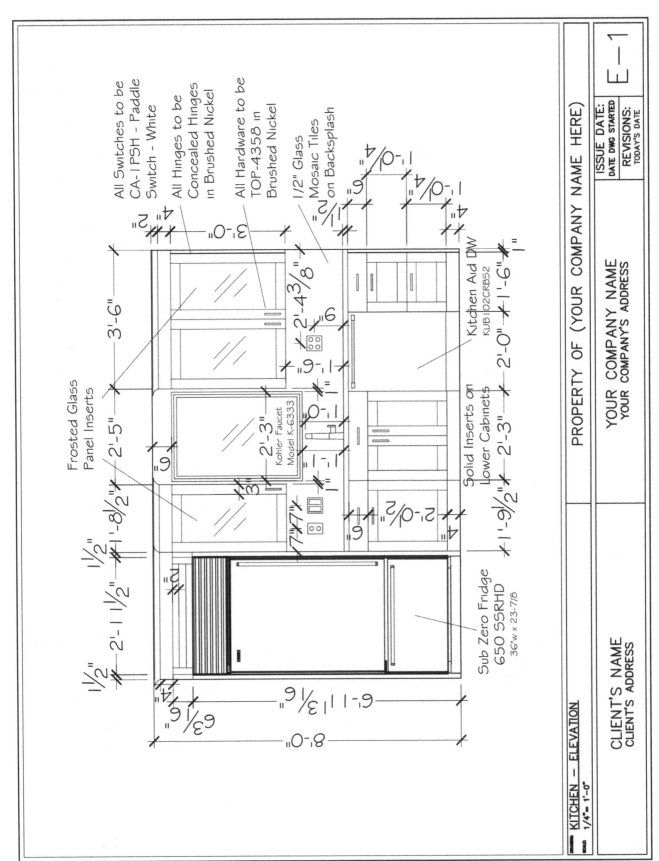

All Switches to be CA-1PSH - Paddle Switch - White

All Hinges to be Concealed Hinges in Brushed Nickel

All Hardware to be TOP-4358 in Brushed Nickel

1/2" Glass Mosaic Tiles on Backsplash

Frosted Glass Panel Inserts

Kohler Faucet Model K-6333

Kitchen Aid DW KUB102CRBS2

Solid Inserts on Lower Cabinets

Sub Zero Fridge 650 SSRHD 36"w x 23-7/8

PROPERTY OF (YOUR COMPANY NAME HERE)

YOUR COMPANY NAME
YOUR COMPANY'S ADDRESS

CLIENT'S NAME
CLIENT'S ADDRESS

ISSUE DATE:
DATE DWG STARTED
REVISIONS:
TODAY'S DATE

E—1

Figure 3.31 Kitchen—Elevation

Kitchen 3D Sketch Examples

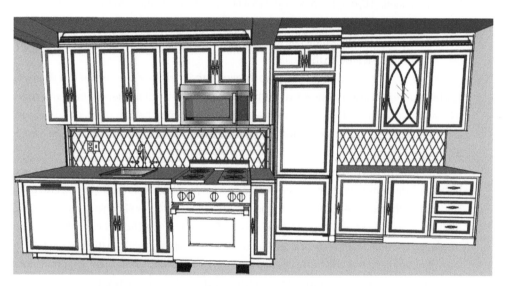

Figure 3.32 Kitchen3D Sketch Examples

Custom Cabinetry Drawings

Whether designing a built-in media unit, a library with intricate millwork (moldings, specialty woodwork), a custom vanity for a bathroom, or a desk, the drawings must be extremely clear.

Of course, the client will review them with the design team, but ultimately they will be sent to the cabinetmaker. The detail and quality of the drawing set depends on the complexity of the project.

When designing built-in cabinetry, the set of drawings should include a plan view, front and side elevations, sections, and, if possible, 3D views, which are quite helpful to the client and all involved in the project.

Detailed notes on finish, specified molding details, door style, panel details, base, crown, fillers, and other important information should be duly noted on the drawing set. Also important to note is whether shelving is adjustable or fixed. If adjustable, what type of supports will be utilized and what is the finish? Will the cabinetry be fabricated in a paint grade or a wood finish? What is the sheen—high gloss, semi-gloss, or satin? What is the edge detail? Has the direction of the laminate or wood pattern been indicated? Have you indicated any seaming?

Then there is lighting. Many custom cabinetry projects include a lighting element. Recessed lighting, halogen, LED, or perhaps xenon? What finish is the fixture trim? How many watts/lumens does the lamp put out? Is there a diffuser? Is the fixture line voltage or low voltage and, if low voltage, where will the transformer be located? Will you require a switch to be integrated into the cabinetry itself or will it be on the wall?

Perhaps you are using strip lighting to illuminate the shelves of a bookcase in a library. Or maybe you are specifying sconces that will be mounted on a stile or pilaster of a built-in or over a mirror on a wood panel of a custom vanity. All of these details must be documented and reviewed with the cabinetmaker and the electrician to be sure everyone on the design/build team is in the loop.

Attention must be given to audiovisual (AV) components when designing a media unit. Custom media units or built-ins require electrical access panels to be cut and grommets to guide cords down through the countertop to the cabinet below or to a wall behind. Internet access, modems, system racks, and so on, must all be specified and planned from the very beginning of the design phase so that the client's needs and wishes are fully addressed in the end result.

We recommend that you create detailed notes on each drawing. Some of the important notes will relate to finish, hardware, and lighting. Even though this information will appear on other drawings, the more detail you can give to the cabinetmaker, the better. In addition, detailed drawings inform the client of your design intent in a more robust manner. Figures 3.33 to 3.37 show examples of custom cabinetry drawings.

DRAWINGS   **CUSTOM CABINETRY CHECKLIST**

Plan View

- ☐ **Show door swing and drawers open.** (Show the swing or path of the door or drawer using a dashed or lighter line weight.)
- ☐ **Show HVAC.** (Note floor/ceiling vents, and ducts/soffits using a dashed line.)
- ☐ **Show overall dimensions of the room, surrounding walls, and cabinetry.**
- ☐ **Show all clearance dimensions.**
- ☐ **Draw, label, and dimension all cabinet features and lighting within cabinetry.**
- ☐ **Show all ceiling lighting using dashed lines, notations, and dimensions.**
- ☐ **Note and dimension outlets, cable, Internet, and phone near or integral to cabinetry.**
- ☐ **Note and dimension outlets and switches.**
- ☐ **Note type** (duplex, quad, dimmers, etc.).
- ☐ **Note and dimension vents, radiators, HVAC, and ductwork/soffits near or integral to the cabinet.** (Call out the location if on the floor; should be a dashed line if on the ceiling.)
- ☐ **Show all lighting, including wall sconces and under-cabinet lighting.**
- ☐ **Call out all materials/finishes being used.** (Note on the drawing or in a finish schedule.)
- ☐ **Draw hardware.** (Note it on the drawing or in a schedule.)
- ☐ **Draw and label any existing and new equipment when building the cabinet so you know that the equipment will fit where you intend within the cabinet you design.**

Switching Plan

- ☐ **Show a curved dashed line going from the switch to the coordinating light fixture or outlet.** (See Figure 3.34 for Switching Plan example.)
- ☐ **Make sure to create a coordinating legend.**

Elevations

- ☐ **Be sure to show the entire wall elevation, or enough to get a sense of the cabinetry within the space** (including all architectural details, and label where necessary).
- ☐ **Show sections** (include any shelves, drawers, and other details inside the cabinet).
- ☐ **Be sure to show baseboards and crown or fascia on the cabinet, where applicable.**
- ☐ **Show and note hardware and hinges** (manufacturer, item number, finish).
- ☐ **Draw and dimension sconces and wall lighting.**
- ☐ **Dimension ceiling heights, window dimensions, and wall widths.**
- ☐ **Provide overall dimensions for the cabinet as well as detailed dimensions for doors, drawer, fillers, wood, stone or solid surface top thickness, cabinet feet or kick base, crown, and all other details needed to build the cabinet to your specifications.**
- ☐ **Draw and label any existing equipment or new equipment that the client may want to purchase when building the cabinet so you know that the dimensions of this equipment will fit where you intend within the cabinet you design.**
- ☐ **Show and note the outlets and switches, near or integral to the cabinet. Not type of switch and/or outlet. Include the following details where applicable: dimmer, lazy switch, slide, color and finish, etc.**

Detail Drawings

- ☐ **Show blow-up details of any areas that may be hard to read in the plan or that need to be explained in further detail.**

Hours Spent

Date Completed: ____/____/____

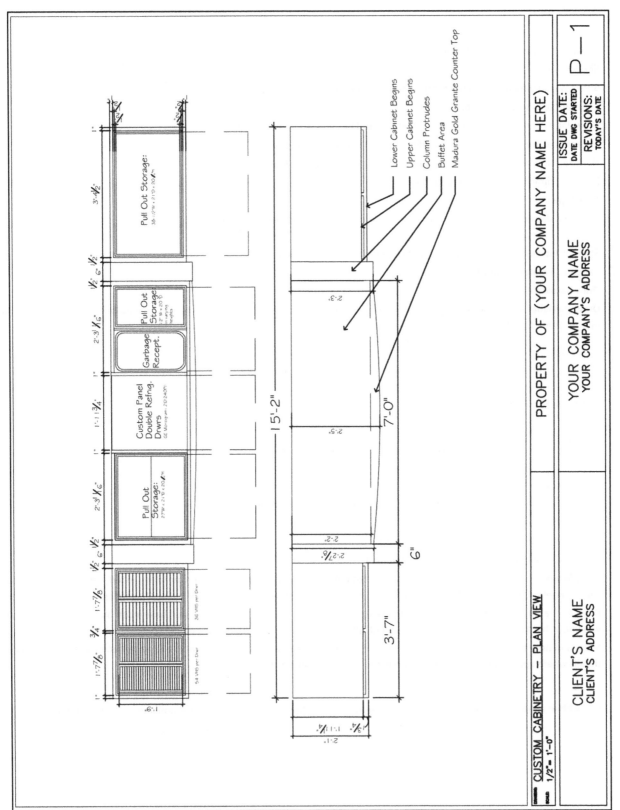

Figure 3.33 Custom Cabinetry—Plan View

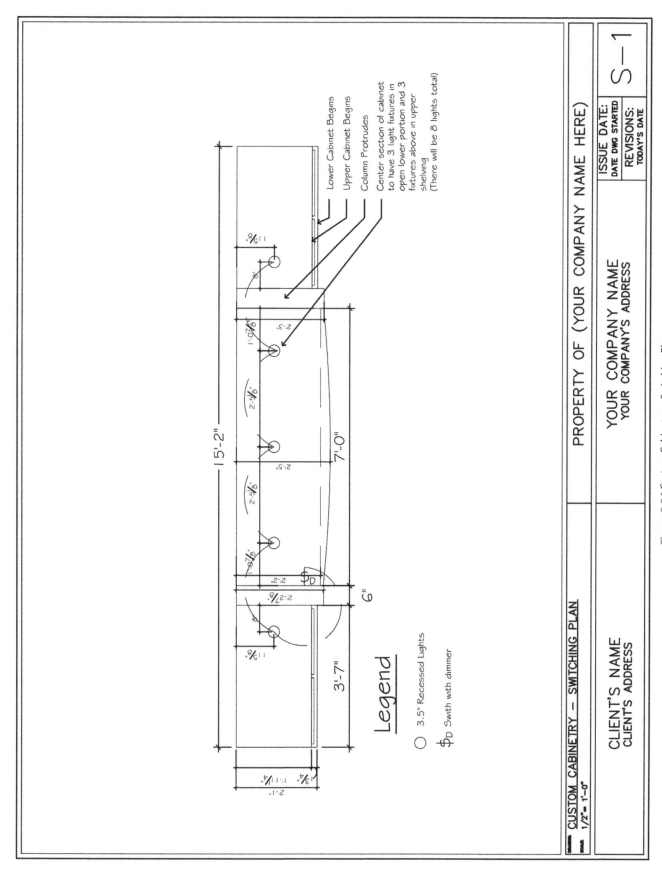

Figure 3.34 Custom Cabinetry—Switching Plan

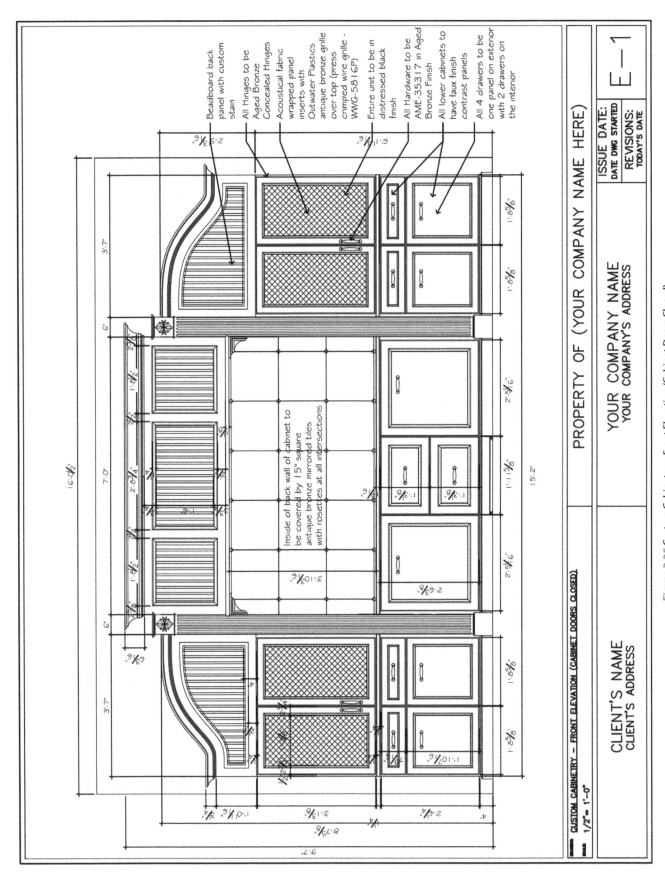

Figure 3.35 Custom Cabinetry—Front Elevation (Cabinet Doors Closed)

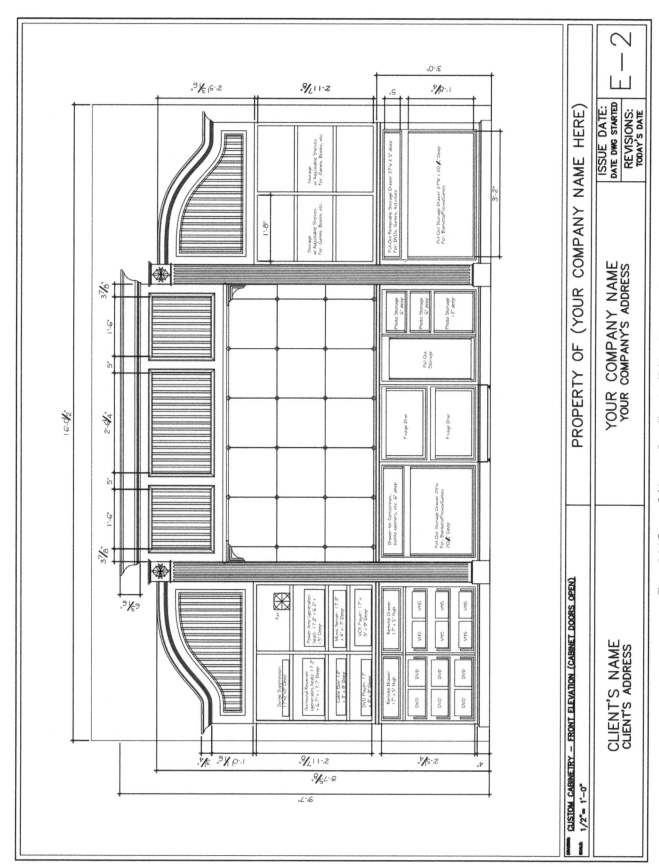

Figure 3.36 Custom Cabinetry—Front Elevation (Cabinet Doors Open)

81

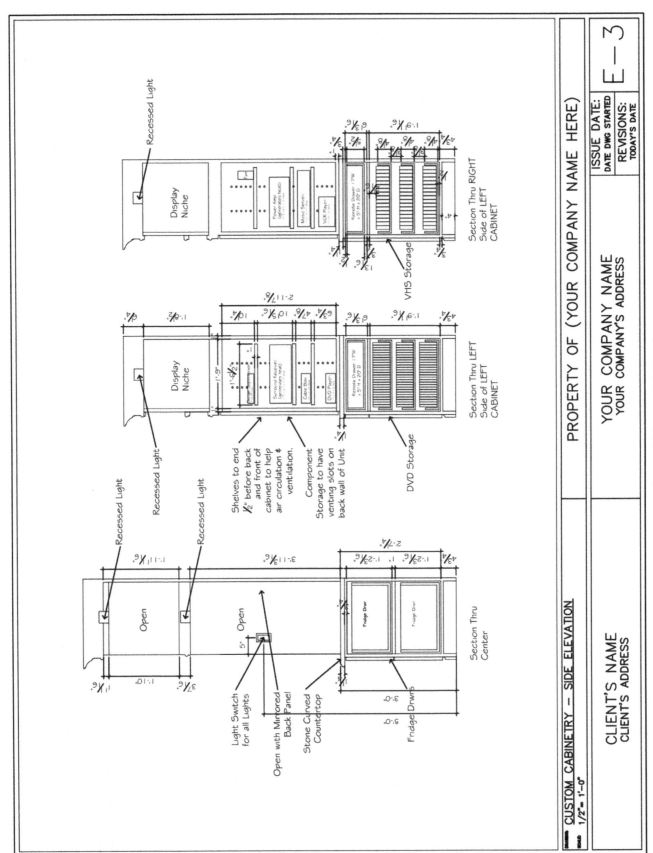

Figure 3.37 **Custom Cabinetry—Side Elevation**

PART III

Specifications

CHAPTER **4**

Residential Specifications

General Notes

Specification is one of the most important and time consuming tasks for an interior designer. Most clients do not realize how much time and energy goes into the specification phase of a project, nor can they comprehend the attention to detail necessary to write a specification, create a request for proposal (RFP), or generate a purchase order.

This section has been designed to give you the necessary tools to streamline this process and allow you to be sure you are not missing vital information that could make or break the success of your project.

Each space is designed with a multitude of layers. The specifications take us through all of the components of a space from electrical to furnishings, cabinetry, and fixtures to window and wall treatments.

When you are specifying products for the residential market, you should look to the purpose of the space. Who will be using the space? What type of traffic will it get? What hours of the day will it be in use? Are there kids or pets involved? Generally speaking, a space is designed to have a life span of 15 to 20 years, which might guide you to the most appropriate options in terms of materials, textiles, and finishes. All of these factors will weigh on your specification decisions.

Residential designers rely on showrooms or manufacturers' sales representatives to communicate their preferences. Sometimes, you will shop online or even at a retail store when necessary or requested by a client. In all cases, you must generate paperwork that details what exactly you will be specifying and purchasing for your client. I also suggest you include a photo of each item (a color photo is best) as part of your purchase order. Both Studio I.T/Studio Webware™ and Design Manager project management tools include this feature in their software programs. It has been a huge help in our practice and a great source for quick reference. (See "Ordering and Deliveries" in Chapter 6 for more in-depth information on purchase orders. Figure 6.1 shows an example of a purchase order.)

Budget is always an important factor. In contract design, you are generally given a firm budget. Many residential projects do not have the same parameters, and the scope of the project generally creeps during the design process. It is strongly suggested that you create a budget with your clients and try to stick to it. You can use the Cost Budgeting System that accompanies this book to track the expenditures on a project.

As discussed in previous sections, you should always perform an access measurement with the delivery company to be certain all selected items are deliverable. This should be done *prior* to placement of an order. This is critical, and it is a part of your scope of work and your responsibility as a designer.

Included here is a newer player in the field: the luxury space. Here you will find detailed info to help you design the man (or woman) cave, the billiard room, the home spa and gym.

While residential projects are not required to be green or sustainable, today's interior designer has a responsibility to educate the client on the environmental impact of the items specified. For example, in New York City 50 percent of the lighting specified on a project must be energy efficient. While you might not care to specify fluorescent fixtures, you must comply with code and perhaps use LED or other more energy-efficient luminaires. Sustainably designed products are more widely available now. They are more aesthetically pleasing and well-designed than ever, so be mindful of your environmental responsibility and integrate this specification into your practice. You should make this part of an initial discussion with your client. In residential environments, especially with the onslaught of chemical sensitivities, and rising asthma and allergy rates, the specification of nontoxic and low-VOC (volatile organic compound) paints and wallcoverings is more important than ever. We can create healthier living spaces that are indeed functional *and* beautiful while simultaneously protecting the earth for future generations.

Bathroom Specifications

A residential bathroom is one of the most complex spaces we design within a home or apartment. It requires an extraordinary amount of planning and attention to detail. The specification checklists provided in this chapter give you the tools to appropriately plan any bathroom in the home.

Planning bathrooms offers today's designer the opportunity to think outside the box. From a freestanding tub to a floating vanity, the possibilities are endless. However, the most important factor is *function*. Will this design work for the end users, your clients, and their lifestyle? For example, are the clients empty nesters wishing to age in place? If so, you will probably want to anticipate their future needs and install grab bars, include a curbless shower, and make the space as accessible as possible. We recently specified a fabulous freestanding oval tub, which had grab bars integrated into the design. It is trés chic and practical all at once!

If you happen to be designing an ADA-compliant bath, be mindful that you specify only ADA-compliant fixtures and give thought to employing universal design and sustainable design principles. You should specify lavatory faucets that have automatic sensors, which are easier for a physically challenged person to use and are more sanitary for all. At the very least, if sensors are not in the budget, specify levers or single-lever faucets over handles. They are easier to operate.

Bathroom fixtures actually have many parts and fall into two categories. The rough-in components, which are the plumbing valves, are the parts that remain behind the wall. The trims for the fixtures, the parts you see, generally have longer lead times and are sent to the job site at a later date, when needed. The rough-in components need to be on-site after demolition is complete so the plumber can rough in all the fittings for the shower/tub/lav fixtures.

When considering fixtures, look for durability. Some finishes are more prone to pitting and staining, while others are easier to maintain. Even when a fixture offers a "lifetime" finish, the warranty generally does not cover the fixture for natural aging and patina. Adding a protective finish such as silver oxide on hardware and other surfaces prevents the growth of germs and should be considered when specifying fixtures.

New offerings on the market include sinks and toilets with inherent antimicrobial finishes. This is especially helpful with young children who do not wash their hands as effectively as adults. The finish also facilitates cleaning and limits the spread of germs.

When specifying toilets, many manufacturers offer wall-mounted as well as floor-mounted options. They also offer dual flush options, heated seats, built-in bidet options, and many more bells and whistles. Some toilets are tankless, making them elegant and more like a work of art. The price points are, of course, higher, so perhaps these options are best reserved for the higher-end powder room.

In the shower, you should work with a plumbing specialist to be sure you are specifying the correct system. Do you want pressure balance or thermostatic control? What kind of water pressure does the client have? Does the client want steam or body sprays? Does the client require a hand shower? A rain head? All of this needs to be taken into account.

Remember to specify shower drains. Sometimes floor drains are a great idea to include in the design, in case of a leak. Do you wish to install a linear, square, or round drain? Many manufacturers now offer terrific options with regard to design, shape, and finish. The new linear shower drains are less conspicuous and have a more modern look.

As in all areas of the home, accessories play an important role in the bathroom. You must coordinate all of the accessories to create a cohesive look. Accessories of critical importance for proper functionality of the space are the toilet tissue holder, robe hooks, towel bars and rings, shower baskets, soap dishes or dispensers, and waste bins. For example, if you are using a polished chrome lavatory faucet and drain, you should be consistent with all fixtures and accessories and be sure the styles and finishes relate for a more harmonious and well-thought-out design.

When specifying mirrors or medicine cabinets, you must look at the type of wall construction. Medicine cabinets can be specified as surface-mounted or recessed into a cavity for a cleaner look if there is room in the partition to accommodate the recess. If you are going for a mirror that can segue into an ADA-compliant bathroom, you may want to select a pivot mirror. There are many elegant options that look terrific and offer the versatility should the need arise for a more universal design. The tilt of the wall mirror can help people of smaller stature and those in a wheelchair to view themselves more easily.

Bathroom tile specification is quite complex. Will you specify stone or porcelain or perhaps a ceramic tile? Will it be handmade or machine made? What color and texture will you specify? Glass tiles present unique opportunities for great design as well, but you must understand how they can best be used. A shower floor is more functional with a honed/matte or textured finish. If you are using natural stone, you can also opt for a mosaic, which offers more traction because of the small scale of the tile and the amount of grout that is used.

At the showroom, you will probably want to connect with a knowledgeable salesperson, who will be able to guide you in making the appropriate selections based on function and design. This person can be an invaluable member of your support team.

SPECIFICATIONS   **BATH FIXTURES CHECKLIST**

NOTE: Always have the rough-in components sent by the plumbing and electrical supplier/vendor *PRIOR* to the trims and fixtures.

Vanity

- ☐ Specify lavatory faucet and handles: **widespread, center-set, single-lever, wall-mounted, or vessel faucet** (circle one).
- ☐ Faucet manufacturer/model number _____ Specify finish _____
- ☐ Specify valve and trim for lavatory faucet and handles.
- ☐ Specify trap: **classic P-trap or concealed trap** (circle one). **Specify stop (hot and cold): exposed or in-wall** (circle one).
- ☐ Specify drain: **pop-up or twist stop** (circle one).
- ☐ Specify vanity: **custom or ready-made** (circle one), **freestanding or built-in** (circle one), **floor- or wall-mount** (circle one).
- ☐ Vanity manufacturer/model number _____ Specify finish _____
- ☐ Specify sink (basin): **wall-mounted, framed, drop-in, under-mount, vessel, or pedestal** (circle one).
- ☐ Sink manufacturer/model number _____ Specify finish _____
- ☐ Specify medicine cabinet: **recessed or surface-mounted and finished on sides** (circle one).
- ☐ Medicine cabinet manufacturer/model number _____ Specify finish _____

Toilet

- ☐ Specify: **one-piece or two-piece** (circle one). **Comfort height or traditional** (circle one). **Elongated or round** (circle one).
- ☐ Specify trip lever manufacturer/model number _____ Specify finish _____
- ☐ Specify stop: **angle or straight stop** (circle one). **Specify trap: P-trap or concealed trap** (circle one).
- ☐ Toilet manufacturer/model number _____ Specify finish _____

Tub/Shower Combination

- ☐ Specify tub: **freestanding, drop-in, or corner** (circle one).
- ☐ Specify drain location: **left or right** (circle one). **Specify drain with pop-up stop for tub.**
- ☐ Specify tub manufacturer/model number _____ Specify finish _____
- ☐ Specify tub apron: **integral, wood, or tiled** (circle one).
- ☐ Specify tub valve (rough) and trim for the faucet and handle(s).
- ☐ Specify **pressure balance and valve trim or temperature control valve** (circle one).
- ☐ Specify diverter(s)-valve and trim (controls the switching from tub to shower to handheld).
- ☐ Specify diverter manufacturer/model number _____ Specify finish _____
- ☐ Specify hand shower: **on sliding bar or on hook** (circle one).
- ☐ Specify body spray manufacturer/model number _____ Specify finish _____
- ☐ Specify tile flange if needed (metal bead).

Shower Only

- ☐ Specify shower door (type of glass and thickness, color/Starphire®—low-iron) _____
- ☐ Shower door handle manufacturer/model number _____ Specify finish _____
- ☐ Specify **pressure balance and valve trim or temperature control valve** (circle one).
- ☐ Specify shower head manufacturer/model number _____ Specify finish _____
- ☐ Specify body spray manufacturer/model number _____ Specify finish _____
- ☐ Specify catch drain: **square, round, or linear** (circle one).
- ☐ Specify shower pan—rough.

Lighting and Electrical

- ☐ Specify wet location shower fixture: **halogen or LED** (circle one). **Specify finish** _____
- ☐ Specify fan on timer, heat lamp, and vent.
- ☐ Specify GFI outlet (at least one).
- ☐ Specify all lighting on a dimmer (specify the type of dimmer).
- ☐ Specify how the lighting switches will be ganged.
- ☐ Specify color of outlet and switch plates. _____

SPECIFICATIONS   **BATH FIXTURES—ACCESSORIES CHECKLIST**

NOTE: Always have the rough-in components sent by the plumbing and electrical supplier/vendor *PRIOR* to the trims and fixtures.

Towel Warmers

- ☐ Towel warmer manufacturer/model number _____ Specify finish _____
- ☐ Specify dimensions _____

Towel Bars

- ☐ Specify single bar, double bar, or swing arm (circle one).
- ☐ Specify towel bar manufacturer/model number _____ Specify finish _____
- ☐ Specify dimensions _____

Towel Rings

- ☐ Towel ring manufacturer/model number _____ Specify finish _____

Tissue Paper Holders

- ☐ Specify: single post, double post, or freestanding (circle one).
- ☐ Specify orientation: horizontal, vertical, or recessed (circle one).
- ☐ Specify location: on wall, floor, or mounted on vanity (circle one).
- ☐ Tissue paper holder manufacturer/model number _____ Specify finish _____

Shower Baskets

- ☐ Specify rectangular or corner baskets (circle one).
- ☐ Shower basket manufacturer/model number _____ Specify finish _____
- ☐ Quantity _____

Robe Hooks

- ☐ Specify single or double hook (circle one).
- ☐ Specify location: back of door, wall, etc. _____
- ☐ Robe hook manufacturer/model number _____ Specify finish _____
- ☐ Quantity _____

Magnifying Mirror

- ☐ Specify tabletop or wall-mounted (circle one). (Drill grommet in countertop if tabletop model.)
- ☐ Specify location if wall-mounted: hardwired or plug-in (circle one).
- ☐ Magnifying mirror manufacturer/model number _____ Specify finish _____

Shelf

- ☐ Shelf manufacturer/model number _____ Specify finish/material _____
- ☐ Specify shelf location (e.g., above toilet) _____

Accessories

- ☐ Soap dispenser manufacturer/model number _____ Specify finish _____
- ☐ Soap dish manufacturer/model number _____ Specify finish _____

Hardware

- ☐ Vanity hardware style: knob or pull (circle one).
- ☐ Vanity hardware manufacturer/model number _____ Specify finish _____
- ☐ Quantity_____
- ☐ Door and linen closet hardware style: knob or lever (circle one).
- ☐ Door and linen closet hardware manufacturer/model number _____ Specify finish _____
- ☐ Quantity _____

SPECIFICATIONS   **BATH TILE AND STONE CHECKLIST**

Floor Tile #1

- ☐ **Floor tile manufacturer/model number** _____ Specify finish _____
- ☐ **Specify color** _____ Tile location and placement _____
- ☐ **Specify dimensions** _____ Quantity _____

Floor Tile #2 (if applicable: i.e., border)

- ☐ **Floor tile manufacturer/model number** _____ Specify finish _____
- ☐ **Specify color** _____ Tile location and placement _____
- ☐ **Specify dimensions** _____ Quantity _____

Floor Tile Grout

- ☐ **Specify sanded or unsanded** (circle one).
- ☐ **Floor grout manufacturer/model number** _____ Specify color _____ Quantity _____

Wall Field Tile

- ☐ **Wall field tile manufacturer/model number** _____ Specify finish _____
- ☐ **Specify color** _____ Tile location and placement _____
- ☐ **Specify dimensions** _____ Quantity _____

Wall Border/Listello/Chair Rail

- ☐ **Wall border tile manufacturer/model number** _____ Specify finish _____
- ☐ **Specify color** _____ Tile location and placement _____
- ☐ **Specify dimensions** _____ Quantity _____

Pencil/Liner

- ☐ **Specify a standard or decorative pencil liner** (circle one).
- ☐ **Pencil tile manufacturer/model number** _____ Specify finish _____
- ☐ **Specify color** _____ Tile location and placement _____
- ☐ **Specify dimensions** _____ Quantity _____

Decorative Molding Trim

- ☐ **Decorative molding trim tile manufacturer/model number** _____ Specify finish _____
- ☐ **Specify dimensions** _____
- ☐ **Specify color** _____ Tile location and placement _____
- ☐ **Specify dimensions** _____ Quantity _____

Wall Tile Grout

- ☐ **Specify sanded or unsanded** (circle one).
- ☐ **Floor grout manufacturer/model number** _____ Specify color _____ Quantity _____

Countertops

- ☐ **Specify species** (stone type, wood type, concrete, solid surface) _____
- ☐ **Specify finish** (polished, honed, brushed, lacquered) _____
- ☐ **Specify edge detail and thickness** (3/4″ or 11/4 ″) _____
- ☐ **Specify overhang dimension over cabinet edge** (1/4″, 1/2″, 1″, etc.) _____

Saddles and Curbs

- ☐ **Specify species** (stone type, wood type, concrete, solid surface) _____
- ☐ **Specify finish** (polished, honed, brushed, lacquered) _____
- ☐ **Specify edge detail/bevel and thickness** (3/4″ or 11/4″) _____

Custom Bedding and Window Treatments Specification

Custom Bedding Specification

Bedding specifications are an area where designers can really get creative and use their imaginations. There are so many layers to this process. You should start with the style: Is your client more traditional, transitional, or contemporary? This will dictate your course of action. In addition, what type of bed does your client have, or will you be specifying a new model? Will you need a box spring? Will you require a bed skirt? Will there be a headboard, and, if so, will it be upholstered, tufted, or channel quilted? You can see how many decisions need to be made, and we have not even gotten to the pillows and shams!

Generally, we suggest starting with the coverlet or duvet cover. Discuss your client's preferences, noting that some clients would like to have both. One way to customize the coverlet/duvet cover is to use a contrasting fabric on the reverse side and an applied trim on all four sides. This allows the client to have two different looks in one piece. It also brings more pattern and texture to the ensemble.

If you are creating a duvet cover, you may want to specify a concealed zipper rather than buttons, as buttons can come loose and fall off and are more difficult to deal with. With a coverlet, we suggest a layer of batting/interlining to give it more weight. You may also wish to do a channel or box quilted coverlet design for more interest, especially when using a plain fabric. You can take this opportunity to add a self or contrast welt (piping) or an applied trim with flange for a more finished and decorative look. It is advisable not to fabricate the coverlet or duvet until the actual mattress/box spring can be measured by the fabricator to verify exact width, height, and preferred drop for all components.

Shams are also important. Your clients will love to prop themselves on a sham when reading or watching television in bed. Shams can be fabricated to fit your clients' bed, and they can be created in many styles. Some of the most popular are knife-edge (with or without a welt or trim), box/border shape, knife-edge with flange, or a ruffled flange for a more traditional client.

You can also specify a box spring cover in a fabric that coordinates, as well as a bed skirt, which can be fabricated with a tailored kick pleat, with inverted pleats, or may be ruffled or shirred.

SPECIFICATIONS   **CUSTOM BEDDING CHECKLIST**

Prior to Creating Any Custom Bedding

☐ Measure the size of the bed (length and width).

☐ Measure the height of the mattress off the floor (floor to top of mattress/crown).

☐ Measure the height from the floor to the bottom of the mattress (for the drop of the bed skirt).

☐ Discuss with your clients the type of bedding they want: coverlet or duvet cover (circle one).

☐ Send the measurements and details to your fabricator for a price and yardage quote.

☐ Once fabric is specified, send the fabric width and repeat to your fabricator to verify quantities before placing the order.

☐ Once the yardage quote is received, reserve the specified amount of fabric and ask for a CFA (cutting for approval) to match to your sample; make sure the ship-to address is your fabricator's address.

☐ If desired, choose a contrasting lining fabric(s) for the back of the coverlet or duvet cover, or discuss with your fabricator the color/type of contrasting lining fabric(s) you wish to use.

Coverlet

☐ Specify fabric suitable for bedding. (Check the label for content and suggested uses.)

☐ Check to see if the fabric chosen needs to be backed for more stability. (Specify knit or acrylic backing.)

☐ Specify a trim; specify a self-welt or contrast welt (circle one).

Duvet Cover

☐ Specify fabric suitable for bedding. (Check the label for content and suggested uses.)

☐ Check to see if the fabric chosen needs to be backed for more stability. (Specify knit or acrylic backing.)

☐ Specify zipper close or button close access.

☐ Specify that you wish to have tabs or snaps to hold the duvet in place inside the duvet cover.

☐ Specify a trim; specify a self-welt or contrast welt (circle one).

Bed Skirt

☐ Specify type: tailored (straight) or ruffled (gathered), cluster or box-pleated (circle one).

☐ Specify whether you are using an applied trim.

Pillows

☐ Specify shape: shams, bolster, shirred round, or square (circle one).

☐ Specify size _____

☐ Specify a trim; specify a self-welt or contrast welt (circle one).

☐ Specify tassel, frog, or gimp (circle one).

Custom Headboard

☐ Specify shape: square (or straight), camelback, wingback, or other _____

☐ Specify options: tufted, channel quilted, or other _____

☐ Specify any details: nail heads, border, trims, contrast welts, etc. _____

Custom Window Treatment Specification

Drapery and other window coverings represent the finishing layer in a space. They add a level of privacy in addition to being decorative, shielding the interior from light and cold air, and adding drama and life to a space.

The designer must take the pulse of the room and of the client. Some clients prefer to leave their windows unadorned to showcase an ocean or forest view, and perhaps that is acceptable when there are no privacy issues to address. A simple shade can always be specified for privacy and light control.

The shade category covers many options. Architectural shades are offered in different opacity levels from blackout to light filtering at varying degrees. Shading options also help reduce heat, and therefore energy consumption for your client and are better for the environment to boot. While simple fabric shades are the most popular and are offered in a variety of "colorways", widths, and lengths to accommodate most windows without seaming, there are also some fabulous woven grass shades. You may also wish to use a laminated shade, where the fabricator applies your selected fabric to the shade material. Generally this is done on a blackout material, and we have used many different fabrics, from cottons to silk. Pleated shades and honeycomb shades are also popular options in residential design. They stack very high on the window and are available in many colors and textures.

Metal and wood blinds offer light control with a bit more flexibility. You have the option to tilt to block glare and light and gain more privacy without losing sight of the outdoor view completely. There are also options such as the Hunter Douglas Silhouette™ and Vignette™ shade systems, which offer privacy with the feel of a sheer.

You may also want to look at softer coverings that will provide privacy and light control. You may opt for a Roman shade, a balloon shade, or an Austrian shade. These shades are fabricated in a textile of your choice and can be trimmed for an added decorative touch.

Always review fabric selections with your workroom to be sure they are viable for the particular installation you desire. For instance, if you are using a thick, heavy fabric, it might be great for a drapery panel but not for a shade because it might not pleat well.

Many clients, especially those with high ceilings and challenging windows, prefer to have automated controls. Your fabricator should offer this option, which can be hardwired or, in some cases, operated via remote control. The fabricator/installer must work closely with the electrician, and all thoughts of automation should happen in the design phase, before construction, so that all wiring can be completed prior to closing up the walls and ceilings.

Once you have settled on the architectural shading, you may want to look at some top treatments. You may want to add a finishing touch with a top treatment. You can specify a soft valance, such as a box-pleated or scalloped treatment, or you may decide to specify an upholstered shaped or straight cornice, which is fabricated on a board.

Drapery is another design layer where the designer has a multitude of options. First, you must decide on the pleat style. Do you want a hand-pleat or a machine-stitched pleat? Will the pleat be inverted, cartridge, pencil, or goblet style? Will you have contrasting banding on the leading edge or a tassel trim? Will you have a contrasting hem? Will your panels be lined and interlined, or are you specifying a sheer fabric? Will they be stationary side panels or drapery that will close to block light? Perhaps you will do tiebacks?

Now you must think about the hardware. Will you specify a pole with rings, and, if so, will you use wood, and what kind of finish? What will the finials be like? How about the brackets—do you need a deeper projection to clear the windows? Are you using a sheer behind and therefore need a double pole?

Another area in the window coverings category that has been gaining in popularity among designers is window film. When a client opts to leave the windows unadorned, most designers absolutely insist that they at least have window film applied to protect floors and furnishings. Even when there are window treatments specified for a client, it is recommended that you add this layer of protection as well. While window film generally does not eliminate the need for window coverings, it complements this layer by reducing glare and fading of fabrics and furnishings, reflecting ultraviolet (UV) rays and heat and lowering overall energy costs. It works well in both summer and winter and is specified in all climates. It is available in a variety of shades and colors, and each has a different energy quotient. Translucent, frosted, and dusted crystal films are used to provide privacy while still letting in light.

Please refer to the checklist in this section to be sure you have followed the measuring guidelines and are giving your fabricators as much information as possible to provide you with an accurate estimate.

SPECIFICATIONS   **CUSTOM WINDOW TREATMENTS CHECKLIST**

Prior to Creating Any Custom Window Treatment

- ☐ **Take pictures of all window wall elevations. (Include any reveals in the wall and/or ceiling for pocket drapery.)**
- ☐ **Measure wall length and ceiling height above finished floor (AFF).** (Note if no finish floor exists at survey date.)
- ☐ **Measure and note height and projection of baseboards and crown molding.**
- ☐ **Measure HVAC and/or radiators.**
- ☐ **Measure interior and overall window dimensions** (length × width × depth).
- ☐ **Measure and note windowsill height and projection, mullions, and also window trim.**
- ☐ **Measure the height from the top of the window to the ceiling.**
- ☐ **Measure wall and ceiling pocket details for drapery.** (Measure width and height.)
- ☐ **Once you have the window measurements, send the drawing and fabric specifications to your fabricator to get a yardage and price quote.**
- ☐ **Once a yardage quote is received, reserve stock ASAP in the fabric you wish to use to prevent losing the stock. Ask for a CFA (cutting for approval) to match your sample, and make sure the ship-to address is your fabricator's address.**
- ☐ **If necessary, pick a liner fabric or contrasting lining fabric or discuss with the fabricator what type/color of liner fabric you wish to use.** (Ask clients if they want a blackout lining, especially if the window treatment is in a bedroom or media room.)
- ☐ **Consider automation.**

Drapery

- ☐ **Specify fabric suitable for drapery, appropriate for pleating, and not too stiff or thick.** (Check the label for content and suggested uses.)
- ☐ **Specify whether drapery panels will be unlined, lined, and/or interlined** (circle one).
- ☐ **Specify the length of the panels: touching the floor, puddle, or break** (circle one).
- ☐ **Specify the type of header for drapery: goblet pleat, cartridge pleat, French pleat, pinch pleat, or hand-pleated** (circle one).
- ☐ **Discuss how the panels will be hung: from a rod with finials, from a hidden application, on a concealed track, etc.**
- ☐ **If necessary, discuss the finish and style of the hardware, drapery rings, and finials.**
- ☐ **Specify trim, leading edge, tassels and/or tiebacks, and reserve stock with a CFA (cutting for approval) if one is available.**

Top Treatments

- ☐ **Specify the style of top treatment: swags and jabots, scarf valance, stagecoach valance, box-pleat valance, cornice, etc.**
- ☐ **Specify IB (inside bracket) mount or OB (outside bracket) mount** (circle one).
- ☐ **Specify drop and depth of treatment with the fabricator.**
- ☐ **Specify whether you wish to use a trim, self-welt, contrasting welt, etc.**

Shades

- ☐ **Specify style: flat shade, roman shade, roller shade, etc.** _____
- ☐ **Discuss with the client the level of shading desired in each space.** (Recommend heaviest shading in media or conference rooms, medium shading in work areas with computers, and lighter shading in reception area.)
- ☐ **Specify IB (inside bracket) mount or OB (outside bracket) mount** (circle one).
- ☐ **If desired, specify trim and reserve the stock necessary with a CFA (cutting for approval) for trim if one is available.**

Wood Blind

- ☐ **Specify finish** _____
- ☐ **Specify slat size** (typical sizes are 1″, 13/8″, or 2″) _____
- ☐ **Specify cord pull or LiteRise®** (circle one). **Specify ladders or tape** (circle one).
- ☐ **Specify IB (inside bracket) mount or OB (outside bracket) mount** (circle one).
- ☐ **Specify cord locations:** left or right (circle one).
- ☐ **Specify whether your blinds need a self-valance:** Yes or No (circle one).

Window Film

- ☐ **Have your supplier take their own measurements if necessary.**
- ☐ **Discuss with your client the type of film desired and the degree to which the sunlight should be blocked.**

Fabric and Trim Specification

Fabric Specification

This task involves the decorative aspect of the interior designer's role in a project. Textiles greatly impact the end result of your design. Residential design offers literally thousands of choices, from a variety of vendors. If you are fortunate enough to live in or near a large metropolitan area, there is most likely a design building that is home to many of the larger textile showrooms. If not, you can become a dealer and arrange to have all the books in your office library for easy selection.

Although aesthetics is always important, function must be front of mind. How do your clients live? Do they have children and/or pets? These factors must be taken into consideration when specifying fabrics. For example, if kids and pets will frequent the area where the sofa you are specifying will be placed, then make it practical by using a fabric that is durable or heavy-duty (at least 30,000 double rubs) and easily cleaned. There are some very good options available, including Ultrasuede®, other kinds of microfiber, and Crypton® fabrics, which are actually antimicrobial and have a waterproof lining. Think about how happy your client will be when a child or the family dog has an accident and it is easily cleaned up, leaving no residue. Your clients will remember you for your foresight and attention to detail!

In a living room, where the furnishings are not heavily used, you can have a bit more fun and specify silks and other less durable materials. Bedrooms also offer options if pets and children will not be sharing the bed with your clients. Always discuss cleaning options, as most designer fabrics require dry cleaning and special care.

Pay attention to fabric content in children's rooms, and be sure you are complying with all codes related to crib bedding design and other factors intended to protect children. All fabrics must be flame resistant. No material is flameproof. Specify fabrics that resist flame longer, allowing occupants of the space time to exit safely. Did you know that wool is inherently flame retardant, as it possesses natural lanolin? It is also a very durable material.

Reserve yardage of the specified fabric and request that a CFA (cutting for approval) be mailed to your firm to check against your memo sample for color matching. This ensures that the dye lot of the goods that are currently in stock aligns with the color in your memo sample.

Colorfastness and light resistance are also important characteristics for a fabric with longevity. Specify all goods from the same dye lot, and, if that is not an option, order cuttings (CFAs) from all dye lots being considered before you purchase. Be sure there is plenty of stock reserved for your order, as it is a waste of time to have to reselect due to insufficient yardage.

Some applications require that you back the fabric for stability. Some fabrics, especially in the contract realm, are already backed. This is great for upholstery and hard window top treatments but not for drapery.

Always consult your fabricator and upholsterer *prior* to placing an order to be sure the fabrics you specify are appropriate for the use intended. We generally advise sending a cutting or a memo sample of the textiles you are considering to the workroom/fabricator for review and approval.

Passamentarie/Trim Specification

Aaah—the crowning glory, the finishing touch, the sparkle and glam of a project. The category of passamentarie, a word describing embellishment, includes the tassel, moss and other fringes, ribbon gimp, cord, frogs, and other ornamental trims. While many of your clients will be familiar with a tassel fringe or a tieback, most do not know the first thing about incorporating trimmings into a decorative/design project.

The wonderful thing about trim and embellishment is the variety that exists. Glass and wood beads have grown in popularity over the last decade, while intricate tapes and ribbon, tassel, and moss fringes have been around for centuries. The delicate designs and skilled craftsmanship of these treasures can introduce bespoke elements into the interiors you create.

Here in New York, not only do we have the trimmings available at various fabric showrooms but we also have Samuel & Sons, a treasure trove of everything passamentarie. The experience of visiting Samuel & Sons begins with the door pull (metal cast in the shape of a tassel!), after which you enter a room furnished with cherry shelving fashioned in a grid pattern. Each opening contains a different element, all color- and style-coordinated. This is sheer bliss for interior designers, and professionals travel from all over the world to shop here. In addition, Samuel & Sons has an excellent website with photorealistic images of each item to make the virtual shopping experience even easier.

There are some important elements to consider in specifying trimmings. First, if you are specifying a cord to use as a welt, you must be sure it also contains a tape or lip so that the workroom can sew it inside the seam for a clean look. You may wish to use a ribbon for the leading edge of your drapery panels. Ribbons come in a variety of widths and colors, and some have embellishments and embroidery.

Trims are sold by the yard, and most manufacturers will not offer a CFA, so be sure that you check dye lots when you order yardage.

If you are ordering a set of tassel tiebacks, be sure the cord offered is long enough. You can customize this length in some cases.

Buttons, frogs, and other decorative elements can be used to detail a chair back, a skirt on a sofa, or a window treatment such as a cornice.

The possibilities are truly endless in the magical world of passamentarie. Following the checklist in this chapter helps to ensure you are specifying correctly.

SPECIFICATIONS   **FABRICS CHECKLIST**

Fabric #1

- ☐ **Vendor/showroom** _____
- ☐ **Pattern/color name or number** _____
- ☐ **Net price** _____
- ☐ **Stock** _____
- ☐ **Where is it stocked? (Specify United States, United Kingdom, etc.)** _____
- ☐ **Lead time and ETA** _____
- ☐ **Width of goods** _____
- ☐ **Vertical repeat** _____
- ☐ **Horizontal repeat** _____
- ☐ **How many double rubs does it have?** _____
- ☐ **Is the fabric fire rated?** _____
- ☐ **Is it backed for upholstery? If not, will it need to be backed for this particular application?** _____
- ☐ **Is the fabric Teflon-coated?** _____
- ☐ **Amount of yards to reserve** _____
- ☐ **Specify that all yardage reserved is from the same dye lot and all one piece if possible.**
- ☐ **Sidemark for goods** (e.g., your company name/client name/room/item) _____
- ☐ **Request a CFA (cutting for approval) to match to your sample and have it mailed to your firm.**
- ☐ **Specify the ship-to address** (your workroom/fabricator, or another furniture company) _____
- ☐ **Do you need to send a COM tag to the fabric manufacturer to be sent with the goods to the furniture company for upholstery?**

Fabric #2

- ☐ **Vendor/showroom** _____
- ☐ **Pattern/color name or number** _____
- ☐ **Net price** _____
- ☐ **Stock** _____
- ☐ **Where is it stocked? (Specify United States, United Kingdom, etc.)** _____
- ☐ **Lead time and ETA** _____
- ☐ **Width of goods** _____
- ☐ **Vertical repeat** _____
- ☐ **Horizontal repeat** _____
- ☐ **How many double rubs does it have?** _____
- ☐ **Is the fabric fire rated?** _____
- ☐ **Is it backed for upholstery? If not, will it need to be backed for this particular application?** _____
- ☐ **Is the fabric Teflon-coated?** _____
- ☐ **Number of yards to reserve** _____
- ☐ **Specify that all yardage reserved is from the same dye lot and all one piece if possible.**
- ☐ **Sidemark for goods** (e.g., your company name/client name/room/item) _____
- ☐ **Request a CFA (cutting for approval) to match to your sample and have it mailed to your firm.**
- ☐ **Specify the ship-to address** (your workroom/fabricator, or another furniture company) _____
- ☐ **Do you need to send a COM tag to the fabric manufacturer to be sent with the goods to the furniture company for upholstery?**

SPECIFICATIONS   **PASSAMENTARIE/TRIMS CHECKLIST**

Passamentarie/Trim #1

- ☐ **Vendor/showroom** _____
- ☐ **Pattern/color name or number** _____
- ☐ **Trim dimensions** _____
- ☐ **Net price** _____
- ☐ **Stock** _____
- ☐ **Where is it stocked? (Specify United States, United Kingdom, etc.)** _____
- ☐ **Lead time and ETA** _____
- ☐ **Is there a minimum for an order?** _____
- ☐ **What is the content?** _____
- ☐ **What type of trim? (Specify moss fringe, tassel, bead, cord, cord with lip, etc.)** _____
- ☐ **Sidemark for goods** (e.g., your company name/client name/room/item) _____
- ☐ **Request a CFA (cutting for approval), if available, to match to your sample and have it mailed to your firm.**
- ☐ **Specify the ship-to address** (your workroom/fabricator, or another furniture company) _____

Passamentarie/Trim #2

- ☐ **Vendor/showroom** _____
- ☐ **Pattern/color name or number** _____
- ☐ **Trim dimensions** _____
- ☐ **Net price** _____
- ☐ **Stock** _____
- ☐ **Where is it stocked? (Specify United States, United Kingdom, etc.)** _____
- ☐ **Lead time and ETA** _____
- ☐ **Is there a minimum order?** _____
- ☐ **What is the content?** _____
- ☐ **What type of trim? (Specify moss fringe, tassel, bead, cord, cord with lip, etc.)** _____
- ☐ **Sidemark for goods** (e.g., your company name/client name/room/item) _____
- ☐ **Request a CFA (cutting for approval), if available, to match to your sample and have it mailed to your firm.**
- ☐ **Specify the ship-to address** (your workroom/fabricator, or another furniture company) _____

Passamentarie/Trim #3

- ☐ **Vendor/showroom** _____
- ☐ **Pattern/color name or number** _____
- ☐ **Trim dimensions** _____
- ☐ **Net price** _____
- ☐ **Stock** _____
- ☐ **Where is it stocked? (Specify United States, United Kingdom, etc.)** _____
- ☐ **Lead time and ETA** _____
- ☐ **Is there a minimum for an order?** _____
- ☐ **What is the content?** _____
- ☐ **What type of trim? (Specify moss fringe, tassel, bead, cord, cord with lip, etc.)** _____
- ☐ **Sidemark for goods** (e.g., your company name/client name/room/item) _____
- ☐ **Request a CFA (cutting for approval), if available, to match to your sample and have it mailed to your firm.**
- ☐ **Specify the ship-to address** (your workroom/fabricator, or another furniture company) _____

Flooring Specification

Hard Surface and Resilient Flooring Specifications

When you consider a hard surface flooring option, you must consider the function. Are you going to use this in a hallway, an entry foyer, a kitchen, or a bathroom?

While resilient flooring is easier on the body—especially your feet and back—than a hard flooring alternative would be, sometimes hard surfaces are the best option.

If you are specifying a hard flooring alternative such as porcelain, ceramic tile, or natural stone, note that the larger tiles have a tendency to crack more easily. Ask your supplier any and all questions that you may have about the tile you are interested in purchasing. Does the tile have a rectified edge? Is there a cove tile available? Does the color go all the way through the tile (common in porcelain)? Ask the sales associate or your tile mechanic their recommendation for a grout joint. Commercial projects typically use 1/8" grout spacing. In residential projects, the grout joint varies dependent upon the material specified. Try to butt-join stone tiles whenever possible, or leave minimal space. The smaller the grout joint, the cleaner the installation and the less chance dirt and mold have to grow. A tile with a matte, honed, or textured surface offers better traction and slip resistance than a polished surface, so be mindful of this, especially when designing for wet locations.

Stone tiles require more maintenance than a man-made alternative such as porcelain or ceramic. They need to be sealed periodically, and sometimes you need to re-polish to bring the finish back to its original glory. Many clients love the patina that natural stone gets as it ages. Know your client, and manage their expectations.

Resilient flooring most often means carpeting, but there are many other choices available, including cork, wood, bamboo, linoleum, vinyl, rubber, and so forth.

If you are specifying carpet, you will need to decide whether you want a plush cut pile or a low loop pile. Perhaps the client wants a pattern that has a high/low mix. That is also available. Next, decide whether you are going with wool, flax, linen, bamboo, olefin, or a synthetic nylon. If you specify wool, be sure nobody in the home has allergies.

It is best to use a heavy-duty carpet in areas where there are kids, pets, and high traffic. In a basement, you should not use wool but something that stands up to humidity and allows for direct glue-down installation. Low pile works best when you need to facilitate ease of movement. If you are designing a home office, a low-pile carpet or area rug works best and allows for the motion of an office chair.

Carpet tiles have gained in popularity in the residential market partially due to the offerings from FLOR®. They burst onto the market a decade ago with great patterns, mix-and-match options, and easy installation instructions. Designers can have fun with this system, as the carpet tiles are very easy to replace in the event of damage. Replacing one or a few tiles costs a lot less than having to replace wall-to-wall carpeting and extends the life of the installation. We recommend that when you place the order for carpet tiles, you add 20 percent overage to the order for your client to hold in reserve (known as "attic stock"). This ensures that your client will have replacement tiles on hand in the same dye lot as the carpet tiles initially installed.

If you are specifying wood or cork floors, use a resilient finish for heavy traffic areas. Engineered wood floors should also be considered, especially for conditions such as basement levels or other spaces with humidity and water issues. Linoleum, vinyl/rubber tile, and poured acrylic floors are also great options for resilient floors that stand up to heavy wear and tear.

If you are specifying multiple flooring types in one space or transitioning from one space to another, make sure there is little to no difference in the heights of the materials to allow for an easy transition from one space to another and to adhere to ADA and IBC guidelines. If there is a difference in the heights of your flooring, use a saddle or a transition strip between the two areas.

Always remember to consult your clients about whether they are interested in specifying sustainable flooring, which helps protect the environment.

SPECIFICATIONS   **FLOORING—HARD SURFACE AND RESILIENT CHECKLIST**

Flooring #1

- ☐ **Vendor/showroom** _____
- ☐ **Item manufacturer, number, and color** _____
- ☐ **Net price** _____
- ☐ **Stock** _____
- ☐ **Where is it stocked? (Specify United States, United Kingdom, etc.)** _____
- ☐ **Lead time and ETA** _____
- ☐ **Product dimensions** _____
- ☐ **Flooring type (Specify hardwood, tile, rubber, vinyl tile, carpet, area rug, etc.)** _____
- ☐ **Finish** _____
- ☐ **Square footage of space** _____
- ☐ **Amount to be ordered** _____
- ☐ **Sidemark** (e.g., client name/room/item) _____

Flooring #2

- ☐ **Vendor/showroom** _____
- ☐ **Item manufacturer, number, and color** _____
- ☐ **Net price** _____
- ☐ **Stock** _____
- ☐ **Where is it stocked? (Specify United States, United Kingdom, etc.)** _____
- ☐ **Lead time and ETA** _____
- ☐ **Product dimensions** _____
- ☐ **Flooring type (Specify hardwood, tile, rubber, vinyl tile, carpet, area rug, etc.)** _____
- ☐ **Finish** _____
- ☐ **Square footage of space** _____
- ☐ **Amount to be ordered** _____
- ☐ **Sidemark** (e.g., client name/room/item) _____

Flooring #3

- ☐ **Vendor/showroom** _____
- ☐ **Item manufacturer, number, and color** _____
- ☐ **Net price** _____
- ☐ **Stock** _____
- ☐ **Where is it stocked? (Specify United States, United Kingdom, etc.)** _____
- ☐ **Lead time and ETA** _____
- ☐ **Product dimensions** _____
- ☐ **Flooring type (Specify hardwood, tile, rubber, vinyl tile, carpet, area rug, etc.)** _____
- ☐ **Finish** _____
- ☐ **Square footage of space** _____
- ☐ **Amount to be ordered** _____
- ☐ **Sidemark** (e.g., client name/room/item) _____

Furniture Specification

Furniture—Case Goods Specification

Furniture that has a storage component is placed into the category of case goods in the design world.

Some examples of case goods are desks, console tables with drawers or shelves, bookcases, chests of drawers, chests with doors, sideboards, and buffets or credenzas.

When specifying case goods, you need to be concerned with dimensions for access measurement. Be sure the pieces will fit through openings and be able to turn corners, go up a flight of stairs, and so forth. Always ask the salesperson whether the pieces can be delivered unassembled and put together on-site. This will spare you many installation headaches and heartache.

Be sure to ask about the case construction. Hardwood materials and dovetail construction are wonderful. Also look for soft-close glides on drawers and door hinges wherever possible. If the piece has a lacquer finish, is it available in high gloss only or can a satin finish be used? Can you customize the color? These are questions to review with your salesperson along with the choices of hardware finishes and leg options.

A sideboard or buffet that is not custom-built and installed must also be specified with care. It might be wise to specify an item that is modular—that is, available in sections—which facilitates the longevity of a piece if it is moved to another residence, since it has a better chance of fitting into a new space if it can be reworked. One of our clients moved, and we were able to repurpose the existing buffet/server by using one piece in the new dining room, while the other two served as a media cabinet in their new family room.

Designers select all finishes on case goods with the awareness that we are expected to do something different—something clients would not come up with if left to their own devices. As a designer, you have at your fingertips the opportunity to work with a variety of materials, finishes, and color selections to create a personal expression of your client's taste.

Lead time is critical. Are the pieces in stock? Are the projected delivery dates in sync with your project installation timeline? Are the delivery fees in line with your budget? These fees can be steep, depending on the manufacturer.

Upholstered Furniture Specification

Upholstered furniture represents the "bread and butter" of the business for many design professionals. Here you have the opportunity to truly customize a piece for your client. Many designers "white label" an upholstered piece, keeping the manufacturer's name hidden from the clients, so that the clients regard the piece as their own. Other designers buy directly from manufacturers and disclose the details to clients. In some cases, clients will request a certain manufacturer or furniture showroom/designer.

You must perform an access measurement to ensure that all the furniture you are reusing/repurposing, as well as the new items you are specifying, will fit through the building entrance door, the elevator, any corridors, the entry door to the dwelling, any stairwells, individual spaces, and so forth.

When there are children and pets under foot, durability is a paramount consideration. If your clients are looking for longevity in the pieces that they purchase, choose furniture that is geared to high-traffic areas and built to last.

Think about finish options, metal versus wood frames, tight seat and back versus cushions. The fewer movable parts, the easier the piece will be to maintain. Also be mindful of the appropriateness of a piece. A chair or sofa in a family room will probably take much more abuse than one in a private bedroom or a formal living room that does not get much use.

There are so many options to consider when specifying upholstered furnishings. What is the arm style, what type of leg or foot will be specified, and what will the finish be? Will the piece have a skirt, and, if so, will it be a waterfall style? Will the skirt have an inverted pleat? Will it be shirred?

Cushions also must be specified. Many manufacturers offer options. Perhaps you want a bench seat cushion (one long cushion) rather than individual seat cushions. Do you want a box-edge cushion, and will it have a welt or a baseball stitch? Will the cushion be filled with down, a spring-down blend, or foam? The back cushions also need to be specified. Perhaps your client prefers a tight back that is channel quilted or tufted like a Chesterfield sofa. Be as specific as you can.

When considering the fabric to be upholstered on a piece, look at the integrity of the fabric. Silks must be knit-backed for upholstery use, while chenille or other woven fabrics may require an acrylic backing for more structural integrity. Inquire with the manufacturer for new work and with your workroom for reupholstered work. It is best to have a memo sample sent to the manufacturer or workroom to verify what is necessary for upholstery.

You also have to decide on the direction of the fabric. Will you run it "off the bolt," or do you wish to "railroad," or turn the fabric, so that you can avoid seams?

Many times designers opt to use more than one fabric on a particular piece of furniture. The designer might specify trim for the piece as well. Be as specific as you can when writing purchase orders to both the manufacturer and the fabric and trim suppliers. The manufacturer will provide you with a COM (customer's own material) tag. This must be used for *each* fabric and trim being applied to the piece. You may have many COM tags for just one sofa. The details are so important.

SPECIFICATIONS

FURNITURE—CASE GOODS CHECKLIST

NOTE: Be sure to do an access measurement to ensure that the piece you are specifying will fit into all the following areas that apply: the building entrance door, the elevator, the entry door to the space, any stairwells, etc.

Furniture #1

- ☐ **Vendor/showroom** _____
- ☐ **Item name and/or number** _____
- ☐ **Net price** _____
- ☐ **Stock** _____
- ☐ **Where is it stocked? (Specify United States, United Kingdom, etc.)** _____
- ☐ **Lead time and ETA** _____
- ☐ **Overall product dimensions** _____
- ☐ **Finish** _____
- ☐ **Leg/foot/base type** _____
- ☐ **Hardware finish** _____
- ☐ **Sidemark** (e.g., client name/room/item) _____

Furniture #2

- ☐ **Vendor/showroom** _____
- ☐ **Item name and/or number** _____
- ☐ **Net price** _____
- ☐ **Stock** _____
- ☐ **Where is it stocked? (Specify United States, United Kingdom, etc.)** _____
- ☐ **Lead time and ETA** _____
- ☐ **Overall product dimensions** _____
- ☐ **Finish** _____
- ☐ **Leg/foot/base type** _____
- ☐ **Hardware finish** _____
- ☐ **Sidemark** (e.g., client name/room/item) _____

Furniture #3

- ☐ **Vendor/showroom** _____
- ☐ **Item name and/or number** _____
- ☐ **Net price** _____
- ☐ **Stock** _____
- ☐ **Where is it stocked? (Specify United States, United Kingdom, etc.)** _____
- ☐ **Lead time and ETA** _____
- ☐ **Overall product dimensions** _____
- ☐ **Finish** _____
- ☐ **Leg/foot/base type** _____
- ☐ **Hardware finish** _____
- ☐ **Sidemark** (e.g., client name/room/item) _____

NOTE: Be sure to do an access measurement to ensure that the piece you are specifying will fit into all the following areas that apply: the building entrance door, the elevator, the entry door to the space, any stairwells, etc.

Furniture #1

- ☐ Vendor/showroom _____
- ☐ Item name and/or number _____
- ☐ Net price _____
- ☐ Stock _____ Where is it stocked? _____
- ☐ Lead time and ETA _____
- ☐ Overall product dimensions _____
- ☐ Seat height/depth _____ Arm height _____
- ☐ Interior width (inside arms) _____
- ☐ Leg/foot/skirt/base type _____
- ☐ Finish _____
- ☐ Arm style (rolled, panel, pleated, box/tuxedo) _____
- ☐ Back style (plain, tufted, etc.) _____
- ☐ Back type (Dacron®, down, spring-down) _____
- ☐ Back options (tight back, 2 back cushions, 3 back cushions) _____
- ☐ Seat type (Dacron®, down, spring-down) _____
- ☐ Seat options (tight seat, bench seat, 2 seats, 3 seats, vented cushion if leather/vinyl) _____
- ☐ Cushion type (T-cushion, rectangular, etc.) _____
- ☐ Nail heads? If so, choose a size, a finish, and spacing _____
- ☐ Does manufacturer allow COM orders? _____
- ☐ COM yardage needed _____
- ☐ To avoid seams, where appropriate, always railroad the fabric. (Note if railroading fabric.) _____

Furniture #2

- ☐ Vendor/showroom _____
- ☐ Item name and/or number _____
- ☐ Net price _____
- ☐ Stock _____ Where is it stocked? (Specify United States, United Kingdom, etc.) _____
- ☐ Lead time and ETA _____
- ☐ Overall product dimensions _____
- ☐ Seat height/depth _____ Arm height _____
- ☐ Interior width (inside arms) _____
- ☐ Leg/foot/skirt/base type _____
- ☐ Finish _____
- ☐ Arm style (rolled, panel, pleated, box/tuxedo) _____
- ☐ Back style (plain, tufted, etc.) _____
- ☐ Back type (Dacron®, down, spring-down) _____
- ☐ Back options (tight back, 2 back cushions, 3 back cushions) _____
- ☐ Seat type (Dacron®, down, spring-down) _____
- ☐ Seat options (tight seat, bench seat, 2 seats, 3 seats, vented cushion if leather/vinyl) _____
- ☐ Cushion type (T-cushion, rectangular, etc.) _____
- ☐ Nail heads? If so choose a size, a finish, and spacing _____
- ☐ Do they allow COM orders? _____
- ☐ COM yardage needed _____
- ☐ To avoid seams, where appropriate, always railroad the fabric. (Note if railroading fabric.) _____

Kitchen Specification

Let's begin with the kitchen cabinet selection, which is generally where you will start your specifications after the plan has been approved.

Many designers work with a cabinet sales representative, or they may opt to work with a showroom. It is generally a good idea to educate your client on the options.

The first item to discuss is the finish. Do the clients want wood or a laminate/composite? Do they prefer a stain, painted, or lacquer finish? What style will the door be—modern or traditional? You may want to have the client create an idea book in the cloud on Pinterest.com or Houzz.com, or create an Evernote.com file and share it with you. This is a great way to begin the dialogue.

Once the door style and color/finish have been selected, you can move to more detailed elevations. This is when the kitchen begins to come to life. You can work out the details of the upper and lower cabinetry, whether or not you will have a peninsula or an island in a contrasting or matching finish. You also should discuss any glass door inserts, pull-out drawers and shelves, corner cabinet inserts, silverware drawers, and other bells and whistles available in each cabinet line.

Cabinets can be specified from the low end to the high end and everywhere in between. Always get a general budget for the cabinetry so that the specifications you are suggesting are realistic and in line with the client's and your vision for the project.

Once the cabinetry has been selected, you need to tackle the appliances and fixtures. Appliances are integral to the functionality of a kitchen. There are a number of factors to consider before specification can take place. First, is there gas or electric fuel for cooking? Will you use a slide-in range or a cooktop and wall oven combo?

Do you need a warming drawer, double ovens, refrigerator or dishwasher drawers, or a wine refrigerator? Again, specifications are important.

Refrigerators and dishwashers can be slide-in models or they can be integral and have face panels that match the cabinetry doors/drawers. This needs to be worked out in advance of your cabinet order so that if a panel is required, the correct model of the appliance is ordered and the specs are given to the manufacturer/representative.

If you are using a slide-in model, perhaps in stainless steel, you must also consider the specifications with regard to depth and height and the fillers needed on the cabinetry. Again, coordinate with your rep to be sure that all cabinetry is ordered correctly and that your drawings and the shop drawings are correct. Measure twice, cut once!

Now to the fixtures: In a kitchen, you must, of course, consider the sink. Will it be an undermount or perhaps a farmhouse style? How wide will it be and of what shape? How about the finish? Will it be stainless or porcelain or another precious metal? You also need to specify the stopper and drain.

You may be designing a kitchen that requires a bar/prep sink for the island. Will this be round or square? This type of sink is generally smaller than the main sink. You may also want to specify an instant hot water dispenser and/or a soap dispenser at the sink.

Many designers are being asked to install pot fillers over the range or cooktop to facilitate filling large pots for soup or cooking pasta. These are not only functional but also very decorative. Always be consistent with your finish selection as well.

The hardware is also an important component and constitutes the finishing touch on the cabinetry. Be sure to coordinate the style and finish so that they harmonize with both the cabinetry style and the finish of the fixtures you have selected.

Floor tile should be carefully selected for function and durability. Try to work with a tile that has texture, which constitutes a safer surface when wet. Also, a larger-scale tile means fewer grout lines and less area for food to stain when it is spilled. The kitchen is the area with the most traffic in the home, so the kitchen floor takes a great deal of abuse. A porcelain tile with integral color wears better in the event of chipping. Natural stone is always a durable option, but it requires more maintenance.

While wood floors are showing up in more kitchens these days, tile is still found on the majority of kitchen floors. There are newer options, including porcelain tile with a photo-realistic image of wood, that offer a more functional alternative to a hardwood floor in a wet location.

You may specify any number of materials for a backsplash—stone, porcelain, glass, metal, tin, and so on. You can choose subway tiles, mosaics, or squares. You can create attractive designs and switch things up behind a range or sink to add more interest. The possibilities are endless and should be thoroughly explored with your client.

SPECIFICATIONS   **KITCHEN CABINETRY CHECKLIST**

Cabinets

- ☐ Specify cabinet door style (Shaker, flat panel, raised panel, arch raised panel, etc.) _____
- ☐ Specify cabinet material/wood species _____
- ☐ Specify finish and material of cabinet exterior _____
- ☐ Specify finish and material of cabinet interior/shelves _____
- ☐ Specify any panel inserts (clear glass, frosted glass, stainless, bead board, etc.) _____
- ☐ Specify style of crown if applicable _____
- ☐ Specify soft close on all drawers.
- ☐ Specify soft close hinges on all doors: concealed or exposed (circle one).
- ☐ Specify base and trim molding to coordinate with cabinetry if applicable.
- ☐ Specify interior elements of cabinetry (lazy susan, pull-out drawers behind doors, etc.) _____
- ☐ Are your appliances to receive a panel? Yes or No (circle one).
- ☐ Are any exposed sides of cabinetry to receive a panel? Yes or No (circle one).

Hardware

- ☐ Specify and order hardware for doors (any knobs, pulls, etc.).
- ☐ Manufacturer/model number _____ Specify finish _____
- ☐ Specify and order hardware for drawers (any knobs, pulls, etc.).
- ☐ Manufacturer/model number _____ Specify finish _____

Countertops

- ☐ Specify species (stone type, wood type, concrete, solid surface) _____
- ☐ Specify finish (polished, honed, brushed, lacquered) _____
- ☐ Specify thickness (3/4″ or 1 1/4″) _____
- ☐ Specify edge detail (bullnose, eased, ogee, etc.) _____
- ☐ Specify overhang dimension over cabinet edge (1/4″, 1/2″, 1″, etc.) _____
- ☐ Discuss with your vendor any seaming and cuts that may need to be made within the surface and where this seaming should occur. (Try to seam in the least noticeable places.)
- ☐ Set up a time for the vendor to template, and have one of your staff on-site to explain design intent and answer any questions.
- ☐ Make sure the templater is aware of any extensions to the countertop and templates accordingly (e.g., overhangs for barstool seating).

SPECIFICATIONS   **APPLIANCES CHECKLIST**

NOTE: Before placing an order for any appliance, re-measure the space allotted for the appliance to make sure the model you specified fits within the parameters of the space. Be sure to send all appliance specs to the kitchen cabinet maker/supplier.

Refrigerator

☐ **Specify size** (If in a small apartment setting, you may want to suggest a slim refrigerator to save space.) _____

☐ **Specify whether refrigerator is built-in, receiving a panel, or freestanding** (circle one).

☐ **Specify whether client wants refrigerator drawers in place of or in addition to full size refrigerator.**

☐ **Discuss with the client door/drawer options and their configuration (side-by-side, French door–bottom freezer, etc.).**

☐ **Discuss and note features: icemaker, adjustable shelves, etc.** _____

☐ **Manufacturer/model number** _____ **Specify finish** _____

☐ **Get all the necessary specs from the manufacturer for filler dimensions needed on either side of the appliance.**

☐ **If the refrigerator is to receive a panel, get those specs as well.**

Range

☐ **Specify gas, electric, or dual fuel** (circle one).

☐ **Specify width** (if in a small apartment setting, you may want to use a 24″ range) _____

☐ **Specify freestanding or frameless range** (circle one). **Specify number of burners: 4, 5, 6, or 8** (circle one).

☐ **Specify single or double oven configuration** (circle one). **Specify with or without warming drawer** (circle one).

☐ **Manufacturer/model number** _____ **Specify finish** _____

☐ **Get all the necessary specs from the manufacturer for filler dimensions needed on either side of the appliance.**

Cooktop

☐ **Specify gas, electric, or induction cooktop** (circle one).

☐ **Specify drop-in or slide-in** (circle one). **Specify number of burners: 4, 5, 6, or 8** (circle one).

☐ **Specify size** _____

☐ **Manufacturer/model number** _____ **Specify finish** _____

Range Hood

☐ **Specify size** _____

☐ **Manufacturer/model number** _____ **Specify finish** _____

Wall Oven

☐ **Specify size** _____

☐ **Specify single or double oven** (circle one). **Specify whether client wants oven/microwave combination unit: Yes or No** (circle one).

☐ **Manufacturer/model number** _____ **Specify finish** _____

☐ **Get all the necessary specs from the manufacturer for filler dimensions needed on either side of the appliance.**

Microwave Oven

☐ **Specify standard microwave, microwave recirculating range hood (good solution for a small apartment setting to eliminate the need for a separate range hood), or microwave drawer** (circle one).

☐ **Manufacturer/model number** _____ **Specify finish** _____

☐ **Get all the necessary specs from the manufacturer for filler dimensions needed on either side of the appliance.**

Dishwasher

☐ **Specify size** _____

☐ **Specify with or without a handle** (consider interfering doors/drawers on perpendicular cabinetry planes) (circle one).

☐ **Manufacturer/model number** _____ **Specify finish** _____

☐ **Get all the necessary specs from the manufacturer for filler dimensions needed on either side of the appliance.**

SPECIFICATIONS   **KITCHEN FIXTURES CHECKLIST**

NOTE: Always have the rough-in components sent by the plumbing and electrical supplier/vendor *PRIOR* to the trims and fixtures. Be sure to send all appliance specs to the kitchen cabinet maker/supplier.

Sink

☐ Specify sink (basin): framed, drop-in, apron-front, or under-mount (circle one).

☐ Specify single, double, or triple bowl sink (circle one).

☐ Specify sink shape: circular, oval, D-shape, rectangular, or square (circle one).

☐ Sink manufacturer/model number _____ Specify finish _____

☐ Sink dimensions _____

☐ Specify sink grate if necessary (recommended for stainless steel sinks).

☐ Sink grate manufacturer/model number _____ Specify finish _____

Faucet

☐ Specify faucet and handles: single-handle, single-handle with pull-out spray, two-handle, bridge, wall-mounted, or water filtration (circle all that apply).

☐ Specify faucet location: left side of sink, right side of sink, or center (circle one).

☐ Specify valve (rough-in) and trim for faucet and/or handles.

☐ Faucet manufacturer/model number _____ Specify finish _____

Sprayer

☐ Specify sprayer manufacturer/model number _____ Specify finish _____

☐ Specify sprayer parts kit. You will need a hose and trim kit.

Soap Dispenser

☐ Specify soap dispenser manufacturer/model number _____ Specify finish _____

Pot Filler

☐ Specify deck mounted or wall mounted (circle one).

☐ Shower pot filler manufacturer/model number _____ Specify finish _____

Lighting and Electrical

☐ Specify GFI outlets (for all wet locations).

☐ Specify under-cabinet lighting manufacturer/model number _____

☐ Specify overhead lighting fixture on dimmer (specify type of dimmer).

☐ Specify overhead lighting fixture manufacturer/model number _____ Specify finish _____

☐ Specify how the lighting switches will be ganged and the color of outlets and switch plates _____

Hardware

☐ Specify door hardware manufacturer/model number _____ Specify finish _____

☐ Specify drawer hardware manufacturer/model number _____ Specify finish _____

Floor Tile

☐ Floor tile manufacturer/model number _____ Specify finish _____
☐ Tile location and placement _____
☐ Specify dimensions _____ Quantity _____

Floor Tile Grout

☐ Floor grout manufacturer/model number _____ Specify color _____
☐ Quantity _____

Wall/Backsplash Field Tile

☐ Wall field tile manufacturer/model number _____ Specify finish _____
☐ Specify dimensions _____ Quantity _____
☐ Tile location and placement _____

Wall/Backsplash Border Tile or Decorative Molding

☐ Wall border tile manufacturer/model number _____ Specify finish _____
☐ Tile location and placement _____
☐ Specify dimensions _____ Quantity _____

Pencil/Liner Tile

☐ Specify simple or decorative pencil/liner (circle one).
☐ Pencil/liner tile manufacturer/model number _____ Specify finish _____
☐ Tile location and placement _____
☐ Specify dimensions _____ Quantity _____

Wall Tile Grout

☐ Wall grout manufacturer/model number _____ Specify color _____
☐ Quantity _____

Saddles

☐ Specify species (stone type, wood type, concrete, solid surface) _____
☐ Specify edge detail and thickness (3/4″ or 11/4″) _____
☐ Specify finish (polished, honed, brushed, lacquered, etc.) _____

Lighting Specification

Lighting is integral to the success of your project. First, you must address the three main lighting solutions:

- Ambient or general illumination—how you move through and illuminate the space for way finding
- Task lighting—illumination required for a specific purpose such as reading, writing, or general work
- Accent or "key" lighting—which adds drama, creates emphasis and focus, highlights architectural details, and illuminates artwork and sculpture

Let's start with the general or ambient lighting solution. Many residential spaces have drywall ceilings, so you may think that recessed lighting or pendant lighting with direct/indirect illumination is a better fit for the space. If you are designing a space with an exposed ceiling, you need to think differently.

Track lighting is a very efficient way to illuminate your space and provides you with many options for both general, task, and accent lighting. Clients enjoy the flexibility provided by track lighting.

You need to do the research and be specific about the source of electric light. Are you planning to specify fluorescent, halogen, high-intensity discharge (HID), or light-emitting diode (LED) lamping?

If you are blending electric light sources, how will the various color temperatures work together in harmony? These different lamp types vary in their energy consumption and affect the efficiency and efficacy of the fixture.

Also be mindful that if designing an ADA-compliant residence, all wall-mounted luminaires (sconces) must not exceed 4" deep.

Whether you are designing a sustainable project or not, many local codes now require that 50 percent of a space be fitted with energy-efficient lighting. Incandescent and halogen lamps do not qualify, so look to other sources. The new favorite is, of course, LED, which is now more readily available in color temperatures of 2700 K and has a color rendition similar to that of an incandescent lamp. LED technology has come a long way in the last few years, and there are many fixtures/luminaires on the market for a variety of installation options.

Many manufacturers have introduced light and motion sensors, which turn on and shut off lights when someone enters or leaves a room. They can now also sense levels of natural light entering a space and calculate when a fixture turns on and off based on the natural daylight quotient. This can contribute toward your LEED credits if you are working on a sustainable project.

When budgets permit, it is strongly suggested that you work with a professional lighting designer to ensure that you give your clients the best lighting solution that reduces their energy consumption and works within their budget, while also supplying a balance of functional lighting and mood lighting.

Lighting #1

- ☐ **Vendor/showroom** _____
- ☐ **Item name and/or model number** _____
- ☐ **Net price** _____
- ☐ **Stock** _____
- ☐ **Where is it stocked? (Specify United States, United Kingdom, etc.)** _____
- ☐ **Lead time and ETA** _____
- ☐ **Overall product dimensions** _____
- ☐ **Shade dimensions (height and width)** _____
- ☐ **Back-plate dimensions** _____
- ☐ **Bulb type and wattage** _____
- ☐ **Finish** _____
- ☐ **Shade material/finish** _____
- ☐ **Sidemark** _____
- ☐ **Quantity** _____

Lighting #2

- ☐ **Vendor/showroom** _____
- ☐ **Item name and/or model number** _____
- ☐ **Net price** _____
- ☐ **Stock** _____
- ☐ **Where is it stocked? (Specify United States, United Kingdom, etc.)** _____
- ☐ **Lead time and ETA** _____
- ☐ **Overall product dimensions** _____
- ☐ **Shade dimensions (height and width)** _____
- ☐ **Back-plate dimensions** _____
- ☐ **Bulb type and wattage** _____
- ☐ **Finish** _____
- ☐ **Shade material/finish** _____
- ☐ **Sidemark** _____
- ☐ **Quantity** _____

Lighting #3

- ☐ **Vendor/showroom** _____
- ☐ **Item name and/or model number** _____
- ☐ **Net price** _____
- ☐ **Stock** _____
- ☐ **Where is it stocked? (Specify United States, United Kingdom, etc.)** _____
- ☐ **Lead time and ETA** _____
- ☐ **Overall product dimensions** _____
- ☐ **Shade dimensions (height and width)** _____
- ☐ **Back-plate dimensions** _____
- ☐ **Bulb type and wattage** _____
- ☐ **Finish** _____
- ☐ **Shade material/finish** _____
- ☐ **Sidemark** _____
- ☐ **Quantity** _____

Luxury Spaces Specification

Many of you will work on residential projects where clients request designs for spaces such as wine cellars, billiard rooms, home theaters, and home gyms. We call these *luxury spaces*.

These can be complex spaces. You need to be mindful of the function of each space, coordinating audiovisual components and engineering with specific furnishings, fixtures, finishes, and equipment.

Luxury spaces require you to work with a multitude of other trade professionals to be sure that the outcome is what your client desires. Hiring an audiovisual specialist is critical for a home theater, but other professionals likewise play important roles in luxury space design. For example, the designer of a home gym will benefit from consulting with the client's personal trainer. Since a wine cellar should be designed with cooling and temperature control in mind, the designer should consult with an HVAC professional as well as a wine cellar consultant. Do the clients wish to have a tasting table in the cellar or outside? Their answer to this question affects the overall size of the cellar, the lighting solution, and the ambiance.

The checklists in this section provide you with a road map for navigating this relatively new area in single-family luxury home design. Technology changes rapidly, and innovations appear each day. Now your client can program multiple functions from an iPad® or a wall-mounted keypad. Lighting, music, and many other functions can be automated and controlled from one or multiple devices, giving your clients more control of their environment

SPECIFICATIONS   **BILLIARD/GAME ROOM ITEMS/FIXTURES CHECKLIST**

Audiovisual Equipment

☐ TV manufacturer/model number _____

☐ Media player manufacturer/model number _____

☐ Stereo manufacturer/model number _____

☐ Game console _____

Equipment, Lighting, and Electrical

☐ Specify whether overhead lighting fixtures will be on a dimmer. (Specify type of dimmer.) _____

☐ Specify overhead lighting manufacturer/model number _____ Specify finish _____ Quantity _____

☐ Specify billiards light manufacturer/model number _____ Specify finish _____ Quantity _____

☐ Specify ceiling fan(s) manufacturer/model number _____ Specify finish _____ Quantity _____

☐ Specify how the lighting switches will be ganged and the color of outlets and switch plates _____

Billiards Items

☐ Billiards table manufacturer/model number _____ Specify finish/felt color _____

☐ Specify dimensions _____ Quantity _____

☐ Specify freestanding or wall-mounted pool cue rack (circle one)

☐ Pool cue rack manufacturer/model number _____ Specify color/finish _____

☐ Specify dimensions _____ Quantity _____

☐ Specify cue sticks, balls, racks (triangle), cue chalk, cue chalk holders, at least one bridge stick, pool table cover, etc.

☐ Dartboard manufacturer/model number _____ Specify color/finish _____

☐ Specify dimensions _____ Quantity _____

☐ Air hockey table manufacturer/model number _____ Specify color/finish _____

☐ Specify dimensions _____ Quantity _____

☐ Foosball table manufacturer/model number _____ Specify color/finish _____

☐ Specify dimensions _____ Quantity _____

☐ Ping-Pong table manufacturer/model number _____ Specify color/finish _____

☐ Specify dimensions _____ Quantity _____

☐ Pinball machine manufacturer/model number _____ Specify color/finish _____

☐ Specify dimensions _____ Quantity _____

Furniture

☐ Pub table manufacturer/model number _____ Specify color/finish _____

☐ Specify dimensions _____ Quantity _____

☐ Bar stools manufacturer/model number _____ Specify color/finish _____

☐ Specify dimensions _____ Quantity _____

☐ Sofa manufacturer/model number _____ Specify color/finish _____

☐ Specify dimensions _____ Quantity _____

☐ Loveseat manufacturer/model number _____ Specify color/finish _____

☐ Specify dimensions _____ Quantity _____

☐ Club chair manufacturer/model number _____ Specify color/finish _____

☐ Specify dimensions _____ Quantity _____

☐ Cocktail table manufacturer/model number _____ Specify color/finish _____

☐ Specify dimensions _____ Quantity _____

☐ Media unit manufacturer/model number _____ Specify color/finish _____

☐ Specify dimensions _____ Quantity _____

☐ Card table manufacturer/model number _____ Specify color/finish _____

☐ Specify dimensions _____ Quantity _____

SPECIFICATIONS   **HOME GYM CHECKLIST**

Flooring

- ☐ Flooring manufacturer/model number _____ Specify finish _____
- ☐ Specify dimensions _____ Quantity _____
- ☐ Flooring location and placement instructions _____
- ☐ Mats for use under equipment: manufacturer/model number _____ Specify color _____ Quantity _____

Equipment

- ☐ Treadmill manufacturer/model number _____ Specify color _____
- ☐ Specify dimensions _____ Quantity _____
- ☐ Elliptical/cross-trainer manufacturer/model number _____ Specify color _____
- ☐ Specify dimensions _____ Quantity _____
- ☐ Stair climber manufacturer/model number _____ Specify color _____
- ☐ Specify dimensions _____ Quantity _____
- ☐ Exercise bike manufacturer/model number _____ Specify color _____
- ☐ Specify dimensions _____ Quantity _____
- ☐ Home gym manufacturer/model number _____ Specify color_____
- ☐ Specify dimensions _____ Quantity _____
- ☐ Weight bench manufacturer/model number _____ Specify color _____
- ☐ Specify dimensions _____ Quantity _____

Accessories

- ☐ Exercise mat manufacturer/model number _____ Specify color _____ Quantity _____
- ☐ Stabilization ball manufacturer/model number _____ Specify color _____ Quantity _____
- ☐ Free weights manufacturer/model number _____ Specify color _____ Quantity _____
- ☐ Jump rope manufacturer/model number _____ Specify color _____ Quantity_____
- ☐ Resistance bands manufacturer/model number _____ Specify color _____ Quantity _____
- ☐ Kettlebell manufacturer/model number _____ Specify color _____ Quantity _____
- ☐ Medicine ball manufacturer/model number _____ Specify color _____ Quantity _____
- ☐ Mini trampoline manufacturer/model number _____ Specify color _____ Quantity _____
- ☐ Pull-up bar manufacturer/model number _____ Specify color _____ Quantity _____
- ☐ Speed bag manufacturer/model number _____ Specify color _____ Quantity _____
- ☐ Punching bag manufacturer/model number _____ Specify color _____ Quantity _____
- ☐ Incline step manufacturer/model number _____ Specify color _____ Quantity _____
- ☐ Foam rollers manufacturer/model number _____ Specify color _____ Quantity _____
- ☐ Specify whether you are using any mirror for the walls and how much? _____

Audiovisual Equipment

- ☐ TV manufacturer/model number _____
- ☐ Media player manufacturer/model number _____
- ☐ Cable/satellite provider _____
- ☐ Stereo manufacturer/model number _____
- ☐ Game console _____

Equipment, Lighting, and Electrical

- ☐ Mini fridge manufacturer/model number _____ Specify finish _____
- ☐ Specify whether overhead lighting fixtures will be on a dimmer. (Specify type of dimmer.) _____
- ☐ Specify overhead lighting manufacturer/model number _____ Specify finish _____
- ☐ Specify ceiling fan(s) manufacturer/model number _____ Specify finish _____ Quantity _____
- ☐ Specify how the lighting switches will be ganged and the color of the outlets and switch plates _____

Flooring

- ☐ Flooring #1 manufacturer/model number _____ Specify finish _____
- ☐ Specify dimensions _____ Quantity _____
- ☐ Flooring location and placement instructions _____
- ☐ Flooring #2 manufacturer/model number _____ Specify finish _____
- ☐ Specify dimensions _____ Quantity _____
- ☐ Flooring location and placement instructions _____

Fixtures

- ☐ Specify a straight, corner, or freestanding air tub/hot tub (circle one).
- ☐ Air tub/hot tub manufacturer/model number _____ Specify color _____
- ☐ Specify dimensions _____
- ☐ Steam shower manufacturer/model number _____ Specify color _____
- ☐ Specify dimensions _____
- ☐ Shower jets manufacturer/model number _____ Specify finish _____ Quantity _____
- ☐ Dry sauna manufacturer/model number _____ Specify color _____
- ☐ Specify dimensions _____
- ☐ Vanity manufacturer/model number _____ Specify color _____
- ☐ Specify dimensions _____ Quantity _____
- ☐ Sink/basin manufacturer/model number _____ Specify color _____
- ☐ Specify dimensions _____ Quantity _____

Accessories

- ☐ Massage table manufacturer/model number _____ Specify finish _____
- ☐ Specify dimensions _____
- ☐ Chair manufacturer/model number _____ Specify finish _____ Quantity _____
- ☐ Towel warmer manufacturer/model number _____ Specify finish _____ Quantity _____
- ☐ Specify dimensions _____
- ☐ Towel bar manufacturer/model number _____ Specify finish _____ Quantity _____
- ☐ Specify dimensions _____
- ☐ Robe hook manufacturer/model number _____ Specify finish _____ Quantity _____
- ☐ Specify single or double hook (circle one).
- ☐ Specify robe hook location(s): back of door, wall, etc. _____
- ☐ Specify custom cabinetry or shelving for towels, oils, etc.

Audiovisual Equipment

- ☐ TV manufacturer/model number _____
- ☐ Media player manufacturer/model number _____
- ☐ Cable/satellite provider _____
- ☐ Stereo manufacturer/model number _____
- ☐ Sound system manufacturer/model number _____

Equipment, Lighting, and Electrical

- ☐ Consider specifying a fireplace.
- ☐ Specify overhead lighting fixtures on a dimmer. (Specify type of dimmer.)
- ☐ Specify overhead lighting manufacturer/model number _____ Specify finish _____
- ☐ Specify ceiling fan(s) manufacturer/model number _____ Specify finish _____ Quantity _____
- ☐ Specify how the lighting switches will be ganged and the color of the outlets and switch plates _____

SPECIFICATIONS   **HOME THEATER CHECKLIST**

Flooring

- ☐ Flooring manufacturer/model number _____ Specify finish _____
- ☐ Specify dimensions _____ Quantity _____
- ☐ Flooring location and placement instructions _____

Seating

- ☐ Specify the type of seating your client would like to use: **ganged theater-style seating or sofas/loveseats** (circle one).
- ☐ Seating #1 manufacturer/model number _____ Specify color/finish _____
- ☐ Specify dimensions _____ Quantity _____
- ☐ Seating #2 manufacturer/model number _____ Specify color/finish _____
- ☐ Specify dimensions _____ Quantity _____
- ☐ Specify a platform(s) if necessary
- ☐ Platform manufacturer/model number _____ Specify color/finish _____
- ☐ Specify dimensions _____ Quantity _____

Candy Counter/Snack Stand

- ☐ Specify cabinetry finish _____
- ☐ Specify cabinetry countertop supplier _____
- ☐ Specify cabinetry countertop material and color _____
- ☐ Specify countertop edge: eased, bullnose, ogee, bevel, or other. (Circle one or write in.) _____
- ☐ Specify door/drawer hardware manufacturer/model number _____ Specify finish _____

Kitchenette

- ☐ Specify cabinetry finish _____
- ☐ Specify cabinetry countertop supplier _____
- ☐ Specify cabinetry countertop material and color _____
- ☐ Specify countertop edge: eased, bullnose, ogee, bevel, or other. (Circle one or write in.) _____
- ☐ Specify door/drawer hardware manufacturer/model number _____ Specify finish _____
- ☐ Specify microwave manufacturer/model number _____ Specify finish _____
- ☐ Specify refrigerator manufacturer/model number _____ Specify finish _____
- ☐ Specify trash bin manufacturer/model number _____ Specify color _____ Quantity _____

Audiovisual Equipment

- ☐ Projector or TV manufacturer/model number _____
- ☐ Screen manufacturer/model number (if applicable) _____
- ☐ Speakers/surround sound/subwoofer manufacturer/model number _____
- ☐ Media player manufacturer/model number _____
- ☐ Cable/satellite provider _____
- ☐ Universal remote manufacturer/model number _____

Lighting and Electrical

- ☐ Specify overhead lighting fixtures on a dimmer. (Specify type of dimmer.)
- ☐ Specify overhead lighting fixture(s) manufacturer/model number _____ Specify finish _____
- ☐ Specify wall sconce on a dimmer. (Specify type of dimmer.)
- ☐ Specify wall sconce manufacturer/model number _____ Specify finish ____ Quantity _____
- ☐ Specify how the lighting switches will be ganged and the color of the outlets and switch plates _____
- ☐ Specify GFI outlets (for all wet locations).

SPECIFICATIONS

Audiovisual Equipment

☐ TV manufacturer/model number _____

☐ Media player manufacturer/model number _____

☐ Stereo manufacturer/model number _____

Lighting and Electrical

☐ Specify overhead lighting fixtures on a dimmer. (Specify type of dimmer.)

☐ Specify overhead lighting manufacturer/model number _____ Specify finish _____ Quantity _____

☐ Specify under-cabinet lighting manufacturer/model number _____ Quantity _____

☐ Specify pendant lighting manufacturer/model number _____ Specify finish _____ Quantity _____

☐ Specify floor/table lamp manufacturer/model number _____ Specify finish _____ Quantity_____

☐ Specify ceiling fan(s) manufacturer/model number _____ Specify finish _____ Quantity _____

☐ Specify GFI outlets (for all wet locations).

☐ Specify how the lighting switches will be ganged and the color of the outlets and switch plates _____

Bar Fixtures

☐ Specify mini or full-size refrigerator (circle one).

☐ Fridge manufacturer/model number _____ Specify finish _____

☐ Specify sink (basin): framed, drop-in, or under-mount (circle one).

☐ Sink dimensions _____

☐ Specify sink grate if necessary (recommended for stainless steel sinks).

☐ Sink grate manufacturer/model number _____ Specify finish _____

☐ Specify faucet and handles: single-handle, single-handle with pull-out spray, two-handle, bridge, wall-mounted, or water filtration (circle all that apply).

☐ Specify faucet location: left side of sink, right side of sink, or center (circle one).

☐ Faucet manufacturer/model number _____ Specify finish _____

☐ Specify door hardware manufacturer/model number _____ Specify finish _____ Quantity _____

☐ Specify drawer hardware manufacturer/model number _____ Specify finish _____ Quantity _____

Furniture

☐ Pub table manufacturer/model number _____ Specify color/finish _____

☐ Specify dimensions _____ Quantity _____

☐ Bar stools manufacturer/model number _____ Specify color/finish _____

☐ Specify dimensions _____ Quantity _____

☐ Sofa manufacturer/model number _____ Specify color/finish _____

☐ Specify dimensions _____ Quantity _____

☐ Loveseat manufacturer/model number _____ Specify color/finish _____

☐ Specify dimensions _____ Quantity _____

☐ Armchair manufacturer/model number _____ Specify color/finish _____

☐ Specify dimensions _____ Quantity _____

☐ Cocktail table manufacturer/model number _____ Specify color/finish _____

☐ Specify dimensions _____ Quantity _____

☐ End table manufacturer/model number _____ Specify color/finish _____

☐ Specify dimensions _____ Quantity _____

☐ Media unit manufacturer/model number _____ Specify color/finish _____

☐ Specify dimensions _____ Quantity _____

SPECIFICATIONS   **WINE CELLAR CHECKLIST**

Cooling System

- ☐ **Specify through-the-wall system, split system, or self-contained system** (circle one).
- ☐ **Cooling system manufacturer/model number** _____ **Specify color/finish** _____
- ☐ **Cooling system dimensions** _____

Door

- ☐ **Specify an exterior-rated door. (If specifying a door with a glass panel insert, be sure to specify tempered double-pane glass for insulation purposes.)**
- ☐ **Specify weather stripping on all four sides of the door to keep the cellar temperature regulated.**
- ☐ **Door manufacturer/model number** _____ **Specify finish** _____
- ☐ **Specify a saddle for under the door to keep a tight seal in the room.**
- ☐ **Saddle manufacturer** _____ **Specify type/finish** _____

Security/Monitoring System

- ☐ **Specify door hardware with lock: Yes or No** (circle one).
- ☐ **Specify security/monitoring system for the wine cellar: Yes or No** (circle one). (Suggest this to protect your clients' investment from theft, alert them in the event of power failure, and let them know the exact temperature/humidity.)
- ☐ **Security/monitoring system manufacturer/model number** _____

Hardware

- ☐ **Specify door hardware manufacturer/model number** _____ **Specify finish** _____
- ☐ **Specify door hinges manufacturer/model number** _____ **Specify finish** _____

Walls

- ☐ **Wall surface or paint manufacturer/model number** _____ **Specify finish** _____
- ☐ **Location** _____

Wine racks

- ☐ **Specify that the wine racks be constructed using mahogany or redwood. In this cool and possibly damp space, you should choose a wood that is resistant to rotting.**
- ☐ **Wine rack location and placement instructions** _____

Tasting Table

- ☐ **If you are having a tasting table custom-built using wood, specify that it be constructed using mahogany or redwood.**
- ☐ **Tasting table manufacturer/model number** _____ **Specify finish** _____
- ☐ **Specify dimensions** _____

Flooring

- ☐ **Specify flooring type and manufacturer** _____
- ☐ **Specify dimensions** _____ **Quantity** _____
- ☐ **Location and placement instructions** _____

Lighting and Electrical

- ☐ **Specify lights on a timer to prevent excessive heat in cellar.**
- ☐ **Specify overhead lighting fixtures on a dimmer. (Specify type of dimmer.)**
- ☐ **Specify overhead lighting fixture(s) manufacturer/model number** _____ **Specify finish** _____
- ☐ **Specify decorative pendant/sconces (if desired) on a dimmer. (Specify type of dimmer.)**
- ☐ **Specify decorative pendant/sconce manufacturer/model number** _____ **Specify finish** _____
- ☐ **Specify how the lighting switches will be ganged and the color of the outlets and switch plates** _____
- ☐ **Specify GFI outlets (for all wet locations).**

Wall Specification

Paint Specification

The walls account for the largest square footage of space for which an interior designer is responsible. There are a variety of products used to decorate and protect the wall plane.

Paint is the most popular. While solid color and neutral tones are de rigueur many designers also look to newer offerings, including colored, white, and blackboard paints; magnetic paints; faux finishes; and other decorative paint finishes. It is strongly suggested that you look for low-VOC (volatile organic compound) paints to limit the toxic particles and off-gassing.

Most paint manufacturers have architectural reps who will work with you, supplying samples as well as providing you with specifications for your scope of work and construction documents. They are extremely knowledgeable about their product lines and will help you to specify the best product for your particular application. Also, we recommend that you do research on the quality of the paint produced by each manufacturer. The *hide* (how well the product covers new drywall or old paint) is a critical factor in selecting paint. There are many quality brands—you need to educate yourself about them. Also ascertain the correct primer needed for the walls in question and the paint you will be applying. For example, darker colors need a tinted primer and sometimes additional coats, whereas certain product lines do the same job with a primer and one coat and are more environmentally friendly. Do your homework!

You will find an example of a paint schedule that we use in our office following the checklist in this section (see Figure 4.1).

Wallcovering Specification

While paint adds color, wallcovering can add texture, pattern, and interest to walls. Although durability and quality are very important factors, you should also consider the quantity of goods that you will need to order. Residential wallcoverings can range from 21"- to 27"-wide goods up to 54" wide. You might choose paper, vinyl, leather, fabric, or grass cloth, for example. Designers are looking for low-VOC options, which are healthier for the inhabitants of the space and kinder to the environment.

When specifying a wallcovering, always choose one with a high performance rating for your space. If designing a wet location, be sure to specify the appropriate type of wallcovering to stand up to water and steam.

Using a 54-inch-wide wallcovering when possible minimizes seams on the walls and offers a cleaner look. In addition, the labor costs are significantly lower, as the workers are hanging half the number of sheets and the job gets done more quickly.

Computer graphics have impacted the wallcovering industry. More intricate patterns and options for customization are more readily available now than ever. Textural qualities and the opportunity to custom-color a pattern are available to your clients. Always ask for a strike-off sample to check the color and pattern when doing custom work.

As the industry moves toward more of a green initiative, consult your clients about their interest in specifying an eco-friendly wallcovering. Important items to discuss are the recycled content of materials, off-gassing, product life span and recyclability.

Paint Schedule Example

SMITH RESIDENCE FIRST FLOOR PAINT SCHEDULE

FOYER	Treatment	Finish	Item Number	Qty	Vendor
Walls	Wall Covering	NA	4482D Vertical Stripe	All Walls	Vendor Name
Ceilings	Paint	Flat	Ceiling White	All	Vendor Name
Molding/Baseboards	Paint	Semi-Gloss	Super White	All	Vendor Name

LIVING ROOM		Finish	Paint Number	Qty	Vendor
Walls	Paint	Washable Flat	2161-20 Canary Yellow	All Walls	Vendor Name
Ceiling	Paint	Flat	Ceiling White	All	Vendor Name
Molding/Baseboards	Paint	Semi-Gloss	Super White	All	Vendor Name

KITCHEN		Finish	Paint Number	Qty	Vendor
Walls	Paint	Washable Flat	2433-60 Rich Tan	All Walls	Vendor Name
Ceiling	Paint	Flat	Ceiling White	All	Vendor Name
Molding/Baseboards	Paint	Semi-Gloss	Super White	All	Vendor Name

FRONT PORCH		Finish	Paint Number	Qty	Vendor
Walls	Paint	Washable Flat	2161-20 Canary Yellow	All Walls	Vendor Name
Ceiling	Leave as is	NA	NA	NA	NA
Molding/Baseboards/Step	Paint	Semi-Gloss	Super White	All	Vendor Name

DINING ROOM		Finish	Paint Number	Qty	Vendor
Walls	Paint	Washable Flat	2161-20 Canary Yellow	All Walls	Vendor Name
Ceiling	Paint	Flat	Ceiling White	All	Vendor Name
Molding/Baseboards	Paint	Semi-Gloss	Super White	All	Vendor Name

POWDER ROOM		Finish	Paint Number	Qty	Vendor
Walls	Paint	High Gloss	3232-20 Black Ebony	All Walls	Vendor Name
Ceiling	Paint	High Gloss	Ceiling White	All	Vendor Name
Molding/Baseboards	Paint	Semi-Gloss	Super White	All	Vendor Name

Figure 4.1 Paint Schedule

SPECIFICATIONS   **WALLCOVERING CHECKLIST**

Wallcovering #1

- ☐ **Vendor/showroom** _____
- ☐ **Pattern/color name or number** _____
- ☐ **Net price** _____
- ☐ **Stock** _____
- ☐ **Where is it stocked? (Specify United States, United Kingdom, etc.)** _____
- ☐ **Lead time and ETA** _____
- ☐ **Width of goods** _____
- ☐ **Length of goods** _____
- ☐ **Vertical repeat** _____
- ☐ **Horizontal repeat** _____
- ☐ **How is it sold: by the yard, roll, or double roll** (circle one) _____
- ☐ **Is lining paper required? Yes or No** (circle one) _____
- ☐ **What is the content?** _____
- ☐ **Is there a minimum order?** _____
- ☐ **Sidemark for goods** (e.g., your company name/client name/room/item) _____
- ☐ **Request a CFA (cutting for approval), if possible, to match to your sample and have it mailed to your firm.**
- ☐ **Specify the ship-to address** (your workroom, the fabricator, or directly to the client) _____

Wallcovering #2

- ☐ **Vendor/showroom** _____
- ☐ **Pattern/color name or number** _____
- ☐ **Net price** _____
- ☐ **Stock** _____
- ☐ **Where is it stocked? (Specify United States, United Kingdom, etc.)** _____
- ☐ **Lead time and ETA** _____
- ☐ **Width of goods** _____
- ☐ **Length of goods** _____
- ☐ **Vertical repeat** _____
- ☐ **Horizontal repeat** _____
- ☐ **How is it sold: by the yard, roll, or double roll** (circle one) _____
- ☐ **Is lining paper required? Yes or No** (circle one) _____
- ☐ **What is the content?** _____
- ☐ **Is there a minimum order?** _____
- ☐ **Sidemark for goods** (e.g, your company name/client name/room/item) _____
- ☐ **Request a CFA (cutting for approval), if possible, to match to your sample and have it mailed to your firm.**
- ☐ **Specify the ship-to address** (your workroom, the fabricator, or directly to the client) _____

CHAPTER 5

Contract Specifications

General Notes

In contrast to the selection of residential furniture, specifying contract furniture is a "layered" process. While residential designers generally select each and every detail on a case good or upholstered piece, they are generally ordering a single piece or a smaller quantity of goods, whereas in contract work the volumes are considerably higher.

Furthermore, residential designers rely on showrooms or manufacturers' sales representatives to communicate their preferences, while contract furniture is ordered through a third-party provider referred to as a *dealer*. Manufacturers such as Steelcase™, Herman Miller®, Allsteel®, and Knoll® have fantastic showrooms in major markets, where designers can go to see product, but you must then place your order through your dealer. Dealers cannot represent more than one *major* manufacturer like Steelcase™ or Knoll®, as this would present a conflict of interest, so you need to familiarize yourself with dealers in your area and establish relationships with them. Most dealers also represent a variety of small manufacturers in addition to the top-tier manufacturer that they feature.

Larger commercial/contract clients have a facilities manager or a management team on-site, and someone from that team will usually be your contact on a project.

Of course, durability is a key and critical factor when specifying contract goods. Most manufacturers offer a variety of options based on the intended use of a system or chair, for example. Consideration of high-traffic areas and the need to satisfy a variety of users are both part of contract design work.

Another important factor is budget. Most contract furniture is placed in leased spaces, and has a shorter life span (typically for 5 to 10 years), due to wear and tear and office relocations. It is important to discuss budget and lead times with your client at the outset of the project and also be very clear with your dealers so they can guide you to the most appropriate options in terms of materials, textiles, and finishes.

In residential design, you should always perform an access measurement to be sure all selected items are deliverable. As a commercial designer, you should be aware of this when designing/selecting, but in most cases the dealer is responsible for making sure the items can be delivered to the space being designed.

The issue of sustainability is now more than ever at the forefront of an initial discussion with your clients. Do they require LEED points or just want to reduce the carbon footprint of the project as a whole? We strongly suggest that you gear your specifications to the most eco-friendly offerings. All manufacturers have stepped up to the plate with a variety of options to assist you in this matter. Textiles are available with more earth-friendly components, and carpet manufacturers are offering "cradle-to-cradle" options whereby the carpet can be returned after use for recycling into other materials. Specifying earth-friendly materials is easier than ever before and continues to be a growing trend. Nontoxic and low-VOC paints and wallcoverings are more readily available and actually create a healthier and more productive work environment while protecting the planet for future generations.

Contract Furniture Specification
Contract Case Goods and Other Furnishings

From conference rooms to breakout areas and everything in between, you will be sourcing case goods, tables, and other furnishings to outfit your client's space.

In commercial work, the access measurement is the sole responsibility of the furniture dealer, but as the designer you should be aware of the process. This is a critical component, especially with larger elements such as a long conference table, reception desks, work walls, bookcases, and credenzas. There is always a solution to be found—you just need to be prepared.

When specifying case goods, always look to your dealer to see if the items you are specifying can be delivered unassembled and put together on-site. This will save you from installation headaches and heartache. For example, if you are specifying a very long and wide conference table, it may be best to look for something that comes in two parts and can be locked together. Pedestals are generally preferred over legs, as they allow more space for adding chairs and provide extra legroom. Be sure to specify grommets on the surface of your case goods and tables to ease access to floor and wall outlets or power on the pedestal legs. All of this should be coordinated prior to placing the order because it affects the architect's electrical plan and where the subcontractor will install the outlets. In most cases, the subcontractor will have the furniture dealer mark out all electrical/voice data openings on the wall or floor that relate to the work wall desk opening or conference room legs, for instance.

Credenzas that are not custom-built and installed must also be specified with care. It may be wise to specify an item that is modular—available in parts or sections—which facilitates the longevity of the piece in the event that it is moved to another office. It will have a better chance of fitting into the new space if it is modular.

Finish is another specification. As a designer, you are asked to do something different— something clients could not come up with on their own. Integrating their brand and office culture with a variety of textiles, materials, finishes, and color selections creates a fluid design. Be sure to maintain a flow throughout the space with dominant, subordinate, and accent colors, which serve to create a harmonic environment and enhance the spirit of the client's corporate identity.

Pricing is also done differently in the commercial arena. The furniture dealer gives this information to the designer to review prior to presenting to the client. As a designer, you can figure out the discount percentage the dealer is offering because the list price can be found online most of the time.

In addition, as in all other aspects of contract work, lead time is critical. Are the pieces in stock? Are the projected delivery dates in sync with your timeline? Are the delivery fees in line with your budget? The manufacturer or the furniture dealer will provide you with stock and lead time information as well. When you create a furniture request for proposal (RFP), include the time frame you need for delivery of all furniture so the dealer can let you know whether some items require longer lead times.

SPECIFICATIONS   **CONTRACT CASE GOODS AND OTHER FURNISHINGS CHECKLIST**

Furniture Item #1

☐ **Client name/floor #/room #/item** _____

☐ **Showroom** _____

☐ **Dealer** _____

☐ **Item name and/or number** _____

☐ **Color** _____

☐ **Finish** _____

☐ **Price** _____

☐ **Stock** _____

☐ **Where is it stocked? (Specify United States, United Kingdom, etc.)** _____

☐ **Lead time and ETA** _____

☐ **Overall product dimensions** _____

☐ **Leg/foot/base type** _____ **Finish** _____

☐ **LEED credits** _____ **Recycled content: Yes or No** (circle one)

☐ **Quantity** _____

Furniture Item #2

☐ **Client name/floor #/room #/item** _____

☐ **Showroom** _____

☐ **Dealer** _____

☐ **Item name and/or number** _____

☐ **Color** _____

☐ **Finish** _____

☐ **Price** _____

☐ **Stock** _____

☐ **Where is it stocked? (Specify United States, United Kingdom, etc.)** _____

☐ **Lead time and ETA** _____

☐ **Overall product dimensions** _____

☐ **Leg/foot/base type** _____ **Finish** _____

☐ **LEED credits** _____ **Recycled content: Yes or No** (circle one)

☐ **Quantity** _____

Furniture Item #3

☐ **Client name/floor #/room #/item** _____

☐ **Showroom** _____

☐ **Dealer** _____

☐ **Item name and/or number** _____

☐ **Color** _____

☐ **Finish** _____

☐ **Price** _____

☐ **Stock** _____

☐ **Where is it stocked? (Specify United States, United Kingdom, etc.)** _____

☐ **Lead time and ETA** _____

☐ **Overall product dimensions** _____

☐ **Leg/foot/base type** _____ **Finish** _____

☐ **LEED credits** _____ **Recycled content: Yes or No** (circle one)

☐ **Quantity** _____

Contract Upholstered Furniture

When specifying contract upholstered furniture, you must be mindful of a few things. Again, you or your furniture dealer must perform an access measurement to ensure that all of the furniture you are reusing/repurposing in addition to the new items you are specifying will fit into the building entrance door, the elevator, the entry door to the space, any stairwells, individual offices, and any other such areas that may apply.

Durability is paramount here. Your clients are looking for longevity in the pieces they purchase, so specify furniture that is geared to high-traffic areas and is built to last.

Think about finish options, metal versus wood frames, and tight seat and back versus cushions. The fewer movable parts, the easier the piece will be to maintain. Also be mindful of the appropriateness of a piece. A chair or sofa in a reception area or lobby will probably take much more abuse than one in a private office. For instance, in commercial reception areas you generally would not select any textile that has less than 100,000 double rubs and has passed several National Fire Protection Association (NFPA) tests.

You should contact the manufacturer or dealer for information on stock and lead time so you can be sure the item fits within your delivery window for the project.

Ergonomic Chairs

There are some important elements to consider when specifying ergonomic chairs. You have a plethora of options to choose from. In general, ergonomic chairs are easy to adjust and reconfigure for each person's body type and preferences. In a true ergonomic task chair, the arms are connected to the seat and not the back, for ultimate movement and flexibility without affecting the position of the user's arms and hands. Versatility and adjustability are key!

Color choices should reflect the corporate culture. In addition, you can select from various finish options for arms, knobs, casters, and so forth. You also should specify whether the chairs will be used on a carpeted surface or a hard flooring surface.

Does your client prefer a chair with a mesh back or something fully upholstered? Are you going to specify a hierarchy of seating for different levels of management? You may want a chair with a higher back for a president/vice president or director and one with a lower back for salespersons and reception/administrative personnel. Many manufacturers now suggest utilizing the same task chair throughout an office culture but adding a "jacket" or removable cover in leather, vinyl, or other very durable textiles to elevate the look.

Durability and quality are also very important factors to consider. Of course, your clients will be looking for longevity in the pieces they purchase, so you should choose a quality ergonomic chair that is built to last. Many chairs on the market today are offered in a variety of sizes to accommodate different user types. If your client is tall with long legs, he or she may not be comfortable in the same chair you would specify for a person of short stature. As a rule of thumb, a medium-size chair is a good compromise for an office culture where staff changes occur on a regular basis. You are purchasing expensive seating for your client, and you want it to work for many users—one never knows who will come and go in a corporate culture.

Systems Furniture

Almost all specification of quality systems furniture is done through a dealer representative. Much like kitchen cabinet showroom reps, dealers are fully versed in all of their product offerings and will likely have the best and most creative ideas in terms of getting the most functional layout and appropriate offerings for your budget.

Ascertain that an access measurement is performed to ensure that the piece(s) you specify will fit into the building entrance door, the elevator, the entry door to the space, any stairwells, and any other such areas that may apply. This ensures that all components can be delivered to the appropriate spaces for installation.

Consult with the clients about their need for electrical capacity on the units that you specify. Does the systems furniture you are specifying meet these needs? Adding grommets and power options is critical to the success of the system. There are a variety of power options from which to choose, and you must think about providing access in individual offices, office systems, conference rooms, breakout areas, and the like.

There are also a myriad of choices when selecting finish options for both vertical and horizontal surfaces. It is recommended that you visit the manufacturer's showroom to review the options or have your rep bring samples to you for review. Tying into the branding and colors of your client's firm can be an important way to integrate the systems furnishings into the corporate identity and reinforce the branding message in the interior space.

It is a good idea to specify systems furniture that is easily reconfigured, as a company's needs may change over time, necessitating a change in the physical layout. Versatility is important! Durability and quality are likewise very important factors to consider. Your client is looking for longevity in the pieces they purchase, so choose a system that is built to last and can be easily added to even after it has been moved and reconfigured multiple times.

SPECIFICATIONS   **CONTRACT—UPHOLSTERED FURNITURE CHECKLIST**

Furniture

- ☐ **Client name/floor #/room #/item** _____
- ☐ **Showroom** _____
- ☐ **Dealer** _____
- ☐ **Item name and/or number** _____
- ☐ **Net price** _____
- ☐ **Stock** _____
- ☐ **Where is it stocked? (Specify United States, United Kingdom, etc.)** _____
- ☐ **Lead time and ETA** _____
- ☐ **Overall product dimensions** _____
- ☐ **Seat height/depth** _____ **Arm height** _____ **Interior width (inside arms)** _____
- ☐ **Leg/foot/base type** _____ **Finish** _____
- ☐ **Arm style** _____ **Back style** _____
- ☐ **Cushion type** _____ **Trim type** _____
- ☐ **Do they allow COM (customer's own material)? Yes or No** (circle one) **COM yardage needed** _____
- ☐ **Fabric A Pattern #** _____ **Fabric A Location** _____
- ☐ **Fabric B Pattern #** _____ **Fabric B Location** _____
- ☐ **To avoid seams, where appropriate, always railroad the fabric. (Note if railroading fabric.)** _____
- ☐ **Quantity** _____

Fabric A

Place photo of furniture here

Place photo of fabric A here

Fabric B

Place photo of fabric B here

SPECIFICATIONS   **ERGONOMIC CHAIRS CHECKLIST**

Ergonomic Chair #1

- ☐ **Client name/floor #/room #/item** _____
- ☐ **Manufacturer** _____
- ☐ **Dealer** _____
- ☐ **Item name and/or number** _____
- ☐ **Frame color** _____
- ☐ **Wheel base to be used on carpet or hard surface** (circle one)
- ☐ **Price** _____
- ☐ **Lead time and ETA** _____
- ☐ **Overall product dimensions** _____
- ☐ **Fabric type and color/finish** _____ **Yardage** _____
- ☐ **Special elements (stitching, welt, detail)** _____
- ☐ **Base color/finish** _____
- ☐ **Arm type/finish** _____
- ☐ **Arm: Adjustable arm height: Yes or No (circle one) Adjustable arm angle: Yes or No** (circle one)
- ☐ **Back: Adjustable back pitch: Yes or No (circle one) Adjustable lumbar: Yes or No** (circle one) **Tilt control Yes or No** (circle one)
- ☐ **Seat: Adjustable seat height: Yes or No (circle one) Adjustable seat depth: Yes or No** (circle one)
- ☐ **LEED credits** _____ **Recycled content: Yes or No** (circle one)
- ☐ **Quantity** _____

Ergonomic Chair #2

- ☐ **Client name/floor #/room #/item** _____
- ☐ **Manufacturer** _____
- ☐ **Dealer** _____
- ☐ **Item name and/or number** _____
- ☐ **Frame color** _____
- ☐ **Wheel base to be used on carpet or hard surface** (circle one).
- ☐ **Price** _____
- ☐ **Lead time and ETA** _____
- ☐ **Overall product dimensions** _____
- ☐ **Fabric type and color/finish** _____
- ☐ **Base color/finish** _____
- ☐ **Arm type/finish** _____
- ☐ **Arm: Adjustable arm height: Yes or No (circle one) Adjustable arm angle: Yes or No** (circle one)
- ☐ **Back: Adjustable back pitch: Yes or No (circle one) Adjustable lumbar: Yes or No** (circle one) **Tilt control: Yes or No** (circle one)
- ☐ **Seat: Adjustable seat height: Yes or No (circle one) Adjustable seat depth: Yes or No** (circle one)
- ☐ **LEED credits** _____ **Recycled content: Yes or No** (circle one)
- ☐ **Quantity** _____

SPECIFICATIONS

CONTRACT—SYSTEMS FURNITURE CHECKLIST

Furniture System #1

- ☐ Client name/floor #/room #/item _____
- ☐ Manufacturer/showroom _____
- ☐ Dealer _____
- ☐ System name _____
- ☐ Specify individual component dimensions/configurations
- ☐ Specify height of privacy panels _____
- ☐ Specify wiring and cabling locations _____
- ☐ Specify work surface material _____
- ☐ Body _____ Base _____
- ☐ Frame style and finish _____
- ☐ Leg/foot/base type _____
- ☐ Specify any windows or bins.
- ☐ Specify hardware and finish _____
- ☐ Specify tack-boards: Yes or No (circle one) _____
- ☐ Specify task lighting (integral to components): Yes or No (circle one)
- ☐ Specify tiles or panel system (circle one).
- ☐ Specify tile/panel type (glass, fabric, whiteboard, etc.) (circle one).
- ☐ Specify fabric pattern/color _____ Yardage _____
- ☐ Specify accessories (keyboard tray, monitor slide, etc.) _____
- ☐ Specify number/orientation of file cabinets and number of drawers _____

Contract Bath Fixture Specification

Corporate or contract bathrooms require a great deal of planning. The checklist provided in this chapter will assist you in navigating the multitude of components necessary to equip this space so that it functions well and meets ADA guidelines.

Whereas residential bathrooms are generally unisex in nature, larger corporate interiors usually provide separate facilities for men and women. Furthermore, some fixtures and accessories used in a corporate men's room are different from what we specify for a ladies' room. While it would be wonderful to opt for unisex facilities, most firms still rely on the traditional model and have separate spaces for men and women. The reason is that there is a specific fixture count required for the certificate of occupancy for each floor of each building. For example, many buildings require several fixtures for each gender, which would then not allow for a unisex ADA-compliant single bathroom for each because it would take up too much space.

Be mindful that you specify only ADA-compliant fixtures, and endeavor to incorporate universal design and sustainable design principles. Code requires that you specify lavatory faucets that have automatic sensors, which are easier for a physically challenged person to use and are more sanitary for all. They constitute a green option, as they have automatic settings to turn them off after a certain amount of time, thus conserving water resources. If you are designing an executive bathroom that is an additional ADA-compliant restroom on the floor, then you would typically select a faucet with a lever handle option to give a more residential feeling.

The newer sinks and toilets on the market come complete with antimicrobial finishes. This facilitates cleaning and limits the spread of germs. In terms of finish, silver oxide on hardware and other surfaces prevents the growth of germs and should be considered when specifying fixtures.

In addition, look for toilets with automatic flush sensors and, at the very least, the dual flush option to save water and keep things sanitary. Again, follow the ADA guidelines when specifying grab bars and wall-hung versus floor-mounted toilets. A wall-mounted toilet saves 3" of floor space, but the wall depth is increased.

Remember, in each stall or each ADA-compliant bathroom you must have two grab bars, one that is 36" wide and one that is 42" wide. Consult local codes; these dimensions may change as guidelines are renewed.

Accessories are also an important component in corporate bathrooms. When considering waste receptacles, ask: Are they wall or floor-mounted? Are they located adjacent to the lavatory or near the door? Recessed towel dispensers located close to the exit door with waste receptacles below have become extremely popular in public bathrooms. Automatic hand dryers are a terrific option. They generally operate on a sensor and are timed to turn off, saving energy. They are clean and efficient, and they reduce waste.

If you are using a polished chrome lavatory faucet and drain, you may want to be consistent with all fixtures and accessories for a more harmonious and well-thought-out design. When considering a paper towel dispenser or a hand dryer, think about the finish and coordinate it with that of the other fixtures.

When specifying mirrors, keep in mind that the tilt of a wall mirror can help people of smaller stature and those in wheelchairs view themselves more easily.

Also remember to take into account depth and ease of use. If a restroom accessory is in the path of travel it can project only 4" from the wall to still be code-compliant.

Many bathrooms provide seat covers and sanitary waste receptacles in the individual stalls. This is a good amenity. Although it does add depth that must be considered when planning the stalls, especially for an ADA-compliant compartment, it is important to the use of the space.

Remember to specify floor drains in case of a leak or toilet or sink overflow in the finish used for all fixtures. The new linear drains are less conspicuous and look more modern.

SPECIFICATIONS   **CONTRACT BATH FIXTURES CHECKLIST**

Client/floor #/room #/bathroom name: _____

Lavatory

☐ Specify lavatory faucet and handles: **widespread, center-set, single-lever, wall-mounted, or vessel faucet** (circle one).

☐ **Faucet manufacturer/model number** _____ **Specify finish** _____ **Quantity** _____

☐ Specify trap: **classic P-trap or concealed trap** (circle one). **Specify stop (hot and cold): exposed or in-wall** (circle one).

☐ Specify **drain: pop-up or twist stop** (circle one).

☐ Specify **sink/lavatory (basin): wall-mounted, pedestal, under-mount, drop-in, or integral** (circle one).

☐ **Sink/lavatory manufacturer/model number** _____ **Specify finish** _____ **Quantity** _____

☐ Specify **soap dispenser: wall-mounted or deck-mounted** (circle one).

☐ **Soap dispenser manufacturer/model number** _____ **Specify finish** _____ **Quantity** _____

Toilet

☐ **Specify stall manufacturer/model number** _____

☐ **Specify material/finish** _____

☐ **Standard stall quantity** _____ **ADA compliant stall quantity** _____

☐ Specify: **one-piece or two-piece** (circle one). **Specify wall-mounted or floor-mounted** (circle one).

☐ Specify **flushing method: pressure (flushometer), gravity, or pressure-assist** (circle one).

☐ Specify: **manual handle, timed flush, dual flush, or automatic flush** (circle one).

☐ Specify **stop: angle or straight stop** (circle one). **Specify trap: P-trap or concealed trap** (circle one).

☐ **Toilet manufacturer/model number** _____ **Specify finish** _____ **Quantity** _____

☐ Specify **grab bars in ADA-compliant stalls.**

☐ **Grab bar manufacturer/model number** _____ **Specify finish** _____ **Quantity** _____

Urinal

☐ Specify: **standard or waterless** (circle one).

☐ Specify: **Manual handle, timed flush, or automatic flush** (circle one).

☐ **Urinal manufacturer/model number** _____ **Specify finish** _____ **Quantity** _____

Accessories

☐ **Waste receptacle manufacturer/model number** _____ **Specify finish** _____ **Quantity** _____

☐ Specify: **paper towel dispenser or hand dryer** (circle one).

☐ **Towel dispenser manufacturer/model number** _____ **Specify finish** _____ **Quantity** _____

☐ Specify **hand dryer: push-button or sensor** (circle one).

☐ **Hand dryer manufacturer/model number** _____ **Specify finish** _____ **Quantity** _____

☐ Specify **combination waste receptacle/paper towel unit if desired.**

☐ **Combination waste receptacle/paper towel unit manufacturer/model number** _____

☐ **Specify finish** _____ **Quantity** _____

☐ **Sanitary waste receptacle manufacturer/model number** _____ **Specify finish** _____ **Quantity** _____

☐ **Mirror/medicine cabinet manufacturer/model number** _____ **Specify finish** _____ **Quantity** _____

☐ **Seat cover dispenser manufacturer/model number** _____ **Specify finish** _____ **Quantity** _____

☐ **Toilet paper holder manufacturer/model number** _____ **Specify finish** _____ **Quantity** _____

☐ **Tissue dispenser holder manufacturer/model number** _____ **Specify finish** _____ **Quantity** _____

☐ **Hooks for stall doors manufacturer/model number** _____ **Specify finish** _____ **Quantity** _____

Lighting and Electrical

☐ Specify **GFI outlet(s) for wet locations.**

☐ Specify **architectural and/or decorative lighting.**

☐ Specify **how the lighting switches will be ganged.**

☐ Specify **manufacturer and color/finish of the outlets and switch plates** _____

Contract Flooring Specification

There are some important tips we want to share with you to help with specifying contract flooring. It is your job as the designer to think about durability—the materials you select must stand up to high traffic.

Try whenever possible to specify resilient flooring, as it is easier on the body, especially your feet and back, than a hard flooring alternative. Some examples of resilient flooring are carpet, cork, vinyl, linoleum, and rubber flooring.

If you are specifying a hard flooring alternative such as tile, note that the larger tiles have a tendency to crack more easily, so ask your supplier any and all questions that you may have about the tile you are interested in purchasing. Does the tile have a rectified edge? Is there a cove tile available? Does the color go all the way through the tile (common in porcelain)? What is the recommended grout joint? In commercial settings, you would typically specify 1/8" grout spacing. Of course, a tile with a matte, honed, or textured surface offers better traction and slip resistance than a polished surface.

When specifying carpet, opt for a heavy-duty contract carpet with a low pile to facilitate ease of movement of office chairs, wheelchairs, walkers, and/or canes. It is customary to use broadloom carpeting in executive offices and conference rooms, as it is a more luxurious product. Consider using carpet tiles in corridors, workstations, and other gathering areas where there is heavy traffic and use, as they are very easy to replace in the event of damage. Replacing one or a few tiles costs a lot less than having to replace wall-to-wall carpeting and extends the life of the installation. We recommend that when you place the order for the carpet tiles, you add 20 percent overage to the order for your client to hold in reserve (known as *attic stock*). This ensures that your client has replacement tiles on hand in the same dye lot as the carpet tiles you installed during construction.

If you are specifying wood or cork floors, use a resilient finish for heavy traffic. Engineered wood floors can also be considered, especially for conditions such as basement levels or other spaces with humidity and water issues. Engineered wood flooring is often used in commercial settings because it helps offset the height difference between carpet and wood flooring. When using hardwood flooring, in most cases you have to flash patch because you generally do not add padding under the broadloom or carpet tiles.

Linoleum, vinyl, VCT (vinyl composition tile), rubber tile, and acrylic flooring are also great options for resilient floors that stand up to heavy wear and tear.

If you are specifying multiple flooring types in one space or transitioning from one space to another, be sure there is little to no difference between the heights of the materials to allow for an easier transition from one space to another and to adhere to ADA and IBC guidelines. If there is a difference in the heights of the flooring, use a transition strip or a saddle for a cleaner look when ramping from one type of flooring to another.

Typically the subcontractor verifies square footage and tile takeoffs for the designer and also verifies these items for RFPs.

Always encourage your clients to consider specifying sustainable flooring, which can accrue LEED credits in addition to protecting the environment.

SPECIFICATIONS   **CONTRACT FLOORING CHECKLIST**

Flooring #1

- [ ] Client name/floor #/room #/item _____
- [ ] Vendor/showroom _____
- [ ] Item manufacturer _____
- [ ] Number and color _____
- [ ] Price _____
- [ ] Stock _____
- [ ] Where is it stocked? (Specify United States, United Kingdom, etc.) _____
- [ ] Lead time and ETA _____
- [ ] Product dimensions _____
- [ ] Flooring type (rubber, vinyl tile, wood floors, carpet, area rug, etc.) _____
- [ ] Available options (edge detail, cove tile, etc.) _____
- [ ] Square footage of space _____
- [ ] Quantity to be ordered_____
- [ ] LEED credits _____ Recycled content: Yes or No (circle one).

Flooring #2

- [ ] Client name/floor #/room #/item _____
- [ ] Vendor/showroom _____
- [ ] Item manufacturer _____
- [ ] Number and color _____
- [ ] Price _____
- [ ] Stock _____
- [ ] Where is it stocked? (Specify United States, United Kingdom, etc.) _____
- [ ] Lead time and ETA _____
- [ ] Product dimensions _____
- [ ] Flooring type (rubber, vinyl tile, wood floors, carpet, area rug, etc.) _____
- [ ] Available options (edge detail, cove tile, etc.) _____
- [ ] Square footage of space _____
- [ ] Quantity to be ordered _____
- [ ] LEED credits _____ Recycled content: Yes or No (circle one).

Flooring #3

- [ ] Client name/floor #/room #/item _____
- [ ] Vendor/showroom _____
- [ ] Item manufacturer _____
- [ ] Number and color _____
- [ ] Price _____
- [ ] Stock _____
- [ ] Where is it stocked? (Specify United States, United Kingdom, etc.) _____
- [ ] Lead time and ETA _____
- [ ] Product dimensions _____
- [ ] Flooring type (rubber, vinyl tile, wood floors, carpet, area rug, etc.) _____
- [ ] Available options (edge detail, cove tile, etc.) _____
- [ ] Square footage of space _____
- [ ] Quantity to be ordered _____
- [ ] LEED credits _____ Recycled content: Yes or No (circle one)

Contract Lighting Specification

There are so many lighting layers in a contract/commercial setting that should be discussed. Always channel back to the three main lighting solutions:

- Ambient or general illumination—how you move through and illuminate the space for way finding
- Task lighting—illumination required for a specific purpose such as reading, writing, or general work
- Accent or "key" lighting—which adds drama, creates emphasis and focus, highlights architectural details, and illuminates artwork and sculpture

In an office environment, you first must plan the general or ambient lighting solution. There are so many choices. If there is a dropped ceiling, you may wish to use a lighting system that fits flush with the ceiling tiles. With a drywall ceiling, you may feel that recessed lighting or pendant lighting with direct/indirect illumination is a better fit for the space. Track lighting is also a very efficient way to illuminate a space, and it provides many options for both general, task, and accent lighting. Clients enjoy the flexibility provided by track lighting.

You must do the research and be specific about the source of electric light. Are you planning to specify fluorescent, HID, or LED lamping?

If you are mixing light sources, how will the various color temperatures work together in harmony? These different lamp types also vary in their energy consumption, and they affect the efficiency and efficacy of the fixture.

With regard to ADA compliance, both the IBC and local regulations will require specific dimensions be held for clearance in all spaces. With respect to these regulations, it is important to remember that all wall-mounted luminaires (sconces) must be a maximum of 4" deep.

Energy codes are constantly changing, so consult the local jurisdiction for the number of watts per square foot that are now required to be LED or some other source of energy-efficient lighting. Local codes are requiring that contract interiors be fitted with energy-efficient lighting. Incandescent and halogen lamps do not qualify, so look for other sources. The new favorite is, of course, LED, which is now more readily available in a variety of color temperatures. LED technology has come a long way in the last few years, and there are many fixtures/luminaires on the market for a variety of installation options.

Many manufacturers have introduced light and motion sensors, which can turn on and shut off lights when someone enters or leaves a space. They can now also sense levels of natural light entering a space and calculate when a fixture turns on and off based on the natural daylight quotient. This can contribute toward your LEED credits on a project.

On most contract projects, a professional lighting designer is retained to ensure that you give your clients the best lighting solution that reduces their energy consumption and works within their budget. Please note that every space that is built in a commercial setting needs to pass a COMcheck™, which is a calculation of wattage for lighting that must be completed and included in a construction drawing set before it goes out to bid or is filed.

Luminaire #1

- ☐ **Client name/floor #/room #/item** _____
- ☐ **Architectural or decorative?** (circle one)
- ☐ **Vendor/showroom** _____
- ☐ **Item name and/or model number** _____
- ☐ **Get pricing from subcontractor** _____
- ☐ **Stock** _____
- ☐ **Lead time and ETA** _____
- ☐ **Overall product dimensions** _____
- ☐ **Download specification file.**
- ☐ **Lamp type and wattage** _____
- ☐ **Lumen output** _____
- ☐ **Finish** _____
- ☐ **Quantity** _____

Luminaire #2

- ☐ **Client name/floor #/room #/item** _____
- ☐ **Architectural or decorative?** (circle one)
- ☐ **Vendor/showroom** _____
- ☐ **Item name and/or model number** _____
- ☐ **Get pricing from subcontractor** _____
- ☐ **Stock** _____
- ☐ **Lead time and ETA** _____
- ☐ **Overall product dimensions** _____
- ☐ **Download specification file.**
- ☐ **Lamp type and wattage** _____
- ☐ **Lumen output** _____
- ☐ **Finish** _____
- ☐ **Quantity** _____

Luminaire #3

- ☐ **Client name/floor #/room #/item** _____
- ☐ **Architectural or decorative?** (circle one)
- ☐ **Vendor/showroom** _____
- ☐ **Item name and/or model number** _____
- ☐ **Get pricing from subcontractor** _____
- ☐ **Stock** _____
- ☐ **Lead time and ETA** _____
- ☐ **Overall product dimensions** _____
- ☐ **Download specification file.**
- ☐ **Lamp type and wattage** _____
- ☐ **Lumen output** _____
- ☐ **Finish** _____
- ☐ **Quantity** _____

Contract Textiles Specification

Contract textile offerings have come a long way in terms of style, pattern, texture, and durability. In fact, some can even be considered luxury textiles, especially the new mohairs, velvets, and suedes. There are functional *and* aesthetically pleasing options that meet the requirements of codes for commercial properties. You must be careful to select high-performance fabrics and meet all codes as well, or your client will not be able to obtain a certificate of occupancy.

When specifying a contract fabric, be sure that the material is heavy-duty. A minimum of 30,000 double rubs is suggested, but most design firms prefer 100,000 double rubs.

Some manufacturers specialize in contract textiles, while other companies represent a more residential-oriented product array but carry a commercial line within their overall offerings. Be sure to note whether a fabric you are considering is specified for contract use. The tag generally gives this information.

The back of the memo tag for contract fabrics lists a variety of symbols, and it is important to understand their meaning. This chapter provides a symbol list for your reference following the Contract Textile Specification Checklist, to help familiarize you with these symbols.

All contract fabrics must be flame resistant. No material is flameproof. Specify fabrics that resist flame for a longer period of time, allowing occupants of the space time to exit safely. You may be aware that wool is inherently flame retardant, as it possesses natural lanolin. It is also a very durable material.

When you or your dealer reserve yardage of a fabric, always request that a CFA (cutting for approval) be mailed to your firm to check against your memo sample for color matching. This ensures that the dye lot of the goods that are currently in stock aligns with the color in your memo sample.

Colorfastness and light resistance are important characteristics for fabric longevity. Be sure to specify all goods from the same dye lot, and, if that is not an option, order CFAs from all dye lots being considered before you purchase. The designer requests these cuttings as final sign-offs before the dealer purchases the fabric or leather for a piece of furniture.

Be sure that there is plenty of stock reserved for your order, as it is a waste of time to have to reselect due to insufficient yardage. Investigate any stain-resistant finishes or inherent properties of the textiles you select.

Some applications require that you back the fabric for stability. Some fabrics, especially in the contract realm, are already backed, which is great for upholstery and hard window top treatments but not for drapery.

Always consult your fabricator and upholsterer to be sure the fabrics you are specifying are appropriate for the use intended *prior* to placing an order. We generally advise sending a cutting or a memo sample of the textiles you are considering to the workroom/fabricator for review and approval.

SPECIFICATIONS   **CONTRACT TEXTILES CHECKLIST**

Fabric

- ☐ **Client name/floor #/room #/item** _____
- ☐ **Vendor/showroom** _____
- ☐ **Pattern/color name or number** _____
- ☐ **Price** _____
- ☐ **Stock** _____
- ☐ **Where is it stocked? (Specify United States, United Kingdom, etc.)** _____
- ☐ **Lead time and ETA** _____
- ☐ **Width of goods** _____ **Vertical repeat** _____ **Horizontal repeat** _____
- ☐ **How many double rubs does the fabric have?** _____
- ☐ **Is it backed for upholstery? If not, will it need to be backed for this particular application?** _____
- ☐ **Is the fabric stain resistant? Yes or No** (circle one)
- ☐ **Is it flame resistant? (Look for this icon 🔥) Yes or No** (circle one)
- ☐ **Is the fabric rated for colorfastness to wet and dry crocking? (Look for this icon ❤) Yes or No** (circle one)
- ☐ **Is the fabric rated for colorfastness to light (resistance to fading)? (Look for this icon ✹) Yes or No** (circle one)
- ☐ **Physical properties (Look for this icon ✮)** _____
- ☐ **Abrasion testing rating? (Look for this icon [a] or [A]) Yes or No** (circle one) **List rating:** _____
- ☐ **Is the fabric antimicrobial (very important in hygienic settings such as hospitals)? Yes or No** (circle one)
- ☐ **Is there a yardage minimum for an order?** _____
- ☐ **Number of yards to reserve** _____
- ☐ **Specify that all yardage reserved must come from the same dye lot and be all one piece (or larger pieces).**
- ☐ **Specify the ship-to address** (your workroom, the fabricator, or another furniture company) _____
_____

- ☐ **Do you need to send a COM tag to the fabric manufacturer to be sent with the goods to the furniture company for upholstery? Yes or No** (circle one)
- ☐ **Request a CFA (cutting for approval) to match to your sample and have it mailed to your firm.**
- ☐ **Date cutting was ordered** _____
- ☐ **Check box if cutting was received.**

Place fabric sample here for reference

Specifications—Contract Textiles Symbols Guide

 Flame resistance—A fabric's ability to resist burning.

 Colorfastness to wet and dry crocking—A fabric's ability to retain color and resist color rubbing off when the fabric is abraded in both wet and dry conditions.

 Colorfastness to light—A fabric's resistance to fading in light.

 Physical properties—A fabric's resistance to pilling, tearing, breaking, seam slippage (when a fabric pulls apart at a seam), etc.

a **Abrasion resistance for general contract upholstery**—A contract fabric's resistance to surface wear from rubbing. This is indicated by a number based on how many times the fabric was rubbed back and forth by a machine before the fabric showed signs of breaking down.

A **Abrasion resistance for heavy-duty upholstery**—A heavy-duty fabric's resistance to surface wear from rubbing. This is indicated by a number based on how many times the fabric was rubbed back and forth by a machine before the fabric showed signs of breaking down.

Contract Wall Specifications

Paint

The walls account for the largest square footage of space for which an interior designer is responsible. A variety of products are used to decorate and protect the wall plane.

Paint is the most popular. While solid color and neutral tones are typical, many designers also prefer to use color to create emphasis and focus, for example on a feature wall. Color can also be used to increase work productivity and boost the morale of the employees. Specify low-VOC paints to limit the toxic particles and off-gassing.

Most paint manufacturers have architectural reps who will work with you, supplying samples as well as providing you with specifications for your scope of work and construction documents. They are extremely knowledgeable about their product lines and will help you to specify the best product for your particular application. You should do research on the quality of the paint produced by each manufacturer. The *hide* (how well the product covers new drywall or old paint) is a critical factor in selecting a paint. There are many quality brands, so you need to educate yourself about them. Inquire with the general contractor or the paint mechanic about the correct primer needed for the particular walls you are working with and the paint being applied. For example, darker colors need a tinted primer and sometimes additional coats, whereas certain product lines do the same job with a primer and one coat and are more environmentally friendly. Do your homework!

Wallcoverings

Generally speaking, commercial spaces are substantially larger than residential spaces. While durability and quality are very important factors to consider, you also need to take into account the quantity of goods that you will need to order. Many corporate interior walls are covered in vinyl and other treated materials, and they create a more durable, easier-to-maintain surface for the client.

When specifying a wallcovering, always choose one with a high performance rating that will stand up to wear and tear. Whenever possible, specify a 54-inch-wide wallcovering, which minimizes seams on the walls and offers a cleaner look. Furthermore, the labor costs will be significantly lower, as only half the number of sheets need to be hung and the job gets done more quickly.

Guide your clients in specifying eco-friendly wallcoverings. Important items to discuss are the recycled content of the material, off-gassing, product life span, and recyclability.

SPECIFICATIONS   **CONTRACT WALLCOVERINGS CHECKLIST**

Wallcovering

☐ **Client name/floor #/room #/item** _____

☐ **Vendor/showroom** _____

☐ **Pattern/color name or number** _____

☐ **Price** _____

☐ **Stock** _____

☐ **Where is it stocked? (Specify United States, United Kingdom, etc.)** _____

☐ **Obtain lead time and ETA from subcontractor** _____

☐ **Width of goods** _____

☐ **Vertical repeat** _____ **Horizontal repeat** _____

☐ **How is it sold? By the yard, roll, or double roll** (circle one)

☐ **How many yards are on the roll or bolt?** _____

☐ **Is lining paper required?** _____

☐ **Is it vinyl, paper, etc.?** _____

☐ **Are you specifying a special protective coating? Yes or No** (circle one). **If so, what is the additional cost if any?** _____

☐ **What is the content?** _____

☐ **Does the material need to be backed? Yes or No** (circle one). **If so, what is the additional cost if any?** _____

☐ **Is there a minimum order?** _____

☐ **Request a CFA (cutting for approval), if possible, to match to your sample, and have it mailed to your firm.**

☐ **Specify the ship-to address:** (your workroom, the fabricator, or another furniture company). _____

☐ **LEED credits** _____ **Recycled content: Yes or No** (circle one)

☐ **Quantity** _____

☐ **Order date** _____

☐ **Date received** _____

☐ **Approval date** _____

Place photo of wallcovering here

Contract Window Coverings/Shading

Window coverings are multifunctional in a contract space. We all use computers, tablets, and other electronic devices. Large panes of glass not only allow light to enter the space but also create glare, which affects productivity and causes eye strain. We all benefit from light control, and window coverings can satisfy this requirement.

There are many shading options on the market. Architectural shades are offered in different opacity levels, from blackout to light filtering, at varying degrees. Shading options also help reduce heat, and therefore energy consumption for your client, and help protect the environment to boot. Discuss with your client the desired level of shading in each space. Recommend the heaviest level of shading in media or conference rooms, medium shading in work areas with computers, and lighter shading in reception areas.

Simple woven fabric shades are the most popular and are offered in a variety of colorways. Wide widths, and longer lengths will accommodate most windows without seaming. There are also some fabulous wood shade options for your client to choose from.

Metal and wood blinds offer light control with a bit more flexibility. You have the option to tilt to block glare, control light, and gain more privacy without losing the outdoor view completely.

Many designers advise their clients to use automation to control the window shading in their offices. This can be done in "smart" offices, where the light sensor is programmed so that the shades go up and down according to the desired light level. You can also install a switch that the individual can control in his/her office. There are many options, and all of them should be discussed with your general contractor, client, and your office automation specialist.

Window film has become more popular over the past decade. While it generally does not completely eliminate the need for window coverings, it complements this layer by reducing glare, reflecting UV rays and heat, and lowering your overall energy costs. Window film works well in both summer and winter and is specified for all climates. It is available in a variety of shades and colors, each with a different energy quotient. Translucent frosted and dusted crystal films are used to provide privacy while still letting in light.

In commercial design, the subcontractor is generally responsible for taking all measurements and noting existing conditions, including HVAC and radiator locations, baseboards, soffits, crown molding, and other architectural details such as ceiling pockets and the style of the windows.

The subcontractor/fabricator generates quotes for you and in many instances also supplies you with samples that you can use to show your client and gain approvals.

Not all corporate clients will require top treatments, but some do want to add a bit of personality and softer fabrics to their work environment. Generally, you will see more hard treatments such as cornice valances, rather than drapery in this realm. Refer to the checklist in this section to be sure you have followed the measuring guidelines and are giving your fabricators as much information as possible to provide you with an accurate estimate.

Please note that every building has a standard for shading with which you must comply. The building/facilities management may allow only one particular specification or they may have a few standards from which you can choose. The larger and newer the building, the more likely that a set of standards is in place, so consult with the management at the onset of a project, because window coverings are critical to the success of the space you are designing. Most building managers wish to create a uniform and cohesive look from the outside in. They want the façade to look and feel clean and harmonious, so, although they may let you select from among a few colors, most often they will want the same "TYP" specification for shading.

SPECIFICATIONS   **CONTRACT WINDOW COVERINGS/SHADING CHECKLIST**

Prior to Creating Any Custom Window Treatment Be Sure the Subcontractor Has Performed the Following Tasks

☐ **Measure wall length and ceiling height above finished floor (AFF).** (Note if no finish floor exists at survey date.)

☐ **Measure and note height and projection of baseboards and crown molding.**

☐ **Measure HVAC and/or radiators, and thermostats/detectors, existing switch and outlet locations.**

☐ **Measure overall window interior dimensions** (length × width × depth).

☐ **Measure and note windowsill height and projection and also window frame/trim width.**

☐ **Measure mullions** (width and depth).

☐ **Measure and note height above window to ceiling.**

☐ **Measure wall and ceiling pocket details for drapery.** (Measure width and height.) **Take photos of existing conditions.**

☐ **Note the style of the window.**

☐ **Discuss automation and new switch/outlet and hard wire locations with your contractor.**

☐ **Send the drawings with your fabric info to the fabricator for a quote.**

Top Treatments

☐ **Specify IB (inside bracket) mount or OB (outside bracket) mount** (circle one).

☐ **If specifying a cornice, select a style: straight cornice, stepped cornice, etc.**

☐ **Specify the drop of the top treatment.**

☐ **Specify the depth of the treatment with the fabricator.**

☐ **Specify COM (customer's own material) fabric manufacturer/pattern/width/repeat/content.**

☐ **If fabric has a pattern, specify the direction in which the pattern should run.**

☐ **Specify whether the fabric is backed. If so, specify acrylic or knit** (circle one).

☐ **Specify whether you wish to use a trim, self-welt, contrast welt, etc.**

Shades

☐ **Specify IB (inside bracket) mount or OB (outside bracket) mount** (circle one).

☐ **Specify style** _____ **Specify color** _____

☐ **Discuss with the client the level of shading desired in each space.**

☐ **Specify automation, LiteRise®, cord, or remote** (circle one).

☐ **Specify cord pull location: Right/Left** (circle one).

Wood/Metal Blind

☐ **Specify IB (inside bracket) mount or OB (outside bracket) mount** (circle one).

☐ **Specify type and finish** _____

☐ **Specify slat size** (typical sizes are 1", 1 3/8", or 2") _____

☐ **Specify cord pull or LiteRise®** (circle one). **Specify ladders or tape** (circle one).

☐ **Specify cord location: left or right** (circle one).

☐ **Specify self-valance Yes or No** (circle one).

☐ **Specify automation, LiteRise®, or cord** (circle one).

Window Film

☐ **Send photos, plans, and elevations to your preferred vendor.**

☐ **Discuss film options with client. Color, glare control, light control, heat management, privacy, and security.**

☐ **Manufacturer** _____ **Shade** _____ **Performance** _____ **LEED credits** _____

PART IV

Renovations

Renovations

CHAPTER 6

Residential and Contract Renovations

General Notes

Renovations and additions are the heart of many design practices. While decorating projects represent a large a part of the process, renovations and additions require that systems be put in place for procurement, tracking orders, and organizing/arranging for deliveries. Other responsibilities might include being on site to receive deliveries, and preparing for and supervising installations.

This obviously requires a high level of organization and attention to detail, and the responsibility falls to you and your design team. This chapter focuses primarily on the intricacies of residential design, with a breakdown of the individual components in the process.

There is also a section at the end of the chapter that references special considerations when working on a contract project. Renovations are handled in a unique and different manner in the contract realm and you must be aware of what is expected.

Be aware that we are imperfect beings living in a world where elements are not always in our control. Having this structure and good systems in place will help manage the unforeseen problems that may arise and also keep you and your staff from making expensive mistakes.

Residential Design—Ordering and Deliveries
Purchase Orders and Order Tracking

You have specified elements for your project, and you are ready to place orders. Many firms first send a proposal to the client listing the particulars of the items being ordered, including the sale price, the lead time, the quantity, and any other pertinent information. Proposals, purchase orders, and invoices can be generated from accounting software programs like QuickBooks® or from specific project management programs tailored to our industry such as Design Manager and Studio Webware®, or you can create your own stylized templates.

Once your client has approved your proposal, you move to the ordering phase. The first step is to generate a purchase order for the item(s) you have specified. There are many standards in the interior design industry that you can follow when creating a purchase order. First, you must realize that a purchase order is a legal document. You must be as specific as possible when creating this document. Your firm's contact information, the vendor and receiver/recipient information, and your account number must all appear on the purchase order. You should also include e-mail addresses, if available, as this creates a good paper trail to follow in case of any questions along the way.

A few years back, we ordered an 86" long sofa. The vendor had generated a quote for a 96" long sofa, but our purchase order clearly stated our requested size of 86". To my surprise, many firms do not generate purchase orders for work to be executed and furniture to be produced. They work from the vendor's quotations. Had I not generated this purchase order and had access to the documentation showing that it had been sent and received by my vendor, we would have had a huge issue in terms of errors and omissions. There was insufficient access for a 96" long sofa in this apartment building, not to mention that it would not have worked in our furniture plan.

Our purchase order clearly stated the details, including the request to have the wood base removed and shipped separately from the upholstered portion so that access to the elevator, through the corridors, and entry to the apartment would not be an issue.

Always include all details on your purchase order: furniture dimensions, fabric specified from a different vendor that you are having sent separately, arm style, base or leg style, finish, quilting details, and seat and back cushion details. Be as concise as you can. Some software programs allow you to embed an image into your purchase order. This is an excellent way to create a quick reference for the vendor, your company, and your client as the project progresses. Figure 6.1 shows an example of a purchase order.

If you are ordering fabric, inquire about the lead time if the goods are not in stock. Always request a CFA (cutting for approval). You must be sure the dye lot of the goods being shipped aligns with the sample you have shown and had approved by your client. You should snip a small swatch of this cutting and staple it to the purchase order if image embedding is not possible. Figure 6.2 shows an example of a CFA. Once approved, generate a purchase order.

If you are purchasing fabric from one vendor and having the fabric applied to furniture manufactured by another vendor, then you must generate two distinct purchase orders: The first one is for the furniture and the second for the fabric.

Be sure that when you request a quotation on a furniture item you also request a yardage quote based on the fabric(s) you are specifying to be applied to the furniture. You will need to supply your vendor with the fabric name/number, color name/number, width, repeat, and contents so they can generate a yardage quotation.

When using a fabric from one showroom on an upholstery piece from another showroom, you must use a COM/COL/COV (customer's own material/leather/vinyl) tag. The showroom supplying the furniture will provide you with the tag. All information must be filled out, and the tag must accompany the fabric order. The COM tag provides information such as the purchase order number, the furniture manufacturer's order number, the fabric details, application instructions (railroad or run off the bolt), and any trim to be applied. This is critical information since the factory cannot complete your furniture order without it. Request that a COM tag be sent to you via fax or e-mail and fill it out completely. You should then reserve yardage with the fabric vendor, either by phone or online. Make sure to get a hold/confirmation number for your order.

Send the COM tag along with the purchase order so the vendor can include it with the bolt of fabric. This ensures that once the fabric arrives at the manufacturer or upholsterer's workroom, they will know it is your fabric and for which project it is intended. Figure 6.3 shows an example of a COM tag.

When you send in a purchase order, it is accompanied by either a deposit or payment in full, depending upon how your account is set up and the vendor/manufacturer's policy.

Designers typically have either a *pro forma* or a *net 30* account set up when they begin to do business with a vendor. A pro forma account is the most typical, especially for an emerging professional with little capital and no proven track record with other vendors. This type of account requires payment in full for all fabrics, trims, and so forth, prior to goods being shipped. Furniture on a pro forma account requires a 50 percent deposit upon placement of the order. Net 30 accounts allow designers to float payments, giving them time to collect funds from their clients and saving time writing checks for each individual purchase order.

How do you pay for the items? Designers utilize different methods for collecting monies to pay for the merchandise they order for their clients. Some designers work off a retainer. Some request checks or credit card information from their clients to cover costs. Still others allow their clients to purchase directly from the vendor, eliminating a great deal of bookkeeping time on the designer's end and allowing the clients to see exactly how much an item costs. We call this *cost transparency*. There is no right or wrong way to do this, but be consistent when you set your protocols.

Once you submit a purchase order, you should confirm receipt and be sure there are no questions or concerns on the part of the vendor.

It is a good idea to create a system for following up and tracking items ordered (ship date, etc.). You may select a project management system such as Asana cloud server or Basecamp® so that your design team can be kept up to speed on the status of each order for your client. Other firms use design-specific project management software as previously mentioned (Studio Webware™, Quickbooks®, Design Manager) to track their projects.

Delivery Protocols

As a seasoned designer, I have had my share of delivery sagas. Having started my own firm after only a year of design experience, I had to fly by the seat of my pants and many of the mistakes I made in the infancy of my business could have been avoided if I had had a system in place to provide guidance.

In addition, whenever I have hired new staff, I had to indoctrinate them into the delivery procedures and what to watch for. I needed to spend an inordinate amount of time training them in our protocols, how to handle problems with a delivery or installation, and what to do when something went wrong.

I quickly became tired of this routine and started to formulate a delivery and installation checklist system by which I have been able to steer clear of many delivery dramas. Truth be told, there is always something new and unexpected that can occur, but I have found in my twenty years of experience that forewarned is forearmed. I want to share some important strategies that you, too, can employ in your business.

My best piece of advice is as follows: Try to use only one or two receivers and develop a solid relationship with the person in charge of your account. I have also become well acquainted with the owners of the company, sending them thank-you cards, gifts on holidays, and "just checking in" e-mails to let them know that they are important members of our team. This camaraderie has been worth its weight in gold. Whenever I really need a favor, be it a price check or a quicker ETA, they go to bat for me. I am extremely loyal to my vendors, and that loyalty has made our firm a success.

Whenever possible, you should warehouse all items and deliver everything at once. When your receiver lets you know that your order is ready for delivery, whenever possible, make a trip to the warehouse and personally inspect every item. If there is a problem, you want to know before the item arrives at the client's home so you can troubleshoot and remedy it, thereby managing your client's expectations. This is the key to having a successful reveal and a happy client. If something arrives in less-than-optimum or damaged condition, your client will not be happy, and that reflects poorly on your role as a luxury service provider. Do your homework, find out about warehousing fees, and let your clients know that this is a cost that will be incurred as part of their freight budget. I've found this to be the best way to proceed.

So even the best-laid plans sometimes go awry. Even when you have followed set protocols for years, something can still happen along the way that is beyond your anticipation, preparation, or control.

For example, chairs come in with damaged legs or frames, a sofa is made with the wrong back cushion, a tabletop has a scratch, or a lamp stem is crooked or the shade is dented or stained. There are no glides on the bottom of the chair leg or on a case piece, and the delivery team scratches the floor while moving an item into place. (Always keep a pack of felt glides in your tool box!)

This is another reason for using the Delivery Protocol Checklist. Have this with you to prepare for and receive a delivery so you will be as knowledgeable as possible about all potential pitfalls.

Some of the economic challenges that have impacted the design industry have led to a decrease in quality control and an increase in items being received with defects or missing parts and pieces. This makes our job more difficult and time consuming, as we spend hours trying to right wrongs that are beyond our control.

If an item is scheduled to come via UPS, try to have it delivered to your office, or to the warehouse/receiver, so you can inspect it. When this is not an option, you should follow the protocol directions in the checklist to help you sail through the channels of return and recovery.

As a final note, I would like to add that when we meet with clients to sign a letter of agreement or contract, we educate them and manage their expectations from the very start. We let them know there is the possibility that some items we order may arrive in less than a perfect state and that our function as the designer and purchasing agent is to manage the process of getting this rectified so that the clients will not be bothered with these details. The clients' job is to enjoy the design solution!

☐ **In the upper left-hand corner of the page, including the following:**
  - **Your company name/logo**
  - **Address including city, state, and zip code**
  - **Phone number**
  - **Fax number**
  - **Website (URL)**
  - **E-mail address**

☐ **Add purchasing vendor information, including the following:**
  - **Company name**
  - **Salesperson name**
  - **Address including city, state, and zip code**
  - **Phone number**
  - **Fax number**
  - **E-mail address of your contact**

☐ **Create ship-to information for the item(s), including the following:**
  - **Company name (workroom)**
  - **Recipient name if applicable**
  - **Address including city, state, and zip code**
  - **Phone number**

☐ **Create the purchase order number (P.O. number).**

Your Purchase Order Table Should Include the Following Information

  - **The date the purchase order was generated**
  - **The requisitioner** (the person from your team issuing the purchase order)
  - **How the item(s) is/are to be shipped** (UPS, to a receiver, white-glove delivery, delivered and installed, etc.)
  - **Your account number assigned by the manufacturer/vendor you are ordering from**
  - **The terms of your account** (pro forma, net 30, 50 percent deposit, etc.)
  - **Quantity: List how many of each item you are specifying (units, yard[s], square feet, etc.)**
  - **Description of each item and perhaps a note detailing the room number or the name of the space it is designated for**
  - **Any additional notes you may have for the order including any of the following:**
    - **Reference number**
    - **If specifying fabric or a finish, request a CFA or a strike-off sample,**
    - **A sidemark including your company name, the client name, room/space designation, where fabric is to be applied (drapery, upholstery, walls, etc.). For example: GREATDESIGN/Wilson/Kitchen/Shade.**
  - **Unit price**
  - **Subtotal**
  - **Tax**
  - **Freight/shipping and handling**
  - **Total**

☐ **Include information such as "Deposit Enclosed" and list the amount of the deposit.**

☐ **Add a line for an authorized signature where the client can sign, date, and approve the purchase order prior to sending it to your vendor.**

Purchase Order References

[COMPANY NAME OR LOGO]
[Street Address]
[City, ST ZIP Code]
[Phone Number]
[Fax Number]

PURCHASE ORDER

TO:	SHIP TO:	P.O. NUMBER:
[Company Name]	**[Company Name]**	**[P.O. number]**
[Salesperson Name]	[Recipient Name]	*[The P.O. number must appear on*
[Street Address]	[Street Address]	*all related correspondence,*
[City, ST ZIP Code]	[City, ST ZIP Code]	*shipping papers, and invoices]*
[Phone Number]	[Phone Number]	

P.O DATE	REQUISITIONER	SHIPPED VIA	ACCOUNT #	TERMS
11/6/2013	John Smith	UPS	S-12345	ProForma

QTY	DESCRIPTION	UNIT PRICE	TOTAL
6 yds	Fabric for Roman Shade Pattern: Ledrew/Tide - 54"Width – 9" Horizontal Repeat – 11" Vertical Repeat Ref#: xxxxxxx *** Cutting-for-Approval Required *** **Catalog No.:** fabric **Side Mark:** GreatDesign/Wilson/Kitchen/Shade **Special Instructions:** All one piece	$50.62	$303.72

Deposit Enclosed: $347.12

ITEM TOTAL	303.72
TAX (7.375%)	22.40
FREIGHT/SHIPPING & HANDLING	21.00
GRAND TOTAL	**$347.12**

_____   _____
Authorized Signature   Date

Figure 6.1 Purchase Order Example

RENOVATIONS   **ORDER TRACKING OVERVIEW CHECKLIST**

NOTE: In contract design, the furniture dealer will handle all of the details listed below for fabrics, case goods, and upholstered furniture. The general contractor will handle details for window treatments and provide submittals for designer's approval.

Fabrics

☐ Check all details of the order (yardage, Teflon® coating, knit or acrylic backing, laminating)—before the order is executed.

☐ Be sure to request a COM tag for all fabrics going to furniture manufacturers and workrooms for upholstery.

☐ Make sure the CFA has been received and approved prior to order confirmation and payment.

☐ Follow up on all item(s) ordered: date of order, estimated ship date.

☐ Keep a log of all items that have been ordered, noting when they were shipped and when they were delivered.

☐ Track when the order is complete.

Furniture—Case Goods

☐ Follow up on all item(s) ordered: date of order, estimated ship date.

☐ Check the details of the order—all finishes and features—before the order is executed.

☐ As items are selected by clients, update the drawings to double-check clearances before remaining furniture pieces are purchased/ordered to ensure they still work within the space.

☐ Keep a log of all item(s) that have been ordered, noting when they were shipped and when they were delivered.

☐ Track when the order is complete.

Upholstered Furniture

☐ As items are selected by clients, update the drawings to double-check clearance before remaining furniture pieces are purchased to ensure they still work within the furniture layout your client approved.

☐ Check all details of the order (railroading, welt/trim, wood finish)—before the order is executed.

☐ Make sure the CFA has been received and approved prior to order confirmation and payment.

☐ Check that COM tags were executed and accompanied the purchase order.

☐ Follow up on COM fabrics, trims, etc., to accompany order.

☐ Follow up on all item(s) ordered: date of order, estimated ship date, etc.

☐ Keep a log of when item(s) were ordered, when they were shipped, and when they were delivered.

Window Treatments

☐ Check all details of the order (style, size, trim, wood finish, etc.)—before the order is executed.

☐ Make sure the CFA has been received and approved prior to order confirmation and payment.

☐ Make sure your workroom has received all fabrics and trims to fabricate your order.

☐ Make sure your workroom has sent you a CFA of the goods received to ensure it correlates with your cutting.

☐ Approve the workroom's CFA.

☐ Follow up on all items ordered: date of order, estimated ship date.

☐ Keep a log of when items were ordered, when they were shipped, and when they were delivered.

Order Tracking References

Cutting For Approval   **Kravet, Inc**   01/12/2012 11:44 AM

Please call **1-800-645-9068** or visit our website at **e-designtrade.com** to approve your cutting.
This CFA will expire on **01/26/2012** if not approved.

KRAVET ELITE CONCIERGE

Company- DESIGN CONCEPTS INTERIORS

Sidemark- DCI/MARTINI/FOLDING CHAIRS

PO #
S/O # 3868597   Line # 1.1
Pattern: 27968   Color: 8
Pattern Name KF SMT::JENTRY.ONYX.0
Color Name

Ordered Qty: 2.25
PC & Yds   485064-02   2.250   47-02-C

Mail To: DESIGN CONCEPTS INTERIORS
ATT:PHYLLIS
PHYLLIS HARBINGER
8 DEVONSHIRE COURT
CORTLANDT MANOR, NY 10567
WESTCHESTER
UNITED STATES

UPS-Air-2nd Day Air

Figure 6.2 CFA Example

CUSTOMER'S OWN MATERIAL (C.O.M.) FABRIC ID

Proper identification of your fabric is **VERY** important. If we cannot identify your fabric, your order cannot be put into production. To avoid unnecessary delay, make certain the following information is provided with the shipment of your fabric.

IMPORTANT: Copy this form and attach to your fabric for all C.O.M. ORDERS

Account Name: C.O. Furniture – New York   Fabric Supplier _____

Account Address: 79 Furniture Ave., Suite 20   Fabric Supplier's Address_____

New York, NY 10006/P: 555-555-5555   _____

Order # _____   Pattern Name or Number _____

Frames # _____   # Yards Being Sent _____

Designer Name _____   Special Instructions_____

Date of Order _____   _____

S/M: C.O. FURNITURE NEW YORK/_____
                                         (Designer Name)/(Designer Sidemark)

(Attach swatch if possible)   Return C.O.M. Material

Shipping Address:

FACE OF FABRIC: We will assume that the face side is rolled in. If there can be a question concerning which side is the face side, please either attached a marked cutting or clearly tag the face side of the roll that is being sent to us. Please be certain that all information concerning fabric source and description, and any instructions for the application of your fabric are noted on your order.

NOTE: UNLESS INSTRUCTIONS ARE CLEARLY STATED ON YOUR ORDER, WE RESERVE THE RIGHT TO USE OUR BEST JUDGEMENT CONCERNING CUTTING AND APPLICATION OF YOUR FABRIC.

While we inspect fabrics for mill imperfections, some are difficult to recognize. We cannot be responsible for defects, color, inaccuracies, or other flaws.

Sorry, no C.O.D.'s accepted on C.O.M.

NOTE: We will hold extra COM fabric for 30 days after production of order. If customer does not send a request with the order, or does not contact us within the 30 days in regards to the additional COM to be returned, it will be discarded.

Figure 6.3 COM Tag Example

NOTE: In contract design, the general contractor and the furniture dealer will handle all of the following and will make the designer aware if any problems arise.

Instructions for a White-Glove Delivery

- ☐ If applicable, have the item(s) inspected upon receipt at the warehouse and any repairs made before the delivery date.
- ☐ Before the day scheduled for delivery, be sure that the delivery company has given the building/building management company a copy of the insurance certificate and has filled out any necessary paperwork to gain access to the building on the date of delivery. Make sure that all documents have been approved.
- ☐ Check with the building superintendent to make sure which entrance the delivery person(s) should use and whether there is a freight elevator to be used for deliveries.
- ☐ On install day, bring light bulbs, extension cords, polishing cloths, etc.
- ☐ On install day, wear comfortable clothes and shoes.
- ☐ Have the delivery service bring the item to the exact location you have specified in the home/office.
- ☐ Monitor any on-site unpacking of the item(s). (If you or a member of your design team are not present when the item arrives, instruct the client to monitor the unpacking of the item and send them these instructions to follow.)
- ☐ Inspect every inch of the item, top to bottom, checking for defects, dents, and any imperfections. (See the next section for instructions in case of a damaged or defective item.)
- ☐ If the item has doors or drawers, test all to ensure that they open and close properly with ease. (See the next section for instructions in case of a damaged or defective item.)
- ☐ Make sure all furniture, especially chairs, have glides under the legs to ensure the floor is protected.
- ☐ Ask the delivery service to remove all packaging and debris from the premises.
- ☐ Sign for the delivery and get a copy of the paperwork for your records.

What to Do If There Is Damage to a Delivered Item

- ☐ Notify your supervisor of the problem and ask for specific instructions.
- ☐ Contact the manufacturer and ask for further instructions on whether you should refuse the delivered item or keep it and wait for a replacement or replacement part(s).
- ☐ Document the damage with multiple pictures of the damaged area(s).
- ☐ *Always* add an extremely detailed description of the damage to the paperwork. Make sure you get a copy of this paperwork, or take a photo of the page with a close-up of the damage description that you wrote, for your own protection.
- ☐ If your clients are on-site, notify them of the situation and the course of action being taken to secure a replacement or a repair.
- ☐ Make sure you or your supervisor contacts the client(s) if they are not on-site to notify them of the situation and the course of action being taken to secure a replacement or a repair.

Instructions for a Package Delivery from USPS, UPS, FedEx, or Other Service

- ☐ **Open the box immediately.** (If you are not on-site when the package arrives, instruct the client(s) to open the box immediately and send them these instructions to follow.)
- ☐ **Remove and read the packing list. Match all contents of the box with items listed on the packing list to ensure that you have received everything.**
- ☐ **Remove *all* contents of the box until it is empty.** (This prevents overlooking parts inside the box.)
- ☐ **Check the item(s) for damage, missing parts, etc.**
- ☐ **If an item is damaged, immediately notify the manufacturer of the problem. Then take pictures of the damage to e-mail to the manufacturer for a complete replacement or replacement part(s). Ask the manufacturer for further instructions and procedures for the return of the defective item in order to receive the replacement.** (Will they send you a return authorization (RA) tag to ship back the item? Will they pick up the defective item? Can you dispose of the defective item?) **It is *very* important that you notify your client(s) to keep *all* boxes and packaging until the situation is resolved.**
- ☐ **If a part or item is missing, immediately notify the manufacturer of the problem, so they can ship the missing part/item as soon as possible.**
- ☐ **If necessary, assemble the item, and, if applicable, test the item.** (For example, if the item is a lamp, ensure that the switch works, etc.)

Kitchen and Other Cabinetry Installation

Custom cabinetry is generally delivered and installed by the manufacturer or the cabinetmaker. Stock cabinetry will arrive at the job site, and then the general contractor (GC) or an independent installer will come in and take care of installation.

When cabinetry arrives ahead of the installer, you really must check the packing list and be present to ensure that all components ordered have indeed been delivered. In addition, you need to find out how much time you have to report any damages or missing pieces once the delivery takes place. This is critical, as each manufacturer has a specific policy that must be followed. So, if the installer cannot be on-site for a number of weeks after a delivery is made, then the designer is responsible for making sure the order is complete and correct.

Installation of a kitchen is not a one-day event. It unfolds over several days—the cabinet boxes are brought in and fillers, toe kicks, end panels, and appliance panels/covers are added where required. There are also technical issues involved with wall-hung as opposed to base cabinetry. Shims are used to level cabinets where the floor is not quite even, and fillers are used to disguise uneven ceiling levels and add clearances for appliances.

You need to check the finishes, the interiors of the cabinets, the hinges, the number of shelves and supports, and any other items that should be confirmed. The toe kick is also an important item to check.

Always be sure to inspect all corners during installation and confirm that mitering and edge details are flush and finished smoothly. At this point, you should also make sure that all drawer glides work properly and were installed as per your specifications. For example, if you ordered soft-close glides for the drawers, be sure they were installed.

Once the cabinetry and the countertops are installed, the GC will be able to do the electrical and plumbing hookups and install all of the fixtures, the tile backsplash, and under-cabinet lighting. Coordinate with the GC to set up the various stages of the installation.

Many designers specify and create custom cabinetry for other spaces. Examples include a built-in media unit, a bathroom vanity, a custom desk, or millwork for a library. A representative from your firm should always be on-site to manage the installation and troubleshoot in case of any questions, snafus, or other problems. Always have a copy of the drawing(s) with you so that you can reference the design intent and what was contracted.

Be sure that all decorative hardware/pulls and other accessories are on-site for installation day, and bring your touch-up markers just in case the cabinetmaker misses something. It is best to be prepared!

KITCHEN AND OTHER CABINETRY INSTALLATION CHECKLIST

Before Cabinetry Is Manufactured

☐ Make sure decorative hardware is specified, ordered, and delivered to the job site prior to installation, so that the cabinetmaker can drill holes in the doors and drawers and install the hardware upon completion of the installation.

☐ Make sure the walls and ceiling are painted prior to cabinet installation.

☐ Clear the area of all debris and make it ready for cabinetry installation.

☐ Schedule the electrical and plumbing finish work to coordinate with cabinet installation.

☐ Make sure flooring is complete and protected.

During Cabinetry Installation

☐ When on-site, periodically inspect the work being done.

☐ Check for damage or imperfections on any doors, drawers, crown, base, panels, etc.

☐ If there are any problems on-site that you cannot resolve yourself or on which you need a second opinion, call your supervisor as soon as possible to resolve.

After Cabinetry Is Installed

☐ Inspect the cabinetry, checking for any damages, dings, or imperfections.

☐ Open and close each door and drawer and make sure they function properly and smoothly.

☐ Be sure all shelves are in place inside of cabinets.

Before Countertop Is Installed

☐ Schedule a date for your supplier to template for the new countertop.

☐ Make sure you have seen and approved the available slab (since natural stone goes out of stock quickly and dye lots change).

During Countertop Installation

☐ If you are on-site, periodically inspect the work being done.

☐ Check to make sure any and all seaming is clean and as inconspicuous as possible.

☐ If there are any problems on-site that you cannot resolve yourself or on which you need a second opinion, call your supervisor as soon as possible to resolve and call the supplier if necessary.

After Countertop Installation

☐ Check to make sure any and all seaming is clean looking and as inconspicuous as possible.

☐ Check to see if there are any scratches, dings, or any other installation incidents.

☐ If there are any problems on-site that you cannot resolve yourself or on which you need a second opinion, call your supervisor as soon as possible to resolve and call the supplier if necessary.

Luxury Space Installations

Luxury spaces require special attention to detail. There are generally more "moving parts" in a luxury space and certain considerations that must be dealt with on installation day. Often, more than one vendor is on-site on the same installation since they follow one another as tasks are completed.

Coordination and careful planning of the installation is the job of the designer, working with the GC and the client to provide a seamless and quick turnaround.

Working with a specialist for each of the categories that follows is a great way to be sure that you are covering all the bases. For example, you should always work with audiovisual consultants on home theater and media room installations. Their industry connections and knowledge base on what is available and a good fit for your client's needs will make the design more powerful and more functional as well. In a home theater, you need to be concerned with specialty seating, varying floor levels, acoustics, lighting, technology, screen size, and many other details.

Billiard/Game Room

In a billiard/game room, you need to ensure that there is a proper lighting design in place as well as critical clearances for the span of the cue sticks and movement of people around the table. Although there are adjustable cue sticks on the market, it is best to keep 5' of clearance around all sides of the pool table. Sound and other audiovisual needs are also integral to a successful billiard room, as is light control. Many clients prefer to install flat-screen television(s) to view games that might be airing while they entertain guests or shoot a solitary game. This adds to the appeal and functionality of the space.

A billiard/game room is a recreational space and a staple in the luxury home. It is a place to congregate, compete, and relax. When planning this space, you must take into account the clearances en route and how you will deliver the table. Billiard/pool tables generally come in parts but the top is almost always a single piece, so completing an access measurement to be sure all the parts can be successfully navigated to the destination is of the utmost importance here.

Be sure that all of the accessories are on-site on installation day. For example, confirm that the cue sticks, the storage rack, stools, the cue and the balls, and any other furniture you may have ordered for the space have been delivered. Many people also include a dartboard and a card/poker table. The lighting fixtures may or may not have been installed prior to installation day. It is easier for the electrician to install the pendant(s) prior to installation day, as it is difficult to move a pool table once sited due to the weight.

Beginning Steps

☐ When designing a billiard/game room, be sure that the room you are renovating or constructing has sufficient space to accommodate a pool table in addition to 5' of clearance on all sides. For example, if the table you are specifying is 5' by 9', then the overall space allotted should be at minimum 15' by 19', with no other objects interfering.

☐ It is very important to do a lighting plan/elevation(s) for proper placement, most crucially for the billiard table fixture, and also for any ceiling fans, recessed lights, and/or other ceiling fixtures and wall-mounted fixtures.

☐ Make sure you have the proper wiring done for any flat screens (on a stand or wall-mounted) and stereos/speakers, smart home systems, voice, and data.

After Construction/Electrical Is Finished

☐ Flooring is very important. Sometimes balls hop off the table, so take this into consideration when selecting flooring. Because of this, tile may not be the best option. Appropriate specifications include linoleum, vinyl/vinyl composition tile (VCT), wall-to-wall carpeting, carpet tiles, wood, engineered wood, cork, laminate, or your choice of flooring with a large area rug underneath the billiard table.

☐ If you do choose to specify an area rug, be sure that it is thin and has a low, even pile so that the billiard table stays level, or inset the rug and use a metal bead to finish so there is no level change. Also ensure that it is large enough to extend out past the table on all sides by a considerable amount to prevent having to stand partially on the rug and partially off during play.

☐ If you are specifying a dartboard, it is very important that you specify that it be hung at the proper height. (The regulation height is 5'-8" from finished floor to the center of the bulls-eye.)

☐ Ensure that the throwing line is exactly 7'- 9 1/4" out from the front face of the dartboard.

☐ Discuss with your clients whether they want their AV components exposed or enclosed in a cabinet, closet, or on a rack.

☐ If you have specified a wall-mounted pool cue rack, be sure you note this location (placement on wall and height off the floor) on your elevations so it is installed in the correct location on-site.

Delivery/Installation

☐ All flooring and painting should be completed prior to furniture arrival.

☐ Clear the space of all debris and obstacles.

☐ When delivering, the slate top is all in one piece, so you need to decide on the path of least obstruction prior to delivery.

☐ Be sure the table has been leveled prior to the installer's departure.

☐ Check to be sure all parts have been delivered to the job site (cue sticks, cue, balls, etc.).

Home Gym

When planning a home gym, you may wish to engage other professionals. Consulting an experienced personal trainer and a knowledgeable fitness equipment sales representative would be a great place to start your research.

Your plan will be affected by equipment placement, range of motion, and clearances necessary for each piece of equipment. You must first determine whether the equipment you are specifying will easily get to the space in the home where it is intended to live. An access measurement is a crucial step in the planning process.

While most fitness equipment comes partially or fully unassembled, there are components that are oversized and may not get through a doorway or down a hallway or a flight of stairs with turns, so research all specs before considering a purchase.

Not only is the equipment important, but the flooring in a home gym is key to the success of the space. Be sure that you plan for installation of the floor prior to the delivery of any equipment.

Lighting is also critical in a home gym. Be sure to specify ambient illumination that is diffuse so it is even throughout the space. Fixtures with lamping (bulbs) that simulate natural daylight conditions are preferred.

The use of mirrors is an important specification in a gym. They visually amplify the space, but they also provide motivation for the client to work out more effectively and stay mindful of correct posture and form.

A small refrigerator, a dedicated area for free weights and bands, towels, wipes, and a great AV system will make this a productive space.

Beginning Steps

- ☐ When possible, consider the optimum location for the gym.
- ☐ Keep the gym away from sleeping areas, as a gym can sometimes be a noisy space.
- ☐ If this cannot be avoided, pay special attention to soundproofing materials for the walls and ceiling to absorb noise from AV and gym equipment.
- ☐ Higher ceilings provide much-needed clearance for certain activities such as jumping rope, trampoline jumping, and large-scale gym equipment.
- ☐ Select an area in the home that offers as much natural light as possible, which reduces energy costs. The natural daylight will also give your clients a bit more motivation.
- ☐ Allowing for fresh air to enter the space not only provides much-needed ventilation for cooling but also whisks away perspiration odors that can accumulate in the gym.
- ☐ HVAC considerations should be discussed with your contractor or engineer.
- ☐ You should specify that this room has its own, separate thermostat if possible.
- ☐ Be sure to do a lighting plan for proper placement of any ceiling fans, recessed lights, track, and/or other ceiling fixtures.
- ☐ If you are specifying a ceiling fan, be sure to prepare elevations of the room to cross-check the clearances. Be sure clients have room to lift their arms, with plenty of extra space between the fingertips (at least 18") and the very bottom of the ceiling fan and/or ceiling fan light kit.
- ☐ For lower ceilings, specify a ceiling-hugger fan.
- ☐ Confirm that the fan blades will clear all gym equipment.
- ☐ Discuss electrical considerations for refrigeration/water cooler, etc.
- ☐ Discuss wiring the gym for sound and entertainment.

After Construction/Electrical Is Finished

- ☐ Apply a wallcovering or paint for the walls.
- ☐ Light colors keep the space bright for exercising.
- ☐ Creating a focal wall in an energizing hue such as red or orange will motivate clients to exercise harder.
- ☐ Install flooring that is easy to clean such as rubber tiles, laminate flooring, or foam gym tiles.
- ☐ If not using rubber floor tiles, place rubber mats under each piece of equipment so that the equipment is secure and will not slide or scratch the floor.
- ☐ Indicate mirror locations.
- ☐ Discuss with your client(s) whether they want AV components exposed or enclosed in a cabinet or closet. (Do they want a rack or will they wire back to a central hub?)
- ☐ When planning, leave plenty of clearance surrounding each piece of equipment to prevent collisions and crowding in the gym.
- ☐ Design free spaces for activities such as stretching, yoga, jumping rope, lifting free weights, and other activities that require open floor space. Be sure that in these open spaces there is ample room to swing arms/legs in all directions.

Cabinetry Suggestions

- ☐ Your client may require cabinetry for the space to reflect the function. For example, your cabinet may include an under-counter refrigerator, shelves or a cabinet for fresh towels, a water dispenser, a place for cleaning supplies to wipe down equipment after use or a wipe dispenser, a paper towel holder, and/or a hamper for soiled towels.
- ☐ You may need to design a place to store DVDs and other electronics.
- ☐ You may want to include open shelving as well for easy access to small hand towels and other items and also to serve as a display.

Home Spa

When designing a home spa, there are many facets to consider. First and foremost, what is the function of the space? Does your client want a spa geared toward relaxation, or is it strictly for therapeutic purposes? Does the client require steam, dry sauna, a jetted tub, room for a massage table, or perhaps a private room?

Where will the spa be located? Many clients are now dedicating space in the basement for a home spa, and designers are being asked to work this into the space planning in both new construction and remodeling projects. Other clients wish to incorporate spa features in the master suite or a dedicated room, especially where there is no basement level.

Be sure to design storage for towels, sheets, potions, and lotions. Also include window coverings in your design. Adding blackout lined shades for privacy and light control will enhance the experience.

It is great when the home spa can be located near the gym, but this is not always possible. In any event, make sure that there is space between the wall partitions for great sound attenuation. A quiet place to meditate and enjoy a massage or even a nice soak is always a plus.

Working with a professional audiovisual consultant enhances the overall experience for the client, so be sure to engage the appropriate experts at the start of the project. Arranging for music to be piped into wet locations with high heat levels requires experience and extensive knowledge about available products. Discuss the remote location of the sound system and other equipment. Will you specify cabinetry or a rack or perhaps a closet setup? This allows you to control the music in a closed location, but keeps the clutter out of sight in this tranquil space.

Refrain from using bold pattern in the spa area. You should keep the space as serene as possible. Use natural textures such as wood, stone, cork, bamboo, glass, and other fluid textures to enhance interest and create an atmosphere of peace and serenity.

Beginning Steps

- ☐ Be sure that the surrounding walls and ceiling are properly insulated. This space should be quiet and tranquil and immune to sound from adjoining spaces.
- ☐ Make sure to specify a solid-core door(s).
- ☐ If you are planning new construction, all wiring for lighting and surround sound speakers should be strategically located and properly installed before you close the walls.
- ☐ If the walls already exist, be sure to map out a plan for wiring so your electrician can allocate and snake/install in the exact location on the first try. Measure twice, cut once!
- ☐ Specify all equipment: massage table, spa tub, dry sauna unit or individual custom materials, steam shower, tile, fixtures, etc. (See Home Spa Specifications Checklist in Chapter 4 for more details.)
- ☐ Create a lighting plan for proper placement of any recessed lights or other ceiling and wall-mounted fixtures.
- ☐ Be sure all lighting specified is for wet location use by code.
- ☐ Request that all lighting be put on dimmers. This is super important to enable complete control of the quantity as well as the quality of light.
- ☐ Further specify the type of bulb/lamp to provide the appropriate color of light for the spa experience.
- ☐ If you are specifying ceiling fans, be sure they are ultra-quiet.
- ☐ All elevations should indicate the location of wall-mounted lighting so your electrician will be able to follow your design intent.
- ☐ If windows exist or are designed into the space, determine how they will be addressed. You should have some type of shading in this space for privacy and light control.
- ☐ Make sure that the space is well ventilated and has operable windows if possible.
- ☐ Specify a dedicated thermostat if possible.
- ☐ Specify that radiant heat be installed under the floors. This is a nice feature when stepping barefoot onto the floor as your clients will do often in this space.

After Construction/Electrical Is Finished

- ☐ Specify a wallcovering or paint for the walls. Light and/or neutral colors will keep the space calm and relaxing.
- ☐ Dark tonal values can also work well.
- ☐ Consider using wood or another type of resilient flooring material in the area with the massage tables to add a forgiving surface for the massage therapist to stand on.

Cabinetry Suggestions

- ☐ Create cabinetry for the space to reflect the functions. For example, a cabinet may include a sink, which would be used by a massage therapist for washing hands and other items used during the treatment. Additional counter space would allow the therapist to set up bowls, lotions, hot stones, etc. during treatment.
- ☐ You may include open shelving as well for easy access to massage oils, towels, and other items and also to serve as a display.
- ☐ You also may want to consider using tall towers of closed storage for towels, robes, etc.

Other Items

- ☐ You may want to consider installing a water feature somewhere within the space. The sound is soothing and adds to the user's overall spa experience.
- ☐ Specifying a fireplace within the space adds warmth and ambiance.

Home Theater

The home theater experience knows no boundaries in today's residential market and continues to evolve. While the modest home might simply have a large flat-screen and a nice surround sound system installed in the family room, more upscale residences are opting for dedicated spaces to create a realistic movie theater experience complete with tiered seating, curtains, a fabulous large-scale screen, lighting, Smarthome® system controls, and even a popcorn machine.

Look carefully at the space you have to work with. Can it accommodate tiered seating? This is optimal for viewing purposes but requires more careful planning because you need to consider stairs, risers, platforms, and perhaps even ramping. Be sure to consult the code requirements for your jurisdiction before moving forward. If you do decide to go this route, you should also consider stair riser lighting or another form of illumination for wayfinding and safety in this generally dark environment.

Many clients request that you specify seating with a reclining feature. You can do this with single-chair seating or linked seating, or you may want to use loveseats or sofas. Your client may even wish to purchase seating from an old movie theater for both nostalgic and sustainable rewards. Repurposing and reusing are quite popular approaches, as we have mentioned in previous chapters of this book. Various manufacturers now offer great accessories in their product lines. From cup holders to remote stations to reclining seats with footrests, there is something for everyone!

Many manufacturers now offer theater seating at a variety of price points, so discuss the budget with your clients. Leather is available in varying degrees of quality, or you might want to specify Crypton® or Ultrasuede®, as they are easy to maintain. Although a pricier option, mohair, which has been used for years in many older movie houses and Broadway theaters, is both durable and luxurious.

One of the most important features of a home theater is the sound. Be certain that the room has been soundproofed so that all entertainment can be enjoyed without interruption from adjoining spaces. In addition, the sound inside the space should be fully contained so as not to disturb other areas of the home. While insulation and good-quality materials, thicker walls, solid-core doors, and other factors can go a long way toward mitigating sound transfer, you can also add upholstered wall panels, drapery, and carpet to absorb sound.

Drapery can add a great deal of drama to home theaters. Whether the style is contemporary or traditional or somewhere in between, the right window treatment framing the stage/screen can add a lot of impact while also softening the interior space. It offers a great opportunity to play with color and texture.

Interior designers face special challenges when designing home theaters. We strongly suggest that you engage an audiovisual professional in addition to a lighting designer to facilitate your design process and make your workflow more efficient. Having a qualified group of experts involved from the beginning will enhance the outcome of your project.

Beginning Steps

- [ ] Specify all walls, ceiling, and floor to contribute to sound attenuation/soundproofing.
- [ ] For new construction, all wiring for lighting, AV equipment, and surround sound speakers should be planned and installed before the walls are closed.
- [ ] For renovations of existing space, be sure to map out a wiring plan so the electrician/AV specialist can follow your plan and snake where necessary.
- [ ] Discuss the location of the screen and projector (height, etc.).
- [ ] Discuss with your clients the location and type of enclosure they require for the AV equipment/components. Do they want a rack or shelving? Specify a ventilated space, as the equipment gets hot.
- [ ] Specify all lighting fixtures for the space.
- [ ] Create a lighting plan and an RCP for proper placement of any wall and floor lighting, in addition to recessed lights or other ceiling fixtures.
- [ ] All lighting should be specified with dimmer controls.
- [ ] All elevations should include sconce locations.
- [ ] Windows need to be addressed with blackout shades or drapery.
- [ ] Make sure to specify a solid-core door(s).
- [ ] Specify furniture, and possibly tiered platforms, for the seating.
- [ ] Design all necessary cabinetry for the space, to include a wet bar, refrigeration, microwave, etc. Make sure all lighting and electrical wiring is in the correct location. Be sure to specify decorative hardware and all fixtures needed.
- [ ] Install a water line if necessary for a wet bar.

After Construction/Electrical Wiring Is Complete

- [ ] Specify wall/ceiling treatments: architectural moldings, paint, wallcoverings, or upholstered panels.
- [ ] Darker colors optimize the space for entertainment viewing.
- [ ] Acoustical panels on the walls and possibly on the ceiling contribute to the sound attenuation.
- [ ] Specify a sound-absorbing floor material. Carpeting throughout the majority of the space is suggested.
- [ ] Discuss the idea of utilizing draperies to frame the screen and/or the entry. This also contributes to sound absorption while providing emphasis and focus.

Before Cabinetry Is Created (If Applicable)

- [ ] Discuss all finishes with your client and the cabinetmaker (cabinetry finish, countertop material, etc.).
- [ ] Choose and order hardware for cabinetry (knobs, pulls, etc.).
- [ ] Discuss the location of switches and outlets, etc.
- [ ] Discuss which switches coordinate with which lights.
- [ ] Discuss the type and color of outlets and switches (dimmers, etc.).

Before Cabinetry Is Installed (If Applicable)

- [ ] Make sure the area is cleared of all debris and ready for cabinetry.

During/After Cabinetry Installation (If Applicable)

- [ ] If you are on-site, periodically inspect the work being done.
- [ ] If there are any problems on-site that you cannot resolve yourself or on which you need a second opinion, call your supervisor as soon as possible to resolve and call the supplier if necessary.
- [ ] Inspect the cabinetry, checking for any damage, dings, or imperfections.
- [ ] Open and close each door and drawer and make sure they function properly and smoothly.

The Man Cave

This particular space has become increasingly popular in homes across America in the last few years. Shelter magazines run features detailing the wonderful spaces designers are creating for clients, with budgets ranging from high to low.

Let's look at the origin of the term *cave*. We all know about humans as cave dwellers. We crave cozy, enclosed, and comfortable spaces. With the crazy busy lives we lead, it is satisfying to be able to give clients their own space in which to retreat, enjoy some quiet time, or bond with their friends. Although the space is generally called a "man cave" it is not uncommon for a woman to request such a space of her own for quiet retreat and gathering with friends.

Recently, we designed a man cave for clients who were constructing an addition for their home. This space is an example of design with an element of sustainability. We repurposed a pair of gorgeous walnut and wrought iron antique doors that we had specified for their previous home. They now serve as the entry to the new space. We also reused some of the leather furniture from the previous home, which was a perfect fit!

Five flat-screen TVs line a wall, providing viewing opportunities from the pool table, the bar, and the seating area. The screens were mounted at a height that allows easy viewing whether you are seated or standing.

We designed a full wet bar that seats three, and behind the bar is a full wine cellar, which has a fabulous oak and glass door with custom wrought-iron work to reflect the design of the antique doors at the entry, providing rhythm and repetition.

The room is a multipurpose space, as are most man caves, but this one has the added complexity of a golf simulator. The necessary clearances, sound attenuation, and technology and all the various experts involved in the creation of this space required a great deal of organization, planning, and communication, and most of this went through our office. You should coordinate all efforts in a complex space such as this—drawings, specifications, and installation—sequencing with all team members and specialty contractors.

Beginning Steps

- ☐ Be sure the space you are designing and/or constructing is well insulated for sound attenuation. Specify materials that absorb sound such as carpet and upholstered walls.
- ☐ Locate and confirm that plumbing is in the correct location for the wet bar.
- ☐ If plumbing lines need to be added, collaborate with your plumber to install the necessary components.
- ☐ Create a lighting plan that addresses ambient, task, and accent lighting.
- ☐ Design a furniture plan to accommodate multiple functions and play zones.
- ☐ Specify recessed lighting or mini pendants over the bar, pendants over billiard tables, etc.
- ☐ Specify ceiling fans for movement of air.
- ☐ Specify ceiling light fixtures. Recessed, track lighting, or other sources of ambient illumination should be considered.
- ☐ Specify a door with a lockset so that children cannot get into this space unsupervised. If your client does not wish to have a lockset on the entry door, be sure to design cabinetry where all alcohol can be stored and locked to ensure the safety and welfare of underage household members and/or guests.
- ☐ Work with an AV specialist/engineer to ensure that proper wiring is completed for any TVs (on a stand or wall-mounted), stereos/speakers, and other Smarthome® features such as remotely controlled shades and lighting.
- ☐ Work with other specialists to design specific "play" areas.
- ☐ Leave appropriate clearances for a pool table—5′ on all sides.
- ☐ Be sure to plan appropriate clearances for performing tasks and playing games.
- ☐ Work with the HVAC contractor to ensure that there is adequate ventilation and temperature control.
- ☐ Work with the client and the AV consultant on all Smarthome® features.

Before Cabinetry Is Created (If Applicable)

- ☐ Discuss all finishes—door finish, panel insert material/finish (clear glass, frosted glass, stainless, etc.)—with your client and the cabinetmaker.
- ☐ Choose the style of the crown, the base, and doors, and decide whether you will be installing an AV rack in the cabinetry.
- ☐ Choose and order hardware for cabinetry (knobs, pulls, etc.).
- ☐ Discuss the location of switches and outlets, speakers, etc.
- ☐ Discuss which switches coordinate with which lights.
- ☐ Discuss the type and color of outlets and switches (dimmers, etc.).

Before Installations

- ☐ Check that the walls and ceiling are painted or that wallcoverings are installed prior to installation of cabinetry and electronic equipment.
- ☐ Flooring should be installed prior to cabinet installation in most cases. Install transition strips or saddles where needed.
- ☐ Schedule electrical and plumbing work to be completed prior to cabinet installation.
- ☐ Make sure the area is cleared of all debris and that there is a clear path of entry to the space for all installations and deliveries of furniture.
- ☐ Have someone from the AV team on-site during cabinet installation if possible so they can coordinate efforts.

During Cabinetry and Other Installations

- ☐ If you are on-site, periodically inspect the work being done.
- ☐ If there are any problems on-site that you cannot resolve yourself or on which you need a second opinion, call your supervisor as soon as possible to resolve and call the supplier if necessary.

After Installation

- ☐ Inspect the cabinetry and other furnishings, checking for any damage, dings, or imperfections.
- ☐ Open and close each door and drawer, and make sure they function properly and smoothly.
- ☐ If there are any problems on-site that you cannot resolve yourself or on which you need a second opinion, call your supervisor as soon as possible to resolve and call the supplier if necessary.

Wine Cellars

You need to determine the clients' particular wishes as well as their needs with regard to a wine cellar. For example, will the space be used solely for the storage of the clients' wine collection or will it also serve as a tasting room? Determine the function of the space.

Refrigeration and temperature control are critical here. You should consult with the appropriate HVAC professionals to be sure you take measures to insulate, ventilate, and refrigerate the space effectively.

There are a myriad of materials available for wine storage. You can specify one of many different species of wood, metal racks, custom bins, or a EuroCave™, which is a refrigerator manufactured specifically to store both red and white wine at the appropriate temperatures. Will you design open or closed storage, or a combination of the two?

Next, you must determine the look of the space. Will there be glass enclosures so your clients and their guests can see in and out of the cellar? This is especially nice if you are creating a space where your clients will sit, relax, and do tastings. If glass is specified, be sure to use tempered glass and opt for low iron content so the glass is clear and less green in color. You may want to etch the glass with a design or add a window film detail for safety reasons so that someone does not walk head-on into the glass and get injured.

The type of flooring selected for a wine cellar depends on the location of the cellar. If it will be located in a basement, you may wish to specify an engineered wood, a wood laminate, a tile, or perhaps cork. If possible, specify a floor drain.

Lighting is a critical component. Ambient illumination is necessary for wayfinding, but if the client will use the space to entertain, you must consider accent and task lighting as well. A pendant on a dimmer over the tasting table adds functionality, drama, and the ability to control the light for different mood settings.

It is highly recommended that you consult with a wine cellar design specialist. These professionals have access to the best wine storage product information and will help make the project progress more smoothly.

Beginning Steps

☐ If the existing subfloor is a concrete slab, be sure that it is properly sealed before floor covering is installed.

☐ Specify a vapor barrier to be installed on the walls and the ceiling planes prior to installing insulation and drywall.

☐ It is a good idea when constructing a wine cellar to increase the thickness of the partitions to make room for better insulation.

☐ Work with the contractor/engineer to determine the size of the cooling system you need to specify based on the square footage of the space.

☐ Recommend that your clients install a security/monitoring system. (Suggest this to your clients to protect their investment from theft, to alert them in the event of power failure, and to inform them of the exact temperature/humidity of the wine cellar at all times.)

☐ Make sure you have specified an insulated door with weather stripping to maintain a good seal.

☐ If you are specifying a door with a glass panel insert, be sure to select a thermal door or at the very least, a tempered double-pane glass for insulation purposes.

☐ Especially in new construction, suggest that a floor drain be put in if possible.

Before Cabinetry/Shelving Is Designed and Fabricated

☐ Discuss all finishes—door finish, panel insert material/finish (clear glass, frosted glass, stainless, etc.)—with your client and the cabinetmaker/rack manufacturer's rep.

☐ Discuss the use of open or closed storage.

☐ Design storage for tasting accessories.

☐ Design wine glass storage if tasting will be a function in the space.

☐ Create design drawings to include plan, elevations, lighting plan, and RCP.

☐ Select or design a tasting table if applicable.

☐ Choose the style of the crown and other architectural/trim details for cabinetry.

☐ Choose and order hardware for cabinetry (knobs, pulls, etc.).

☐ Discuss the location of switches and outlets, etc.

☐ Discuss which switches coordinate with which lights.

☐ Discuss the type and color of outlets and switches (dimmers, etc.).

Before Cabinetry/Shelving Is Installed

☐ Make sure walls and ceiling are painted prior to cabinet and rack installation.

☐ Make sure knobs and pulls are on-site so that the cabinetmaker can drill holes in the doors and drawers and install the hardware upon the completion of the installation.

☐ Make sure the area is cleared of all debris and ready for cabinetry.

During Cabinetry/Shelving Installation

☐ If you are on-site, periodically inspect the work being done.

☐ If there are any problems on-site that you cannot resolve yourself or on which you need a second opinion, call your supervisor as soon as possible to resolve and call the supplier if necessary.

After Cabinetry/Shelving Is Installed

☐ Inspect the cabinetry, checking for any damage, dings, or imperfections.

☐ Open and close each door and drawer and make sure they function properly and smoothly.

☐ If there are any problems on-site that you cannot resolve yourself or on which you need a second opinion, call your supervisor as soon as possible to resolve and call the supplier if necessary.

Walls

Once all of the colors have been selected, the finishes have been specified, and wallcoverings have been ordered and received at the job site, you begin to prepare to cover the largest amount of square footage in a space.

In many cases, it is far easier if the clients are not in residence, but that is not always possible. Be very clear about the project parameters with the paint and wallpaper mechanics. Are there pets or small children that will be present while work is being performed?

All of these factors can affect the timetable, in addition to the fact that special precautions may be necessary and the designer should be anticipating potential problems. Pets may need to be gated. (My own little white bichon acquired a red ear when he ran to the front door when it was opened by the paint mechanic so he could paint the inside frame. I learned my lesson early that safety and preparation are everything!)

Be sure that either the clients have moved everything away from the walls or that you have arranged for the paint/wallpaper mechanic to do so. Do not leave this item open, as it can muddy the waters at the start of the project if all parties are not aware of their responsibilities. Better to be crystal clear from the get-go, so there are no surprises.

If you are having paper or any other wallcovering applied to the walls, the wallpaper mechanic needs to review with you whether to install a liner and also how seaming will be handled. All of these details should be worked out prior to ordering the goods. Wallcoverings are available in many different materials, including paper, leather, vinyl, grass cloth, and mother of pearl. Each material has a different hanging requirement, so the designer should have a conference call with the installer and the vendor whenever there is a question with regard to installation procedures.

The paint/wallpaper mechanics need to prep the walls prior to applying the finish coats/papers. A paint schedule such as the one included in this book (see Figure 4.1) is a great way to keep all parties on the same page. This one document catalogs all wall, trim, and ceiling paint colors, wallcoverings, and so on, including finish and manufacturer. This is also very helpful to your clients at the end of the project. They can keep a laminated printout or save a copy to their computer's hard drive, so if repairs are needed in the future, they will know exactly what was applied in each space.

Before Painting

- ☐ Order large paint color samples—one set for the client and one set for the design team.
- ☐ Review the paint samples in the client's space in both natural/daylight and electric light. Color rendering is important.
- ☐ Discuss with the client wall, ceiling, trim colors, and finishes.
- ☐ Have the client approve the color(s).
- ☐ Send drawings of the space to the paint mechanic to get quotes of the square footage.
- ☐ Once colors have been selected, create a paint schedule for the paint mechanic and/or contractor. (See Figure 4.1, for example.)
- ☐ Once the contract has been awarded, e-mail the paint schedule to the paint mechanic and/or contractor and also to the client in advance so that paint and supplies can be purchased prior to the start date.
- ☐ Request that installers wear booties to protect the floors during work.
- ☐ Make sure the installers set up their equipment on drop cloths so as not to damage the surrounding floor area.
- ☐ Drop cloths should be used to cover and protect all flooring and other furnishings remaining on-site during painting.
- ☐ Review all paint purchased to be sure the color matches what was specified.
- ☐ Review the design intent with the paint mechanic/contractor and communicate any special instructions from you or your client so that everyone is on the same page from the beginning.
- ☐ The paint mechanic/contractor should remove electrical outlet and switch plate covers, duct covers, and all hardware/screws prior to prep and painting, and they should be placed in one location so they are easy to find and reinstall after the project is completed.

During the Painting Process

- ☐ If you are on-site, periodically inspect the work being done (about once an hour).
- ☐ After a full wall is completed with primer and one to two coats of the paint, make sure the color matches your sample and that you and your client are satisfied with the result.
- ☐ Check for any inconsistencies in the work; make sure all the walls are coated evenly.
- ☐ If there are any problems on-site that you cannot resolve yourself or on which you need a second opinion, call your supervisor as soon as possible to resolve.

After Painting Is Finished

- ☐ Inspect the painted walls to make sure they are coated evenly.
- ☐ Check to make sure there are no drip marks or streaks.
- ☐ Make sure the paint edges are clean where the ceiling meets the wall and where the wall meets the baseboards.
- ☐ Make sure the floor is clean and does not have any paint on it.
- ☐ Make sure the painters reinstall any electrical plates, switch plates, and/or duct grates after painting is completed.
- ☐ Make sure all debris is removed and the area is as clean as it was before the painters came.

RENOVATIONS   **WALLCOVERING INSTALLATION CHECKLIST**

Before Wallcovering Is Installed

- ☐ Work with the wallpaper mechanic to determine quantities to order.
- ☐ **Research how the goods are sold** (by the roll, by the yard, by the double roll?) **and confirm with the wallpaper mechanic.**
- ☐ Confirm the type of lining paper necessary and determine the installation method.
- ☐ Obtain yardage quotations from the vendor.
- ☐ Request a labor proposal from the wallpaper mechanic.
- ☐ Be sure all walls are prepped, checked for imperfections, and ready to receive the wallcovering.
- ☐ Confirm the seaming of the wallcovering. Should the seams fall at specific locations?
- ☐ If possible, have the wallcovering delivered to your studio first so that you can inspect it prior to installation day and get any replacements if necessary.
- ☐ As the installers set up their equipment, confirm with the client that the area can remain free of traffic.
- ☐ Make sure the installers wear booties upon entering the home.
- ☐ Installers should set up equipment on drop cloths so as not to damage the surrounding floor area.
- ☐ Have installers open all rolls and check/roll out the beginning of each roll to inspect for any damage before any paper is hung.
- ☐ If there are any issues with damage to the wallcovering once it is unpacked, contact your supervisor and the wallcovering vendor immediately to get replacement roll(s) sent.
- ☐ Check inside the boxes to locate any special hanging instructions.
- ☐ Communicate with the installers to clarify which walls are to receive goods and provide any special instructions.

During the Wallcovering Installation

- ☐ **If you are on-site, periodically inspect the work being done** (about once an hour).
- ☐ Check for any air bubbles within the paper.
- ☐ Check to make sure the seams of the paper are straight and lie as flat as possible.
- ☐ If the wallcovering has a pattern, make sure the pattern lines up at the seams.
- ☐ If there are any problems on-site that you cannot answer yourself or on which you need a second opinion, call the principal designer as soon as possible to resolve.
- ☐ If switch plates or outlet covers are present, ask that they be covered if it is part of your design intent.

After Wallcovering Is Installed

- ☐ Carefully inspect the wallcovering, checking for any air bubbles.
- ☐ Inspect the wallcovering at the seams to make sure they are tight and lie as flat as possible.
- ☐ Make sure the ceiling, baseboards, and floor are free of any adhesive residues.
- ☐ If you notice any adhesive residue, have the installers wipe this clean.
- ☐ Make sure all debris is removed and the area is as clean as it was prior to installation.
- ☐ Obtain maintenance information and give to the client (cleaning instructions, etc.).

Window Treatment Installation

We strongly suggest that you or a member of your team be on-site for window treatment installations. Most designers have extremely talented and competent workrooms and installers, and yet there is almost always a question on installation day that requires your input and expertise.

Elements such as mounting heights can be suggested in a drawing, but it is always best to be there and examine the nuances in person. A quarter of an inch up or down can change the entire look of the treatment. You also should make sure the hem touches the floor where you specified it would and that the break or puddle is not too short or too long.

Dressing a top treatment or a soft fabric shade is an art as well as a technical skill, as is pleating a drapery panel or a swag and jabot. Being on-site allows you to really put your stamp on the installation and be sure it is to your liking.

If you are using a new workroom, you may want to review their installation procedures to be sure they meet with your firm's criteria. Do the installers wear booties during installation? Do they carry butterfly clips for casement windows that will be receiving shades? Do they know how to do a quick paint patch for areas where holes were drilled inadvertently? Have they coordinated installation details with the electricians for installing motorized treatments and shading? These are questions to be asked prior to installation day so you are prepared. The more legwork and preparation you do prior to installation, the smoother the day will progress.

RENOVATIONS   **WINDOW TREATMENT INSTALLATION CHECKLIST**

Before Window Treatment Is Installed

☐ All existing window treatments to be rehung should be covered in plastic and hung in a closet if staying on site during construction.

☐ Be sure all walls have been painted or papered.

☐ Arrive early to be sure the client has moved all furnishings away from the window.

☐ If a full day is planned for installation, wear comfortable clothing and shoes.

☐ Get an estimate of the time frame for the installation and discuss with the client.

☐ Prepare a clear path to the area where installers will work.

☐ If window film has been specified, have this applied prior to window treatment installation day.

☐ Confirm installation date(s) with the client and the installer.

☐ Bring a mini steamer and make sure wall and ceiling paint is on-site for touch-ups.

☐ Make sure the installers don booties to protect the floors as soon as they enter the home.

☐ Installers should set up their equipment on drop cloths so they do not damage the surrounding floor area.

☐ Have the installers unpack window treatments so that you can carefully inspect them prior to installation.

☐ While on location, discuss the desired height for mounting the window treatment and review any other special instructions that you and your client have so that everyone is on the same page from the beginning.

☐ If there are any mistakes, issues, or damage to the window treatments upon inspection, contact your supervisor and/or the workroom immediately to rectify the situation before installation takes place.

During the Window Treatment Installation

☐ If you are on-site, periodically inspect the work being done.

☐ Send interim progress photos to the office to keep your supervisor in the loop.

☐ If there are any problems on-site that you cannot resolve yourself or on which you need a second opinion, stop the work and call your supervisor as soon as possible to resolve. FaceTime® and Skype™ can be helpful tools in these instances.

☐ Are the treatments being installed properly (inside bracket [IB] versus outside bracket [OB] mounting)?

After Window Treatment Is Installed

☐ Inspect the work for alignment, draping, steaming of creases and wrinkles, ring placement, pleats, shade details, and leveling, and secure the client's approval. Generally, the installers bring a steamer, so yours is just for backup.

☐ Test all shades to be sure they operate (open and close) with ease.

☐ Be sure that safety hardware and cord cleats have been installed.

☐ Be sure butterfly clips have been installed on casement windows that receive shades. Clips should coordinate in color/finish with window frames and other hardware.

☐ Test all movable drapery and shading to be sure all controls work properly.

☐ Test motorized shades and have the installer review operating procedures with the client.

☐ For motorized installations, have the installer show the client how and where to replace the batteries if remote controls are used.

☐ Have the installer show the client how to operate the treatment. If the client is not on-site, leave a set of detailed instructions behind or send the document via e-mail so the client can save it for future reference on a computer hard drive.

☐ Take scouting shot photographs for reference.

Special Considerations for Contract Renovation

Business is done differently in contract design as opposed to residential design, so there are other protocols to follow. Furniture is specified by the designer, but orders are placed by the furniture dealer in contract design. Contract designers do visit the site periodically during construction and also perform walk-throughs, but many of the tasks that fall to a residential designer are handled in the commercial space by the contractor and his or her subs.

Ordering: Designers working on commercial/contract projects place an order with the furniture dealer rather than with a showroom. They are required to write every specification and select all of the details of each piece of furniture to be ordered. Because the scope of work on a commercial project is generally quite large, a designer might have to place orders for one project with 30 or more manufacturers, which is not cost effective and can be quite time consuming. Therefore, the furniture dealer is responsible for placing all orders on behalf of the designer. This is part of the furniture dealer's fee.

Deliveries: In corporate design, a designer is not required to visit the furniture dealer/receiver's warehouse to check on the condition of furniture prior to delivery as we suggest in residential design. The designer does not work directly with the receivers of case goods and other furnishings. This is the responsibility of the furniture dealer. The furniture dealer typically does not deliver the furniture until everything has arrived at their warehouse. The exception to this rule is when certain items have longer lead times, which do not work with the client's move-in date. These items will then be sent on a separate truck at a later date, and the client will be responsible for the added cost to reserve the freight elevator for a second delivery.

The delivery receivers for construction products (drywall, steel, fixtures, flooring, etc.) are the responsibility of the general contractor.

It is the designer's responsibility to make sure that all deliveries will arrive in time for the installation. The designer is also required to be on-site to execute a punch list at the time of delivery. Unlike residential interior projects, it is not the contract designer's job to arrange for the delivery truck directly. This falls under the furniture dealer's and general contractor's scope of work.

Installation: The designer will always be on-site when the team is installing the furnishings and other products and will complete a punch list prior to the client's move-in date. The actual installation of furniture or millwork is incorporated into the furniture dealer's and general contractor's fee as well.

Many of the smaller details that a residential designer deals with are the responsibility of others in contract design. For example, if felt pads are needed on any of the furnishings, it is the responsibility of the GC to take care of these details.

The contract designer is in charge of making sure the GC and furniture dealer send in their insurance certificates. The designer is not responsible for making them aware of where the freight elevator is located in the building nor the dimensions of the freight elevator. The GC and furniture dealer will coordinate details, as this is their responsibility prior to the delivery so they know everything will fit. Most commercial office buildings will allow delivery personnel to carry the item up the stairs or ride on top of the elevator cab with a building engineer for an additional fee.

Scheduling and coordination of all electrical finish work with the cabinet installation is the responsibility of the superintendent on the job site, who reports to the GC.

Figures 6.4 shows an example of an architectural punch list and Figure 6.5 shows an example of a furniture punch list, both of which are used in contract design work.

Contract Renovation References

ARCHITECTURAL PUNCH LIST

Date

Via: **E-mail**

To: **General Contractor's Name**
Address

RE: Client's name and Address

Attn: Super's Name

FLOOR:

REMARKS:

☐URGENT   ☒FOR YOUR USE   ☐REPLY ASAP   ☐PLEASE COMMENT

The following items were observed on Wednesday June 20th as still open, incomplete or do not meet the requirements and standards set forth in the construction documents. Please complete all items in a timely manner so that we may complete and sign off on this project.

General items:	Open	Completed
Submit as-built drawings.	x	
Submit waivers of lien.	x	
Submit building dept. sign-off.	x	
Submit warranties and instruction manuals were applicable.	x	
All damaged or dirty ceiling tile to be cleaned and/or replaced.	x	
All lenses of light fixtures to be cleaned.	x	
Remove all construction material throughout.	x	
General construction clearing required throughout.	x	
Install door silencers throughout.	x	
Clean all fire extinguisher cabinets.	x	
All sprinkler heads to rest true and flush with ceiling tile.	x	
Install missing pocket door hardware throughout.	x	
Remove temp. loop and finish as req'd all unfinished areas.	x	
Install key ways throughout.	x	
Install missing coat rod and hardware at all closets.	x	
All wood doors and wood base to have nail holes filled and finished.	x	
Confirm with building if fire extinguisher is req'd adjacent to fire stair 1.	x	

Figure 6.4 Architectural Punch List

ARCHITECTURAL PUNCH LIST

Office Doors: To be checked if in working condition. Many doors do not shut properly and cannot be closed without great force.	x	

Hall Capital:

Copy Room #022: Provide blank cover plate over not used junction boxes.	x	
Copy Room #022: Clean glass and frame of existing window.	x	
Copy Room #022: Install missing ceiling tile.	x	
Sand excessive spackle adjacent door number 13.	x	
Butler pantry #024: Bowed ceiling preventing ceiling tile to rest flush.	x	
Large gap in grid above door number 13.	x	
Butler pantry #24: Finish installation of plumbing, tile backsplash, millwork hardware, electrical outlets, and repaint damaged wall around backsplash.	x	
Butler pantry #24:Remove paint on millwork.	x	
Caulk bottom of door frame #13 (large gap).	x	
IT Room #023: Install missing base and ceiling tiles.	x	
Door #9: Door lever needs to be tightened.	x	
Mothering Room #025: Finish installation of plumbing, tile backsplash, millwork hardware, electrical outlets, light fixture, appliances, and wooden blinds.	x	
Mothering Room #025: Ceiling tile above millwork is not resting flush.	x	
Mothering Room #025: Remove paint on side panel of millwork.	x	
Mothering Room #025: Walls need to be cleaned for new look finish.	x	
Door #7: Missing hardware (roller catch). Remove paint on hinges. Color of double wood doors does not match.	x	
Closets at butler pantry: remove surface-mounted wood blocking inside both closets.	x	
Door #6: Paint trimmed opening.	x	
Repair drywall corner across door #6.	x	
Conference Rm. #021: Remove protection throughout.	x	
Conference Rm. #021: Paint touch-up required throughout.	x	

Figure 6.4 Architectural Punch List

ARCHITECTURAL PUNCH LIST

Conference Rm. #021: Finish installation of floating stone shelf.	x	
Door #14: Finish pocket door header.	x	
Conference Rm. #021: Install missing wall base at pocket door #14.	x	
Door #15: Finish pocket door header.	x	
Conference Rm. #020: Clean dirty wall.	x	
Conference Rm. #020: Provide blank cover plate at not used box.	x	
Conference Rm. #020: Large gap at bottom of millwork panel within conference room.	x	
Remove screws in gyp. bd. ceiling in corridor. Finish as req'd.	x	
Men's Room #026: Finish installation of bathroom vanity, plumbing, soap dispenser, door closer, and mirror caulking. All edges of millwork to be finished and neat.	x	
Men's Room #026: Missing grout above entry door.	x	
Men's Room #026: Paint touch-up and/or clean ceiling as req'd.	x	
Men's Room and Women's Room: Install ultrasonic occupancy sensor.	x	
Conference Room #019: Install blank cover plate at not used junction box.	x	
Conference Room #019: Finish pocket door header.	x	
Conference Room #019: Base is peeling away from wall.	x	
Conference Room #019: Tear away bead installation is not complete.	x	
Ada Toilet #027: Finish installation of plumbing and mirror. Patch gyp bd ceiling above sink. ***Additional Items: Install full-length mirror on backside of door. Install new bulb with no visible text at wall sconce.***	x	
Remove gum and stain from carpet outside of women's room.	x	
Door #4: Paint patch.	x	
Door #17: Millwork wrapping into corridor does not rest flush with gyp. bd. ceiling and partition (large gap at reveal).	x	

Figure 6.4 Architectural Punch List (*continues*)

ARCHITECTURAL PUNCH LIST

Door #17: Pocket door paneling is scratched.	x	
Conference Room #018: Install missing floating stone shelf and covers at screws.	x	
Door #18: Finish millwork paneling installation.	x	
Repair required at corner where reception glass side light and millwork panel meet.	x	
Door #35: Finish door installation and remove paint.	x	
Conference Room #17: Blinds do not align when in the half-open position.	x	
Conference Room #17: Paint touch-up req'd where glass meets drywall.	x	
Door #19: Repair damaged nib at base and finish header.	x	
Remove paint from fire strobe at gathering area off reception.	x	
Carry wall covering past glass side light at reception. Provide stop bead at exposed edge.	x	
Column 3;C: Properly finish around outlet. New look finish req'd.	x	
Base at office fronts needs to have a self-return on both sides. Do not return into millwork.	x	
Trimmed openings at all office fronts require paint touch-up.	x	
Column 3;D: Requires paint touch-up.	x	
Column 4;D: Remove stains at top of column.	x	
Door #34: Touch-up req'd.	x	
Install missing ceiling tile above door #34.	x	
Paint touch-up req'd at pocket door #32.	x	
Column 4;D: Replace damaged ceiling tile.	x	

Figure 6.4 Architectural Punch List

ARCHITECTURAL PUNCH LIST

Messy glass caulking at offices 008 and 009.	x	
Open area #016: Light fixture not working.	x	
Paint touch-up req'd at door #'s 32 and 31. Finish door header installation.	x	
Cut base back at pocket door #31. Rubs against door.	x	
Pantry #003: A large number of ceiling tiles are damaged and dirty.	x	
Pantry #003: Painting required. Finish installation of plumbing, electrical outlets, backsplash, appliances, millwork hardware, corner caps at ceiling grid, provide grommet and caulk work counter and install missing ceiling tile.	x	
Office #005: Install missing door hardware. Fix bubble around light switch. Patch gap at data cover plate.	x	
Office #007: Paint touch-up at column.	x	
Door #27: Does not close and drags on rug.	x	
Office #010: Paint touch-up at column.	x	
Office #12: Wall base is peeling off of wall.	x	
Office #15: Remove stain in carpet.	x	
Office #15: Seam at (2) carpets is not straight.	x	
Freight corridor #002: Hold comments until all materials have been removed.	x	
Janitor's closet: Finish installation of flooring, base, and painting of walls.	x	
Base at electrical closet doors needs to return.	x	
Reception #001: Install missing call buttons and lanterns.	x	
Reception #001: Install all security devices at reception area.	x	
Door #2: Finish installation of missing hardware.	x	
Reception #001:Patch gap in cove light.	x	
Reception #001: Patch gap where glass side light and wood paneling meet.		

Figure 6.4 Architectural Punch List (*continues*)

FURNITURE PUNCH LIST

Date: **Via**: **E-mail**

To: **Furniture Dealer's Name**   **RE: Client's name and Address**
      Address

Attn: Furniture Dealer's Project Manager's name   **FLOOR:**

REMARKS:

☐URGENT   ☒FOR YOUR USE   ☐REPLY ASAP   ☐PLEASE COMMENT

The following items were observed on Tuesday June 26th as still open, incomplete, or do not meet the requirements and standards set forth in the construction documents. Please complete all items in a timely manner so that we may complete and sign off on this project.

General items :

	Open	Completed
Open Office		
BBF drawers are not aligned. Align glides.	x	
Work area pods, grommets, sleeves, and covers are missing. (Aluminum)	x	
Return troughs are not finished.	x	
Missing (8) black keyboard trays.	x	
Missing (2) Mobile pedestals with seat cushions.	x	
Missing (1) wood printer station.	x	
Client would like (4) additional 2H 42" files with wood tops near pod 2, 3, 7 & 8.	x	
Private Office		
BBF drawers are not aligned. Align glides.	x	
Return troughs are not finished.	x	
9 private offices (not corner offices) to receive new 3H 30" file cabinets with wood tops.	x	
9 private offices (not corner offices) to receive new wire mold for electric/data cables for printer.	x	
9 private offices (not corner offices) missing (1) wood shelf.	x	
Glass tack boards need the magnets that were supposed to come with them.	x	
Glass tack boards are different shades of white.	x	

Figure 6.5 Furniture Punch List

FURNITURE PUNCH LIST

Hall Capital:

Reception 001: Missing reception desk.	x	
Pantry 003: Client would like to order (2) more chairs. (1) Chair's backplate is missing.	x	
Open Office 004: Pod 5 BBF has a scuff on one of its drawers.	x	
Open Office 004: Pod 6 has a hole in one of the panels, which needs to be replaced.	x	
Private Office 006: There is a scratch on the return wood top.	x	
Private Office 007: Mounted wood wall unit is not aligned with glass tack board. Also, the bottom drawer on the BBF is not closing.	x	
Private Office 008: Glass tack board not aligned.	x	
Private Office 010: There is a scratch on the wood desk top.	x	
Private Office 012: There is a scratch on one of the silea pulls on the return. There is a scratch on the task chair's arm.	x	
Private Office 013: (1) Glass tack board is missing.	x	
Private Office 014: There is a scratch on the top of the desk return.	x	
Private Office 015: There are scratches on the desk and edges. Grommet to be drilled [V.I.F.] on the desk. Wire management channel for the electric outlets. Move the file drawers to the right to accommodate a new 42" wood table to have a keyboard tray and locking casters. There is a crack on the wood file drawers.	x	
Open Office 016: Pod1: BBF has a scratch on it.	x	
Open Office 016: Pod 8 has a scratch on the wood desk. Also, pod 8 has a hole in one of the panels, which needs to be replaced. One of the task chairs has a scratch on it. One of the BBF drawers is not closing.	x	
Open Office 016: Pod 9 BBF drawers are not closing and one of the returns need to be adjusted.	x	
Open Office 016: Files need to be centered between columns. The files joint lines needs to be tightened.	x	
Conference Room 017: The tabletop has three scratches on it and needs to be replaced. There is one extra chair in this room. Verify location.	x	
Conference Room 018: Table end panels are not popped on. The microphones are missing in the table. The credenza and top are missing. One of the chairs has a mark on it.	x	
Conference Room 019 & 020: Tables to be secured. Was not able to do my punch list in these rooms since they were being occupied. Will verify Friday June 29th.	x	
Conference Room 021: Table end panels are not popped on. The credenza and top are missing.	x	

Figure 6.5 Furniture Punch List (*continues*)

FURNITURE PUNCH LIST

Copy Room 022: The Izzy storage unit, which is located in the middle of the room, has a sticky material stuck to one of the drawers. Also, one of the drawers on the unit is not closing. Move (1) of the 5H file cabinets with the pull-out shelf to the other side of the cluster. Therefore, the (2) 5H files with pull-out shelves will be on both ends. One 48" wide portion of the plastic laminate counter has to be lowered to no more than 30" A.F.F. Therefore; the plastic laminate piece will have to be cut. Put the raw edge against the wall. Get new wall brackets to support the 150-pound binding machine, which will now go on the counter. The binding machine is 20" D x 18½" W x 22½" H. The steel-shelving unit below will have to be lowered as well.	x	
Mothering Room 025: The sofa is missing.	x	

Figure 6.5 Furniture Punch List

Glossary

ADA – The Americans With Disabilities Act

AFF – Above Finished Floor – Height measurement taken on site and documented in a survey or dimensioned on a drawing to indicate that the dimension was taken starting above a finished floor height as opposed to an unfinished floor in rough construction.

Ambient Light – In terms of design, ambient light refers to the overall general illumination in a space.

Apron-Front Sink – Also known as a farmhouse sink, an apron-front sink is deeper than a traditional sink. When using this type of sink your base cabinet below is smaller due to the front face of the sink being shown. The front face sits out slightly in front of the cabinetry to allow for any dripping to avoid damaging the cabinets below.

Attic Stock – When you order more of a product than you need to hold in reserve in case of damage to the product that was installed inside the structure.

Baseball Stitch – Often used on upholstery, this double-row accent stitching resembles the red stitching on a baseball where two parallel stitches run on either side of the seam. This decorative detail also strengthens the seam.

Basin – A large bowl/sink used for washing one's hands and face.

Bench Seat – One long cushion on a sofa or a window seat.

Bevel – A type of edge detail on a piece of material that is an angled and cut (usually done on a 45-degree angle) out of the edge where the top of the material meets the side of the material.

Bullnose – A type of edge detail on a piece of material that is rounded where the top of the material meets the side of the material.

Camelback – A name for a specific back style on upholstered furniture that has an arched back with the higher point in the center.

Case Goods – A category of furniture that is made up strictly of hard materials such as wood, glass, plastic, metal, etc. and also has a storage component.

Center-Set Faucet – A type of faucet where the spout and the two controls are all fixed upon the same base unit.

Certificate of Occupancy – A certificate that an owner receives from the building department saying that the building/dwelling/renovation has been constructed to meet all laws and codes and can officially be occupied.

CFA – Cutting for Approval – A cutting that a designer requests from a fabric manufacturer to ensure that the dye lot of the goods being purchased matches the original memo sample that the designer has in their possession. This cutting is a small sample taken from the actual goods being purchased.

Chair Rail – Originally created to keep chairs from damaging expensive wallcoverings, it is a decorative molding that runs around the perimeter of a room on the horizontal plane. This can be made of wood, ceramic, metal, or other materials.

Chamfer – A type of edge detail on a piece of material that is angled and cut (usually done on a 45-degree angle) out of the edge where the top of the material meets the side of the material. (Much like the bevel edge.)

Channel Quilted – A type of stitching that is done either on linens or an upholstered piece of furniture where all of the stitching lines run parallel to one another.

COH–Customer's Own Hardware – When a designer wants to specify hardware for a piece of furniture that is different than what is offered for that particular piece.

COL–Customer's Own Leather – When a designer wants to place an order for a piece of furniture but would like to specify a leather from a different manufacturer.

Color Temperature – A term used to describe the color temperature of light that a luminaire (light fixture) emits.

Color-Fastness – A term used to describe the resistance of the fabric dye to fading or wear when washing.

Colorway(s) – Any and all colors that a fabric or material is available in.

COM–Customer's Own Material – When a designer wants to place an order for a piece of furniture but would like to specify a fabric from a different manufacturer.

COMcheck™ – A product group that makes it easy for building inspectors and officials, architects, builders, designers, and contractors to simplify and determine whether new commercial or high-rise residential buildings, additions, and alterations meet the code requirements and are in compliance.

Concealed Trap – Many toilets possess an exposed trap-way that's often hard to clean because of its location behind the bowl. A toilet with a concealed "trap" will have a smooth surface at the back of the toilet where the trap would normally be visible. Skirted toilets take it a step further and offer a clean line from front to back. Both concealed and skirted traps simplify cleaning and are more aesthetically pleasing.

Contrast Welt – A piping or cording that is created using a different/contrasting textile to the fabric that was used on the body of the piece.

Cornice – A decorative shaped structure that is created and can be upholstered in a textile to dress the top portion of a window. In some cases it is used to hide drapery, blinds, or shade hardware.

COV–Customer's Own Vinyl – When a designer wants to place an order for a piece of furniture but would like to specify a vinyl from a different manufacturer.

Cove Tile – A ceramic tile that looks like a baseboard with a deeply arched or curved bottom edge. You can use a cove tile as a transition from wall to floor.

Coverlet – A light bedspread with a lining between the face and back fabric used more for decorative purposes, rather than a duvet cover/duvet combo, which is used more for warmth.

"Cradle to Cradle" – Certifies that all elements of particular products and furniture can be recycled and/or reused in some way at the end of the product's life. The whole concept of "Cradle to cradle" is certifying products that are essentially waste-free.

Crocking – A term for what happens when the dye on a dry fabric rubs off onto another surface. This generally happens on a fabric that has a dark or intense color.

Crown – A dimensional piece of wood trimming that is used to add decoration where the planes of the walls in a space meet the ceiling plane.

Crown of Mattress – The highest point of the mattress, in the center. Utilized to measure the drop for custom bedding.

Cutting– A small piece that is cut from a large dye lot of fabric.

D

Diverter – A tub/shower plumbing control that allows you to change where the water is flowing to, such as the shower head, body sprays, handheld, etc.

Double Rubs – A result of a test for fabric abrasion and durability. The number rating that a fabric receives is the amount of times a machine has rubbed a fabric, back and forth, before the fabric shows wear and/or breaks down.

Drop-In – A term that can refer to a tub or sink. In a tub application, there would be no apron. The tub would be "dropped-in" to a pre-constructed deck and the rim of the tub will be visible. For a sink, the basin would be "dropped-in" to a pre-drilled hole in the countertop where the rim of the sink is visible.

Duvet Cover – A type of bed cover to encase a feather-filled insert. This can be fabricated with a button or zipper closure for easy removal and cleaning.

Dye Lot – A batch of fabric that was dyed at the same time and has the same exact coloring throughout.

E

Eased Edge – An edge style that, while similar to a bullnose edge with its curved profile, is more of a gradual curve on a small section of the edge.

Efficacy – The amount of light that a luminaire produces in relation to the amount of power it takes to produce that light.

FFF&E – Furniture, Fixtures, Finishes, and Equipment – An acronym used when discussing these items as a whole.

F

Filler – The piece of material (generally wood) that acts as a spacer and offers the correct amount of clearance needed between cabinet doors and appliances, walls, etc.

Flushometer – A metal water-diverter that uses an inline handle to flush toilets or urinals.

Frog – An applied decorative embellishment in passementarie.

G

GC – General contractor

GFI–Ground Fault Interrupt – A type of electrical outlet used in wet locations.

Gimp – An ornamental flat braid or round cord used as a trimming on upholstery, drapery, lamps, bedding, etc.

H

HID – High Intensity Discharge Lamp

"Hide" – How well a coat of paint covers new drywall or old paint

Honed – A stone finish that gives a smooth, even appearance without a high polished gloss.

HVAC–Heating, Ventilation and Air Conditioning – The technology/control of indoor environmental comfort.

I

IB Mount – A term for mounting a window treatment with an inside bracket (inside the window frame).

IBC – International Building Code

Interlining – A thick cotton layer, such as a cotton wool or "bump" between the face fabric and the lining fabric, which insulates a space. Interlining also provides additional weight, helping curtains and draperies to hang well, and provides a thicker, more luxurious appearance.

IT – Information Technology

J

J-Box – Junction box

K

Key Lighting – Accent lighting

Kick Base – Also known as a toe-kick, this is a recess at the bottom of a base cabinet that provides space for your feet so you can get close to the countertop without losing your balance or damaging cabinetry.

L

Lamp – A lighting design term for a light bulb.

LAV – Lavatory or sink/basin for washing one's hands and face.

LED–Light Emitting Diode – An energy efficient source of electric light.

Listello – A decorative border or "thin strip" used to accent a field tile or top a tile backsplash or wall installation, adding interest to an ordinary tile installation.

Luminaire – A designer term for a light fixture used to create electric light. All light fixtures include a fixture body and a light socket that holds the lamp and allows for its replacement.

M

Memo Sample – A swatch or small sample of a textile provided by a vendor or showroom for your project reference or to show to a client for approval.

Miter – A joint made between two materials at an angle of 90 degrees. Picture frame and crown molding joints are good examples of a mitered edge.

Modular – Furniture made up of independent pieces/sections. Can be found in both upholstery and case goods.

Moss Fringe – A thick, dense trim used as a decorative welt in upholstery work.

Mullion – The element that creates a division between parts of a window, door, or screen, or is used decoratively. Most often seen with glass.

N

Nailheads – A decorative tack for upholstery used to beautify and accent furniture, headboards, and doors.

Net Price – Designer's discounted price to purchase an item.

Net 30 – A type of account a designer might select when working with a vendor. A form of trade credit where full payment is expected within 30 days

NFPA – National Fire Protection Agency

O

OB Mount – A term for mounting a window treatment with an outside bracket (outside the window frame).

OC – On Center

Off-Gassing – When volatile chemicals found in building materials are released into the air through evaporation. Examples include certain carpets, vinyl wallcoverings, and paints.

Ogee – A countertop edge detail. A double "S" shaped curve, formed by joining a concave and a convex line.

P

Passementarie – The art of creating intricate trimmings or edge details for furnishings and draperies. Styles include fringes, cords, gimp, frogs, tassels, and rosettes.

Pedestal Sink – A freestanding bathroom sink that sits on a "column" designed to hide the plumbing of the drain and P-trap for a more aesthetically pleasing look.

Pencil/Liner – A trim piece available in a honed or polished finish that may be used as an edge finishing detail on a backsplash, a wainscot, in a shower, or as a detail on a fireplace.

Plumb – Exactly vertical: a (wall) plane that stands perfectly straight and does not lean in any way.

PO – Purchase Order

Pressure-Balance – A valve that provides water at a nearly constant temperature to a shower or a bathtub, despite pressure fluctuations in the hot or cold supply lines. The valve compensates for changes in water pressure and prevents scalding.

Pro Forma – A type of interior design account where you pay for the goods before they are shipped.

Procurement – The acquisition of goods, services, or work from an outside source or vendor.

P-Trap – A wastewater P-shaped drain trap that prevents sewer gas, rodents, and other undesirable elements from entering the home through the plumbing drain.

R

RA Tag – Return Authorization Tag

Railroad – If you turn the bolt on end and roll out the textile from left to right, the pattern would be continuous across the roll. This is especially useful with bench seat cushions and the outside back of a large sofa to eliminate seams. This works best with a plain fabric (no pattern repeat).

RCP – Reflected Ceiling Plan

Rectified Edge – A tile that has had all edges mechanically finished to achieve a more precise facial dimension.

Requisitioner – The person issuing the purchase order.

RFP – Request for Proposal

Rough-In – The elements of plumbing you don't see when the tiles, sinks, faucets, and so on are installed, which generally make up the bulk of the job. All plumbing and electrical rough-in work must be completed to pass inspection before sheet rock or cabinetry can be installed.

S

Self-Welt – The piping/cording around a cushion or pillow that has been created using the cushion or pillow's own fabric.

Sidemark – Each order should be assigned a name, number, or code that cross-references all parties and room designation for each item ordered (Designer/Client/Room/Item).

Soffit – A flat surface or the underside of an architectural element (lower face of a beam, arch, balcony, overhang, etc.).

Sound Attenuation – When sound travels through a medium, its intensity diminishes with distance. In design, we can control sound by adding fiberglass and other sound-dampening insulation between walls, floors, and ceiling planes.

Starphire® – Low-iron glass with improved clarity and color transmission.

T

Tassel – A finishing feature for upholstery and drapery. Fabricated from a tuft of freely hanging threads, cords, or other material, it is then knotted at one end in a decorative and embellished manner.

Template – A shaped piece of metal, wood, cardboard, or other material used to create a pattern for cutting out, shaping, or drilling the surface to receive inserts.

Thermostatic Valve – A mixing valve that blends hot and cold water to provide safe shower and bath temperatures to prevent scalding. The valve temperatures can be set to manage bathing of children, elderly, or mentally challenged bathers.

Tile Flange – A metal bead that sits on top of the tub to hold the tile when you do a three-wall tub (or slide-in tub).

Toe Kick – A recess in the bottom of a cabinet that allows a person to stand closer to a cabinet without hitting the base.

Trip Lever – A toilet tank flush handle and actuating arm. This is also a term used for the lever that opens and closes the drain on the bathtub, regulating waste and overflow.

Tufting/Tufted – An upholstery technique where short U-shaped loops of extra threads are threaded through the textile from the outside so that their ends point inwards. Usually, the tuft yarns form a repetition of dots or buttons, sometimes in a contrasting color (e.g., white on red).

TYP – Typical, general – industry terminology

U

Under-Mount – Refers to installing a sink below a countertop, which makes the sink and the top appear to be one continuous piece.

V

VCT–Vinyl Composition Tile – A resilient flooring material used widely in both residential and commercial building. Tiles are composed of colored polyvinyl chloride (PVC) chips and formed into solid sheets using heat and pressure.

Veneer – A thin decorative covering, generally of wood, applied to a coarser material or other less expensive and more stable substrate material.

Vessel Sink – A sink that sits on top of the counter. Can be fabricated from a myriad of materials.

VOC – Volatile Organic Compound – A large group of carbon-based chemicals that easily evaporate at room temperature. Found in many paints, vinyl wallcoverings, etc.

W

Wayfinding – Signs, maps, and other graphic or audible methodology used to convey location and directions to visitors of a building.

White Label – A product manufactured by one company that is packaged and sold by other companies under different brand names. The end result appears as though it is being made by the designer, when in reality it is being created by a separate manufacturer.

Widespread Faucet – The spout and the hot and cold water handles are all separate pieces. Widespread faucets are available from 6″ to 16″ drillings for three-hole predrilled installation basins/lavatories.

Wingback – A type of upholstered chair, sofa, or headboard having pieces that project forward from the sides of the back. First used in the 1600s in England, to keep the sitter warm and to protect the upper chest, and face from cold drafts. Today it is a more stylized aesthetic piece, used in a variety of interiors.

Wyzenbeek Rating – An abrasion test that examines a fabric's ability to withstand surface wear from rubbing. During the test, the fabric is pulled taut and subjected to rubbing in both the warp and filling (or weft) directions. The number of cycles, or "double rubs", tolerated before the fabric displays "noticeable wear" is calculated and determines the fabric's abrasion rating.

Index